NATIONAL GEOGRAPHIC

Reach™

Language • Literacy • Content

Program Authors
Nancy Frey
Lada Kratky
Nonie K. Lesaux
Sylvia Linan-Thompson
Deborah J. Short
Jennifer D. Turner

NATIONAL GEOGRAPHIC

Hampton-Brown

Literature Reviewers

Carmen Agra Deedy, Grace Lin, Jonda C. McNair, Anastasia Suen

Grade 2 Teacher Reviewers

Blanca L. Campillo
Reading Coach
Chicago Public Schools
Chicago, IL

Carla Chavez
Language Arts Specialist
Galena Park Independent School District
Houston, TX

Annena Z. McCleskey
ELA Consultant/ Regional Literacy Training Center Director
Wayne RESA
Lathrup, MI

Sashi Rayasam
Director of ESL Services K-12
Durham Public Schools
Durham, NC

Robin Rivas
Curriculum Specialist ESL/FL
Milwaukee Public Schools
Milwaukee, WI

Shareeica Roberts
ESL Teacher
Carroll Academy for International Studies
Aldine, TX

Cynthia Rodriguez
Bilingual Teacher
Brill Elementary
Klein ISD, TX

Julie Sanabria
ESOL Teacher
Mamaroneck Avenue School
New Rochelle, NY

Jennifer Slater-Sanchez
Educator
Palmdale School District
Palmdale, CA
Adjunct Professor
Brandman University
Antelope Valley, CA

Georgia Thompson
Literacy Coach
Esperanza Hope Medrano Elementary School
Dallas, TX

Acknowledgments

Grateful acknowledgment is given to the authors, artists, photographers, museums, publishers, and agents for permission to reprint copyrighted material. Every effort has been made to secure the appropriate permission. If any omissions have been made or if corrections are required, please contact the Publisher.

Cover Design and Art Direction:
Visual Asylum

Cover Illustration:
Joel Sotelo

Acknowledgments and credits continue on page 626.

The National Geographic Society
John M. Fahey, Jr., President & Chief Executive Officer
Gilbert M. Grosvenor, Chairman of the Board

Copyright © 2011 The Hampton-Brown Company, Inc., a wholly owned subsidiary of the National Geographic Society, publishing under the imprints National Geographic School Publishing and Hampton-Brown.

National Geographic School Publishing
Hampton-Brown
www.NGSP.com

Printed in the USA.
RR Donnelley, Jefferson City, MO

ISBN: 978-0-7362-7427-2

ISBN (TX): 978-0-7362-7491-3

13 14 15 16 17 18 19

10 9 8

Contents at a Glance

Unit 1

Hello, Neighbor!

(?) BIG QUESTION

What is a community?

Social Studies
- ▸ Community Workers
- ▸ Community Places and Events

Skills & Strategies

Language
Give Information
Key Words
Multiple-Meaning Words
Plural Nouns

Literacy
Characters
Plan & Monitor

Content
Community Workers

Part 1

Skills & Strategies

Language
Ask & Answer Questions
Key Words
Alphabetize Words
Proper & Possessive
  Nouns

Literacy
Details
Plan & Monitor

Content
Community Places &
  Events

Part 2

⬤ NGReach.com   Sing-with-Me MP3s ((MP3)) ▪ Read-with-Me MP3s ((MP3)) ▪ National Geographic Digital Library ▪
Interactive eEdition ▪ Games for learning ▪ My Vocabulary Notebook ▪ Online Resources

Unit 2

Staying Alive

(?) BIG QUESTION

What does it take to survive?

Science
- ▶ Animal Adaptation
- ▶ Animal Needs

🔵 NGReach.com   Sing-with-Me MP3s ((MP3)) ▪ Read-with-Me MP3s ((MP3)) ▪ National Geographic Digital Library ▪
Interactive eEdition ▪ Games for learning ▪ My Vocabulary Notebook ▪ Online Resources

Water for Everyone

(?) BIG QUESTION

Where does water come from?

Science
▸ Water Cycle
▸ Water as a Natural Resource

NGReach.com Sing-with-Me MP3s ((MP3)) ▪ Read-with-Me MP3s ((MP3)) ▪ National Geographic Digital Library ▪ Interactive eEdition ▪ Games for learning ▪ My Vocabulary Notebook ▪ Online Resources

Lend a Hand

(?) BIG QUESTION

What are our responsibilities to each other?

Social Studies
- Good Citizenship
- Making a Difference

Skills & Strategies

Language
Express Feelings & Ideas
Key Words
Suffixes
Complete Sentences

Literacy
Character Traits
Make Connections

Content
Citizenship

Part 1

Skills & Strategies

Language
Express Opinions
Key Words
Synonyms
Subject-Verb Agreement

Literacy
Sequence
Make Connections

Content
Citizenship

Part 2

🌐 **NGReach.com**   Sing-with-Me MP3s (((MP3))) ▪ Read-with-Me MP3s (((MP3))) ▪ National Geographic Digital Library ▪
Interactive eEdition ▪ Games for learning ▪ My Vocabulary Notebook ▪ Online Resources

Everything Changes

(?) **BIG QUESTION**

Why is nature always changing?

Science
▸ Cycles in Nature
▸ Seasons and Weather

⬤ NGReach.com   Sing-with-Me MP3s ((MP3)) ▪ Read-with-Me MP3s ((MP3)) ▪ National Geographic Digital Library ▪
Interactive eEdition ▪ Games for learning ▪ My Vocabulary Notebook ▪ Online Resources

Unit 6

Better Together

(?) BIG QUESTION

Why do people work together?

Social Studies
▶ Cooperation
▶ Working for the Common Good

Skills & Strategies

Language
Give & Carry Out
  Commands
Key Words
Prefixes
Pronouns

Literacy
Story Elements
Determine Importance
Parts of a Play

Content
Working Together

Part 1

Skills & Strategies

Language
Express Needs & Wants
Key Words
Context Clues
Possessive Pronouns

Literacy
Main Idea
Determine Importance

Content
Working Together

Part 2

◉ NGReach.com Sing-with-Me MP3s (((MP3))) ▪ Read-with-Me MP3s (((MP3))) ▪ National Geographic Digital Library ▪
Interactive eEdition ▪ Games for learning ▪ My Vocabulary Notebook ▪ Online Resources

Best Buddies

? BIG QUESTION

How do living things depend on each other?

Science
- ▸ Animal Partnerships
- ▸ Basic Needs

🌐 NGReach.com   Sing-with-Me MP3s (((MP3))) ▪ Read-with-Me MP3s (((MP3))) ▪ National Geographic Digital Library ▪
Interactive eEdition ▪ Games for learning ▪ My Vocabulary Notebook ▪ Online Resources

Unit 8

Our United States

(?) BIG QUESTION

What does America mean to you?

Social Studies
▸ Customs, Symbols, Celebrations, Landmarks
▸ National Identity

Unit Launch Build Background Video **472**

🌐 **NGReach.com**   Sing-with-Me MP3s ((MP3)) ▪ Read-with-Me MP3s ((MP3)) ▪ National Geographic Digital Library ▪ Interactive eEdition ▪ Games for learning ▪ My Vocabulary Notebook ▪ Online Resources

Genres at a Glance

Nonfiction

Hello, Neighbor!

BIG Question

What is a community?

Unit at a Glance
▶ **Language:** Give Information, Ask and Answer Questions
▶ **Literacy:** Plan and Monitor
▶ **Content:** Community

Unit 1

Share What You Know

Do It!

① **Think** of your favorite place in your neighborhood.

② **Draw** a picture of it. Label your picture with the name of the place.

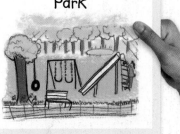

Park

③ **Say** why you like it. Work with your class. Combine your drawings to make a guide book of your neighborhood.

Build Background: Watch a video about communities.
NGReach.com

Give Information

Listen and sing.

Song (((MP3)))

Our Hometown Workers

Here is Nathaniel. **He** is a teacher,
He teaches reading at our school.
Here is his friend, Jae, who cooks
    at Jae's Place.
He makes cooking look so cool.

Here is Maria. **She** is a doctor.
Each year she checks my eyes and ears.
Now here is Vera. She is a good nurse.
When she gives shots there are no tears.

Tune: "La Cucaracha"

Key Words

What **jobs** do people do in a community?

doctor

cook

community workers

teacher

nurse

Talk Together

Act out a job for your class to guess. Tell how it helps people in your community.

5

Character

The **characters** are the people in a story. Use a character map to tell about the characters.

Character Map

Character	Who the character is	What the character's job is
Nathaniel	A community worker	He is a teacher. He teaches reading.
Maria	A community worker	She is a doctor. She checks my eyes and ears.

Write the character's name here.

Write who the character is and what the character does here.

Talk Together

Sing the song on page 4 with a partner. Together, make a character map for Jae and Vera.

More Key Words

belong
(bē-**long**) *verb*

These girls **belong** to a softball team.

build
(**bild**) *verb*

He uses wood and tools to **build** a birdhouse.

care
(**kair**) *verb*

People in families **care** about each other.

community
(ku-**myū**-nu-tē) *noun*

These people live in a small **community**.

neighbor
(**nā**-bur) *noun*

Say "hello" to a **neighbor** who lives next door.

Talk Together

Make a Vocabulary Example Chart for the **Key Words**. Compare your chart with a partner's.

Word	What It Means	Example from My Life
belong	be a part of	I belong to a girls' club.

Add words to My Vocabulary Notebook.
🌐 NGReach.com

Learn to Plan and Monitor

Before you read the cartoon, **preview** it. Look it over. Then make a guess about what might happen next. This is called a **prediction**.

When you read, you can **preview** and **predict**.

How to Preview and Predict

👁	**1.** Scan the text. Study the pictures. Think about what you will read.	I read _____. I see _____.
☁	**2.** Begin to read. Stop and make a prediction.	I predict _____.
🧩	**3.** As you read on, check if your prediction is correct. If it is not, use what you know to make a new prediction.	My prediction is _____.

Language Frames

👁 I read _____ .
I see _____ .
💭 I predict _____ .
🧩 My prediction is
_____ .

Talk Together

Read Kevin's journal entry and the sample prediction. Use **Language Frames** to tell a partner about your predictions.

Journal

September 15, 20__

   Today was both scary and fun! My mom picked me up early from school. "Come on, Kevin," she said. "We have places to go!"

   First, we went to the clinic. I saw my **doctor**. Her name is Dr. Lopez, and she **cares** for kids like me. Years ago, her father helped **build** the clinic! Dr. Lopez said that I am healthy. Yay! No more medicine! I left Dr. Lopez's office with a smile on my face.

   Then we went to a new restaurant called Jae's Place. The food was so good! Mom wanted to thank the **cook**. That's how we met Jae. He is new to our **community**. Mom told him that soon he will feel like he **belongs** here.

Sample Prediction

"I read that Kevin has to leave school early. I see a picture of the doctor.

I predict that Kevin is going to the clinic.

My prediction is correct."

◄ = A good place to preview and predict

Read a Story

Genre

This story tells about things that could really happen. It is **realistic fiction**.

Characters

Characters are the people in the story.

Quinito

Quinito's Neighbors

Quinito's Neighborhood

by **Ina Cumpiano**

illustrated by **José Ramírez**

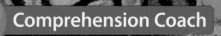
Comprehension Coach

▸ Set a Purpose

Meet some of the people in Quinito's neighborhood. Find out what **jobs** they do.

My *mami* is **a carpenter**. My *papi* is a **nurse**.

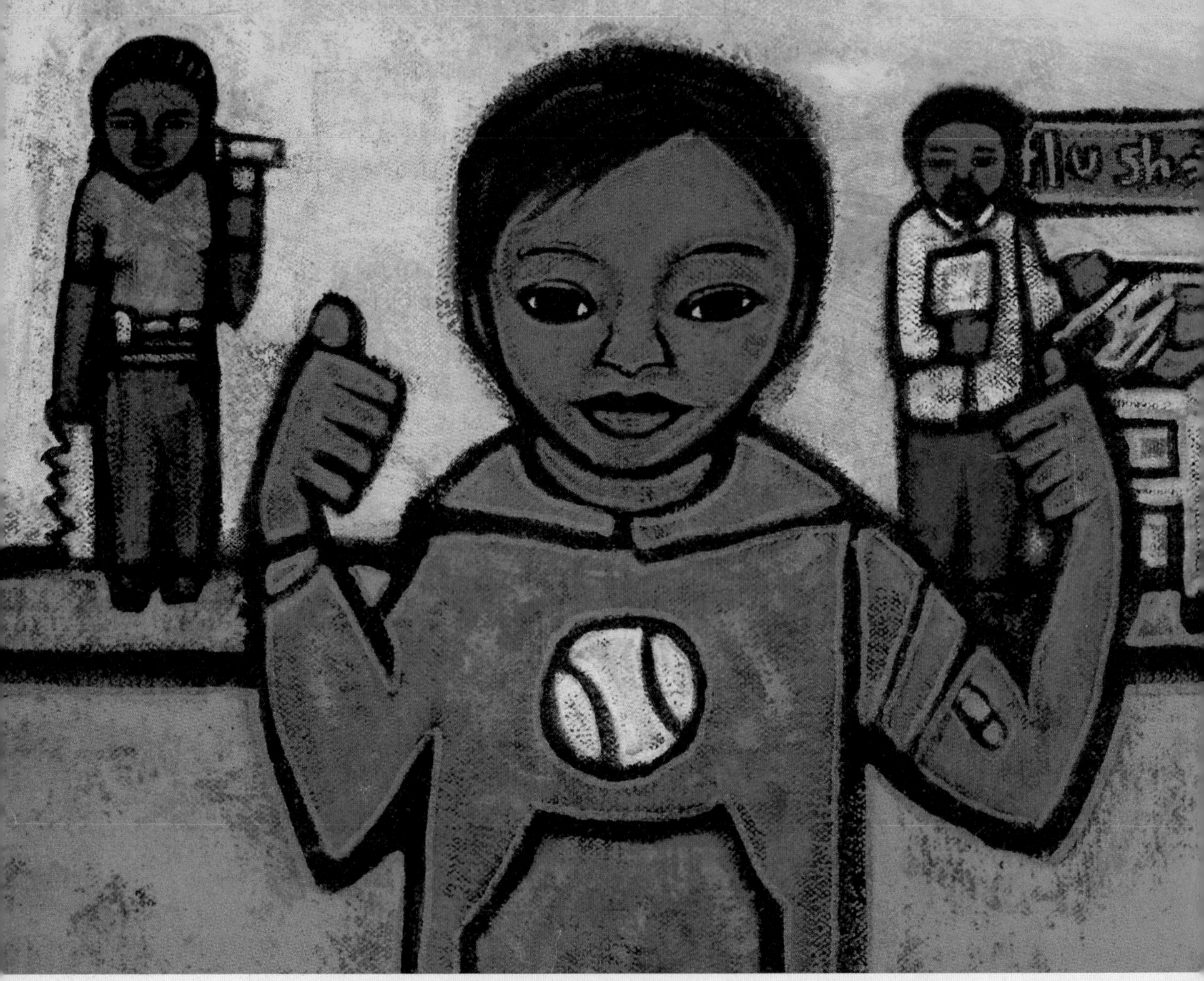

In Other Words

a carpenter someone who **builds** and fixes things made of wood

My **abuela** drives a big truck.
My **abuelo** fixes clocks.

Sometimes my *abuela* brings broken **grandfather clocks** to my *abuelo's* shop.

My *tía* is
a muralist.

My *tío*
teaches
dance.

In Other Words

tía aunt (in Spanish)

a muralist an artist who paints
   large pictures on walls

tío uncle (in Spanish)

My grown-up cousin,
Tita, goes to
clown school.

Her brother, my *primo*
Ruperto, is a dentist.
He **checks** people's teeth.

In Other Words
primo cousin (in Spanish)
checks takes **care** of

▶ **Before You Move On**
1. **Details** Name some of the people in Quinito's family. What **jobs** do they do?
2. **Clarify** What does Ruperto do at his job?

My **neighbor**, Rafi, **bakes** bread.

Mrs. Hernández sells it at her *bodega*.

In Other Words
bakes cooks in an oven
bodega grocery store
(in Spanish)

16

Her daughter, Sonia Isabel, counts the money in the bank **on the corner**.

In Other Words
on the corner at the end of the street

Guillermo is **our mailman**.

Guillermo is going to **marry** Sonia Isabel.

Doña Estrella is a **seamstress**.
She is sewing a wedding dress for Sonia Isabel.

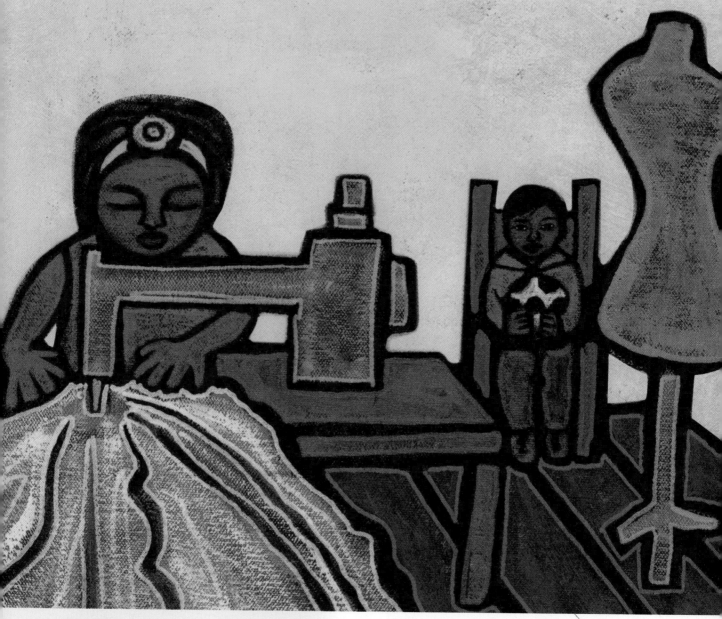

In Other Words

seamstress woman who makes clothes

▶ **Before You Move On**

1. **Confirm Prediction** Who else works in Quinito's community? Tell what they do.

2. **Character** How do Rafi and Mrs. Hernández help each other?

Predict

Look at the picture. Who will Quinito see on the way to school?

Mr. Gómez is Doña Estrella's neighbor.

He is also my **teacher** at school.

Mrs. Gómez is **a crossing guard**.

She helps me cross the street.

In Other Words

a crossing guard someone who helps people
walk across the street safely

I am a very busy person, too.

I have to tell Mr. Gómez
that my *mami* is a carpenter
and my *papi* is a nurse. ❖

▶ **Before You Move On**

1. **Confirm Prediction** Who does Quinito see on the way to school? Was your prediction correct? Explain.

2. **Character** How does Quinito feel about his **community**? How can you tell?

Meet the Author

Ina Cumpiano

AWARD WINNER

Like Quinito and the people in his neighborhood, Ina Cumpiano is very busy. Ms. Cumpiano has had many different jobs. She has been a translator and a poet. She has also written many children's books.

What is her favorite job? "Being a grandmother and playing with my grandchildren," she says.

▲ **Ina Cumpiano lives in a neighborhood in San Francisco, California.**

Writer's Craft

In *Quinito's Neighborhood*, each sentence starts with a capital letter and ends with a period. Draw a picture of someone in your family or neighborhood. Now, write a sentence about that person. Remember to use a capital letter and a period!

Talk About It 🗨

1. **What does Quinito do that you also do in real life?**

    Quinito _____ . I _____ in real life.

2. **Give information** about the people in "Quinito's Neighborhood." Tell about the **jobs** they do.

    Here is _____ . He is _____ . She is _____ .

3. How do Quinito and his **neighbors** help their community?

    They help the community by _____ .

Learn test-taking strategies.
⊘ NGReach.com

Write About It ✏

Do you know people who are like Quinito and his neighbors? Make a list of people you know. Name the jobs that they do.

People I Know	Job
Mom	teacher
Dad	barber
Aunt Laura	nurse

Character

Who are the characters in "Quinito's Neighborhood"?
What do they do?

Character Map

Character	Who the character is	What the character's job is
Mami and Papi	Quinito's parents	She is a carpenter. He is a nurse.
Guillermo		
Doña Estrella		

Now use your character map. Tell
a partner about the characters in
"Quinito's Neighborhood."

Here is _____.
He is _____.
She is _____.

Fluency ◖Comprehension Coach◗

Use the Comprehension Coach to practice reading with
the correct intonation. Rate your reading.

Multiple-Meaning Words

Some words have **more than one meaning**.

The word **cook** can tell about a person or an action.

1. My uncle is a **cook**.

2. I **cook** vegetables in a pan.

Try It Together

Read the sentences above and look at the pictures. Then follow the directions.

1. Read Sentence 1. Does **cook** tell about a person or an action?

2. Read Sentence 2. Does **cook** tell about a person or an action?

3. Choose one of the two meanings for **cook**. Write a new sentence that uses the word.

Connect Across Texts Now learn more about different **communities** and the work people do.

Genre A **photo-essay** is nonfiction. It uses photographs and text to tell about a topic.

WORKING HER WAY
Around the World

By Claire Cavanaugh

Photos by Annie Griffiths Belt, *National Geographic Photographer*

Annie Griffiths Belt **travels** the world and visits many **communities**. Her **job** is to take photos of what she sees.

These women in Rwanda get water for their community.

In Other Words
travels goes to different places in

▶ **Before You Move On**
1. **Predict** Reread the title. What do you think you will learn from this photo-essay?
2. **Clarify** What is Annie Griffiths Belt's **job**?

27

Everybody Works

There are many different jobs in every community. These photos show people at work. Look at all the different jobs people do! ❖

▲ In Nebraska, a cowboy and his horse work hard. They make sure the cattle stay together.

◀ A fisherman in Mozambique, Africa catches fish.

▲ The man is a **teacher** in Pakistan.

▲ This Pai Pai Indian grandmother takes **care** of her grandson in Mexico.

▶ **Before You Move On**

1. **Topic** What is the topic of the photo-essay? How do you know?

2. **Make Connections** Think about the jobs your family does. Describe a photograph you would add to the photo-essay.

Compare Genres

How are stories and photo-essays the same? How are they different?

Realistic Fiction

Doña Estrella is a **seamstress**.
She is sewing a wedding dress for Sonia Isabel.

> tells about things that could really happen

Photo-Essay

◀ A fisherman in Mozambique, Africa catches fish.

▲ The man is a teacher in Pakistan.

▲ This Pai Pai Indian grandmother takes care of her grandson in Mexico.

> uses photographs and text to tell about a topic

Talk Together

What is a **community**? Draw a picture to show people and places in a community. Use **Key Words** as labels. Then share your picture with the class.

Plural Nouns

A **noun** is a word that names a person, place, or thing.
A **singular noun** shows "one." A **plural noun** shows "more than one."

Grammar Rules Plural Nouns

	Singular	Plural
• Add -**s** to most nouns to show more than one.	street job	street**s** job**s**
• Add -**es** to nouns that end in **x**, **ch**, **sh**, **ss**, **z**, and sometimes **o**.	bench class	bench**es** class**es**
• For nouns that end in **y**, change **y** to **i** and then add -**es**.	baby sky	bab**ies** sk**ies**

Read Plural Nouns

Read this sentence from "Quinito's Neighborhood."
Can you find the plural noun?

My *abuelo* fixes clocks.

Write Plural Nouns

Look at the pictures on pages 27–29. Write a sentence about what you see. Be sure to use plural nouns correctly. Share your sentence with a partner.

High Frequency
Words

| it |
| what |
| where |

Ask and Answer Questions

Listen and sing.

New in Town

Song

I am new in town. Can you show me around?

Sure, I've lived in this town for three years.

What is this building? A library?

Yes, and this is my school over here!

And **where** is your home?

Here's my family's home. **It** is next to the hospital.

Will you be my friend in this great town?

Yes, of course. You can bet I will!

Tune: "You're a Grand Old Flag"

library

school

32

Key Words

Look at places in a city.

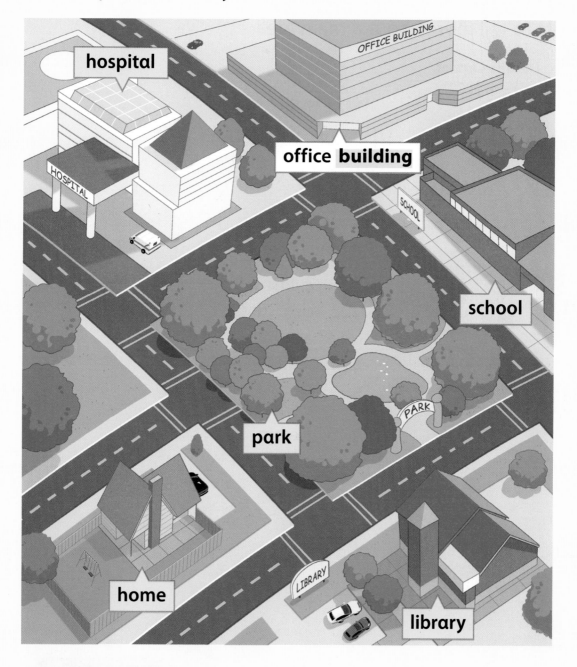

Point to the places that are in your community. What other buildings and places do you know? Tell a partner.

Details

The **main idea** is the big or most important idea. Use **details** to tell more about a main idea.

Details Cluster

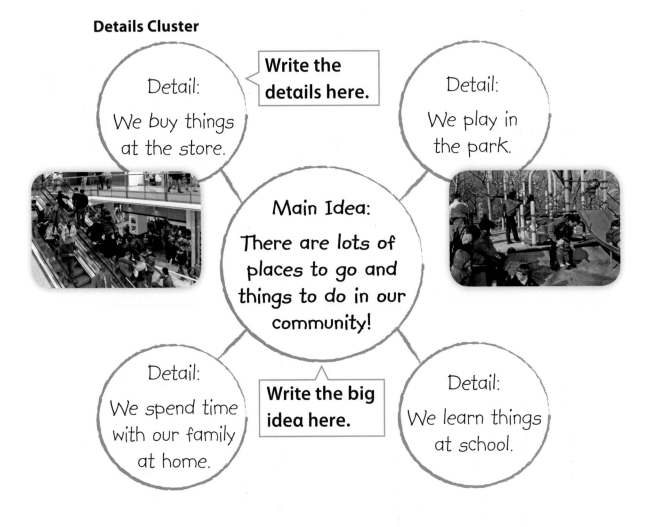

Write the details here.

Detail:
We buy things at the store.

Detail:
We play in the park.

Main Idea:
There are lots of places to go and things to do in our community!

Detail:
We spend time with our family at home.

Write the big idea here.

Detail:
We learn things at school.

Talk Together

Choose picture cards. Create a details cluster for places like these in your community.

More Key Words

area
(**air**-ē-u) *noun*

Water covers a large **area** of earth.

identify
(ī-**den**-tu-fī) *verb*

Mom helps Ana **identify** places on a map.

locate
(**lō**-kāt) *verb*

The girl **locates** the book she is looking for.

place
(**plās**) *noun*

This cabin is in a quiet **place** by a lake.

population
(pah-pyu-**lā**-shun) *noun*

Crowded cities have a very large **population** of people.

Talk Together

Make a Study Card for each **Key Word**. Then compare your cards with a partner's.

> locate
>
> What it means: to find
>
> Example: It is hard to locate a new place in the dark.

Add words to My Vocabulary Notebook.
NGReach.com

35

Learn to Plan and Monitor

When you do not understand something, you can try to **clarify** the meaning. Look at Picture 1. Then look for more information in Picture 2.

1. This man has pomegranates.

2. He sells his fruit at the Farmers' Market.

You can **clarify** ideas when you read, too.

How to Monitor and Clarify

👁	**1.** Read the text.	I read _____ .
❓	**2.** Stop to ask yourself what the text means.	I don't understand _____ .
🧩	**3.** If you do not understand, reread the text. If the meaning still is not clear, read on.	I think that _____ means "_____."

Language Frames

- 👁 I read _____ .
- ❓ I don't understand _____ .
- 🧩 I think that _____ means "_____."

Talk Together

Read Cleo's report about "The Farmers' Market." Then use **Language Frames** to tell a partner about how you figured out the text's meaning.

Report

The Farmers' Market

Sample Clarification

I read the title.

I don't understand what Farmers' Market means.

I think that Farmers' Market means "a place where people buy and sell food."

Are you looking for a great **place** to visit? Try the Farmers' Market. It is **located** in back of the city **park**. It is held every Thursday evening.

Farmers come from farms in rural **areas** about two hours from the city. They pick fresh fruits and vegetables in the morning. Then they drive to our urban park. They set out their food and wait for people to come.

I am there almost every week. It is always crowded. Sometimes it seems like the entire **population** of our city is out shopping and talking. I don't mind the crowds. I love to buy fresh food, but I love to watch people even more!

◀ = A good place to monitor and clarify as you read

Read a Photo-Essay

Genre

A **photo-essay** is nonfiction. It uses words and photos to tell about a topic.

Text Features

Look for **photos** with **captions**. They help you understand the text better.

photo

caption

▲ This neighborhood in Japan has a large population.

Be My Neighbor

by **Maya Ajmera**
and **John D. Ivanko**

▶ **Set a Purpose**
Find out what neighborhoods are
like and why they are special.

A Special Place

A neighborhood is where you live, learn, play, and
work. There are neighborhoods all around the world.

▲ **Children play in a
neighborhood in Israel.**

40

▲ This neighborhood in Japan has a large **population**.

Some neighborhoods have a large **population**. Others have a very small population. Still, every neighborhood is a special **place**.

This neighborhood in Spain has a small **population**.▶

▶ **Before You Move On**

1. **Use Text Features** What do the captions tell about the photos?

2. **Author's Purpose** Why did the authors write this photo-essay? How do the photographs help?

41

Some neighborhoods **are just** a few **buildings** in a **village**. Others **stretch for miles** and are part of a big **city**.

This neighborhood is in a **city** in Brazil.

▲ This small neighborhood is in the countryside of Tanzania.

In Other Words
are just have only
village small town
stretch for miles are large

Many neighborhoods have a town square or a plaza in the middle. It is a good place to meet and **share news**.

A town square in Italy.

In Other Words
share news talk about families and ideas

▶ **Before You Move On**

1. **Clarify** What is a town square? What can you learn about it from this photo and the words?

2. **Make Inferences** Why is a town square in the middle of a neighborhood?

A Place to Live

A **home** can be a place for one family or many families. Home is where people feel safe and **comfortable**.

In Hong Kong, many families live in apartments.

▲ One family lives in this house in the Bahamas.

In Other Words
comfortable happy

▲ Students learn inside
a classroom in Cuba.

These children in Ethiopia
go to **school** outside. ▶

A Place to Learn

Neighborhoods have many kinds of schools.
Some schools have a lot of rooms. Some have
just one room. Some students learn inside a
building. Others learn outside.

▶ **Before You Move On**

1. **Ask Questions** Ask a partner a question
about the text on pages 44–45. How did
your partner know the answer?

2. **Details** How are **schools** the same? How
are they different?

A Place to Play

In many neighborhoods, you can find a **park** or a **playground**. People go there to play.

▼ Children in Finland play baseball in the park.

In Other Words

playground **place** for children to run, jump, and climb

A Place to Shop

Most neighborhoods have markets, **shopping malls**, or **grocery stores**. Families can buy what they need at these places.

Families in Mexico buy food at an outdoor market.

▶ **Before You Move On**

1. **Use Text Features** Look at the photo of the park. What do people do there?
2. **Details** Name three things you can buy at the market shown on page 47.

A Place to Work

People work together to make a neighborhood a better place. Neighbors might clean up a river or a park. Doctors and **firefighters** work to take care of people.

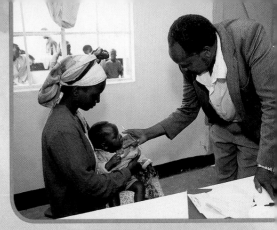

▲ A **doctor** takes care of a sick child at a **hospital** in Kenya.

▲ Neighbors clean up part of a river in the United States.

In Other Words
◀ **firefighters** people who stop fires

A Place to Celebrate

Special **events** bring a community together. **Parades**, parties, and **holidays** are times for fun and great food.

▼ These children in Paris, France, celebrate the Chinese New Year.

In Other Words
events things that happen
Parades Music and dancing in the street
holidays special days

▶ **Before You Move On**

1. **Clarify** What do some people do to make a neighborhood better?
2. **Use Text Features** Look at the photos on page 48 and read the captions. What do they help you remember?

49

We Are Neighbors

Neighbors share the place where they live.
You are a part of your neighborhood and
it's a part of you.

UNITED STATES

MEXICO

BAHAMAS

CUBA

BRAZIL

MAURITAI

N
W E
S

In Other Words

it's a part of you it is
an important part of
your life

It's the place you call home.
Be my neighbor,
wherever you live. ❖

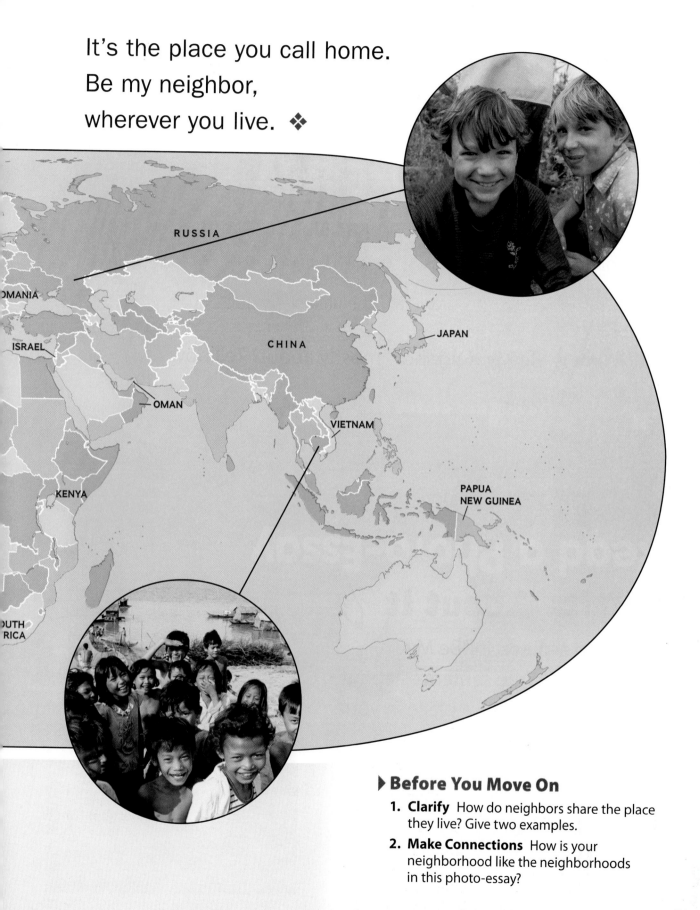

RUSSIA

ROMANIA

ISRAEL

CHINA

JAPAN

OMAN

VIETNAM

KENYA

PAPUA
NEW GUINEA

SOUTH
AFRICA

▶ **Before You Move On**

1. **Clarify** How do neighbors share the place they live? Give two examples.
2. **Make Connections** How is your neighborhood like the neighborhoods in this photo-essay?

Talk About It

1. What do you learn from the photos and captions in the **photo-essay** "Be My Neighbor"?

    The photos show _____ . The captions tell _____ .

2. **Ask a question** about "Be My Neighbor." Look back through the photo-essay to **locate** the **answer**.

    I ask myself, _____ ? I can find the answer by _____ .

3. What is "Be My Neighbor" mostly about? Tell how you know.

    It is mostly about _____ . I know because _____ .

Learn test-taking strategies.
NGReach.com

Write About It

Point to a **place** in "Be My Neighbor." Write sentences about it. Tell how it is like a place in your community.

_____ is like _____ in my community.
The places are alike because _____ .

Details

Make a details cluster for "Be My Neighbor." Look for details that tell more about the main idea.

Details Cluster

Now use your details cluster. Tell a partner about the main ideas and details in "Be My Neighbor."

The main idea is _____ .
One detail is _____ .
Another detail is _____ .

Fluency

Use the Comprehension Coach to practice reading with the correct phrasing. Rate your reading.

Alphabetize Words

To find words in a dictionary, put the **words in order** of the letters of the alphabet.

These words are in order by the **first letter.**

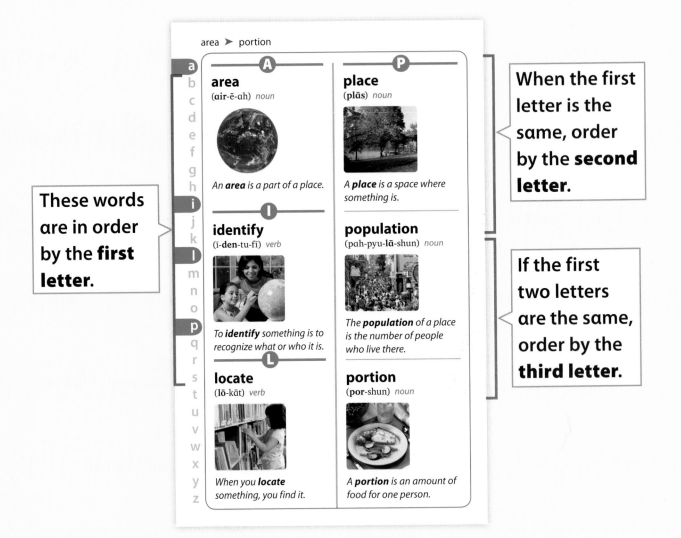

area ➤ portion

area
(air-ē-ah) *noun*

*An **area** is a part of a place.*

identify
(ī-**den**-tu-fī) *verb*

*To **identify** something is to recognize what or who it is.*

locate
(lō-kāt) *verb*

*When you **locate** something, you find it.*

place
(plās) *noun*

*A **place** is a space where something is.*

population
(pah-pyu-**lā**-shun) *noun*

*The **population** of a place is the number of people who live there.*

portion
(**por**-shun) *noun*

*A **portion** is an amount of food for one person.*

When the first letter is the same, order by the **second letter.**

If the first two letters are the same, order by the **third letter.**

Try It Together

place, **park**, **population**

1. List the three words in alphabetical order.

2. Add the words **pole** and **pond** to the list.

My Favorite Place

What Is Your Favorite Place In Your Community?

http://ngreach.com

KidsFavorites

Today's Posts | Calendar | Announcements | News | Search   REGISTER | SIGN IN

| **Question:** | **What is your favorite place in your community?** |

17 Jan, 4:00 PM

Leah

RE: What is your favorite place in your community?

My favorite place is the park. There is room to run and play hide-and-seek or tag. Plus it's a great place to take our dog.

Age: 7

School: Valley View

▶ **Before You Move On**

1. **Details** Why does Leah like the park?
2. **Preview/Predict** Look at the photos on the next two pages. What do you think kids will like about each **place**?

17 Jan, 4:30 PM

Evan

Age: 7

School:
Monte Vista

RE: What is your favorite place in your community?

I like the library. You can read books on the floor and play on the computers. There's a huge tree outside to climb that you can read under too.

17 Jan, 4:35 PM

Zoe

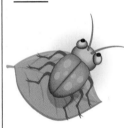

Age: 8

School:
Seaside
Elementary

RE: What is your favorite place in your community?

My favorite place is the river. We can walk there. I like to see all the bugs and nature there.

Thomas

Age: 8

School:
  Valley View

RE: What is your favorite place in your community?

My favorite place is the **zoo**. I love going there. My favorite things are animals. You can learn a lot about animals there. You should **visit** the zoo some time.

Post Reply

In Other Words

zoo **place** where you can see wild animals

visit go to see

▶ **Before You Move On**

1. **Confirm Prediction** What did the kids like about each **place**? How did the photos help you predict what they liked?

2. **Clarify** Why does Evan like the library so much?

Compare Media

"Be My Neighbor" is a photo-essay in a book. "My Favorite Place" is a bulletin board on the Internet. Compare the ways these two types of media give information.

Comparison Chart

	Photo-Essay	Internet Bulletin Board
has photos	✔	✔
has captions	✔	
has more than one writer		
gives facts		
asks and answers questions		
lets people share ideas and communicate		

> This is true for both.

> This is only true for one.

Talk Together

What is a community? Point to photos in "Be My Neighbor." Use **Key Words** to tell a partner something special about the **places** and events you see.

Proper and Possessive Nouns

A **proper noun** is the name of just one person, place, or thing. A **possessive noun** tells who owns something.

Grammar Rules Proper and Possessive Nouns

• Proper nouns begin with a **capital letter**.	**M**arco **N**ew **Y**ork **E**mpire **S**tate **B**uilding
• Titles of people, like Mr. or Mrs., begin with a **capital letter** and end with a **period**.	**M**rs. Gomez **D**r. Foster **M**r. Chang
• Add an **apostrophe** and an **-s** to the name of a person to show that he or she owns something.	Rachel**'s** ball Marco**'s** homework Mr. Chang**'s** bike

Read Proper and Possessive Nouns

Read these sentences. What proper and possessive nouns can you find?

Mr. Powell's house is in the Bahamas.

Families in Mexico buy food at a market.

Write Proper and Possessive Nouns 🖉

Look at the photos in "Be My Neighbor." Rewrite a caption to use proper and possessive nouns. Share your caption with a partner.

Write as a Community Member

Make a Photo-Essay

Think of a person who makes your community special. Use a picture and words to describe the person. Add your description to a class photo-essay.

Study a Model

A photo-essay uses pictures and words to describe something. Look at Miguel's photo essay about his neighbor.

A Good Neighbor
by Miguel Martinez

Kay Hoskins takes care of homeless dogs and cats. She finds homes where they can live. Kay helps each animal stay happy and healthy.

Kay gives each animal a lot of attention.

Kay finds a good home for a cat.

Many families find happy, healthy pets at Kay's animal shelter.

The **topic sentence** gives the main idea. It tells whom the essay is about.

Each picture shows something about the person.

Each **caption** gives details about the person.

The **conclusion** sums up all the ideas.

Prewrite

1. **Choose a Topic** Talk with a partner. Choose an interesting person to describe.

I think _____ really helps our community.

_____ sounds interesting. Tell me what he/she does.

2. **Get Organized** Use a details cluster to show what you know about the person.

Details Cluster

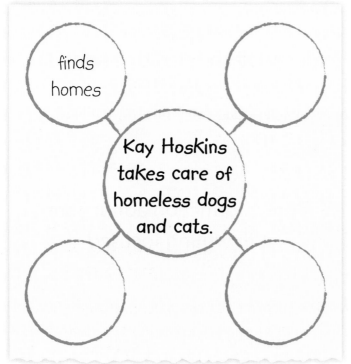

finds homes

Kay Hoskins takes care of homeless dogs and cats.

Draft

Use your details cluster to write a draft.

*   Write a topic sentence that names the person.

*   Turn the details into sentences.

Revise

1. **Read, Retell, Respond** Read your draft aloud to a partner. Your partner retells the ideas. Next, talk about ways to make your writing better.

Your photo-essay is about _____ .

You should tell more about _____ .

2. **Make Changes** Think about your partner's ideas. Then show your changes. Use the Revising Marks on page 563.

   - Take out details that don't tell about your neighbor.

     Kay Hoskins takes care of homeless dogs and cats. ~~My favorite~~ ~~kind of pet is a parakeet.~~

   - Add details that give more information about your main idea. That will keep your writing focused.

     She finds homes where they can live.
     Kay Hoskins takes care of homeless dogs and cats.
     ∧

Edit and Proofread

Work with a partner to edit and proofread your description. Pay special attention to nouns.

Spelling Tip

✔ Use **-s** or **-es** to make most nouns plural.

Capitalize proper nouns.

Publish

On Your Own Make a final copy of your writing. Include your picture and caption. Then show the picture as you tell your classmates about your neighbor.

Presentation Tips	
If you are the speaker…	**If you are the listener…**
Speak slowly and clearly.	Match what you hear to what you see in the picture.
Hold up your picture as you talk.	Think of questions you want to ask.

With a Group Use all the pictures and descriptions to make a photo-essay of the people in your neighborhood.

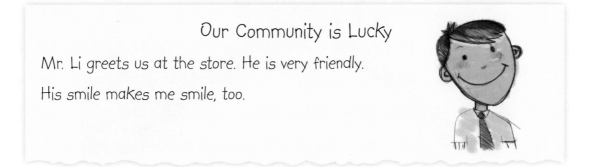

Our Community is Lucky

Mr. Li greets us at the store. He is very friendly. His smile makes me smile, too.

| ? BIG Question | What is a community? |

Talk Together

In this unit, you found lots of answers to the **Big Question**. Now use your concept map to discuss the **Big Question** with the class.

Concept Map

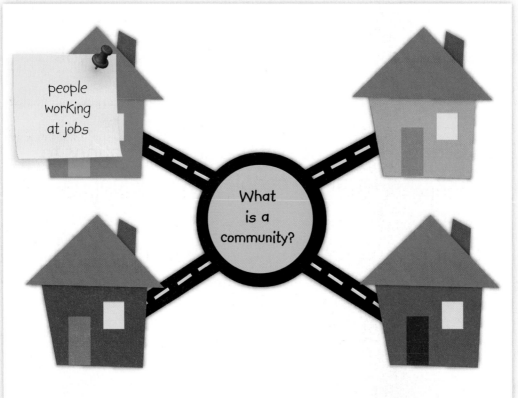

people working at jobs

What is a community?

Share Your Ideas

Choose one of these ways to share your ideas about the **Big Question**.

Write It!

Draw a Map

Imagine a new community. Name it. What places are in it? Draw a map. Label the buildings and streets.

Do It!

Make a Commercial

Pretend it is your job to tell people about your community. Think of the special things you want them to know. Plan a commercial. Work with classmates to present it.

Do It!

Sing a Song

Work with your class to make a new song. Start with the tune for "Old MacDonald." Take turns adding information about a person or place in your town.

Talk About It!

Conduct an Interview

Ask your classmates what job they would like to do in the community. Discuss what they like about the job.

Staying Alive

BIG Question

What does it take to survive?

Unit at a Glance
▶ **Language:** Describe, Explain
▶ **Literacy:** Make Inferences
▶ **Content:** Adaptations, Needs

Unit
2

Share What You Know

Do It!

❶ **Look** at pictures of animals and places in nature.

❷ **Match** the animals with their homes.

❸ **Talk** with a partner about things that might help the animals live in each place.

Build Background: Use this interactive resource to learn how animals survive.
 NGReach.com

Describe

Listen and sing.

Where Can My Butterfly Be? *Song* ((MP3))

Oh where, oh where can my
   butterfly be?
Oh where, oh where did it fly?
It **has** brown wings, and it flew **to**
   this tree.
It's hard to find, but I'll try!

Its wings blend into this habitat.
It flutters down and sits still.
Its wings **look** like the brown leaves
   on this tree.
It's hard to find, but I will!

Tune: "Oh Where, Oh Where Has My Little Dog Gone?"

Key Words

How do **animals** and **insects** look? How does this help them in their **habitat**?

color | The lizard is green.

The polar bear is white.

shape | The fish has an oval spot.

The puffer fish is round.

size | This bear is big.

This ladybug is tiny.

Talk Together

Tell about the animals and insects on this page. How do you think their color, shape, and size help them survive?

Plot

The **plot** is what happens in a story. The story events happen in order. Show this in a story map.

Beginning-Middle-End Chart

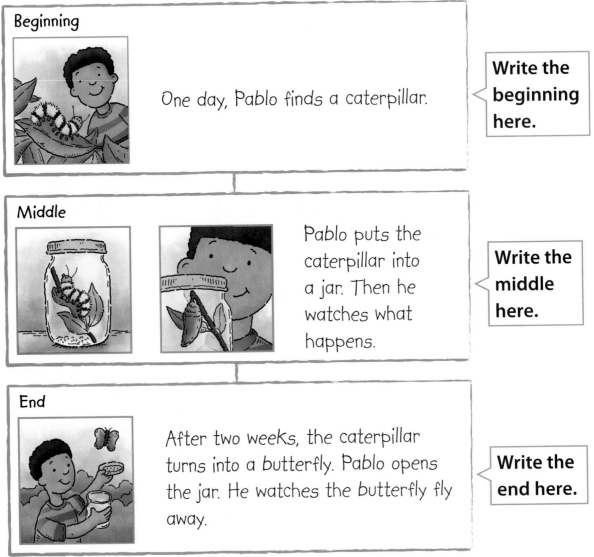

Beginning

One day, Pablo finds a caterpillar.

> Write the beginning here.

Middle

Pablo puts the caterpillar into a jar. Then he watches what happens.

> Write the middle here.

End

After two weeks, the caterpillar turns into a butterfly. Pablo opens the jar. He watches the butterfly fly away.

> Write the end here.

Talk Together

Tell your partner about a nature walk you took or would like to take. Your partner makes a story map.

More Key Words

adaptation
(a-dap-**tā**-shun) *noun*

A turtle's hard shell is an **adaptation** that keeps it safe.

defend
(di-**fend**) *verb*

The mother **defends** her baby so that it does not get hurt.

hide
(**hīd**) *verb*

She **hides** the gift so her dad cannot see it.

safe
(**sāf**) *adjective*

He wears a helmet to keep his head **safe** in case he falls.

survive
(sur-**vīv**) *verb*

Penguins **survive** cold weather by standing together to stay warm.

Talk Together

Work with a partner. Use **Key Words** to ask and answer questions.

How do some animals _defend_ their young?

They _hide_ them to keep them safe.

Add words to My Vocabulary Notebook.
🔵 NGReach.com

Learn to Make Inferences

Look at the cartoon. Pablo is excited. The text does not say why. Look at the picture to figure out, or **make an inference**, about why he is excited.

BUTTERFLY HOUSE

Hurry up, Dad!

You can **make inferences** to help you understand what you read and see.

How to Make Inferences

👁	**1.** Read the text. Look at the pictures.	I read _____ .
☁	**2.** Think about what you already know.	I know _____ .
🧩	**3.** Use what you know and what you read to figure out more.	And so _____ .

Talk Together

Read Pablo's journal. Read the sample inference. Then use **Language Frames** to tell a partner about your inferences.

Journal

Saturday, May 15, 2010

Today Dad brought me to the Butterfly House at the zoo. The Butterfly House has hundreds of butterflies that you can look at.

While we were there, my dad told me all about butterflies. He said that when butterflies land on flowers, they are not playing. They are really getting food. Butterflies need flowers to **survive**. Dad also said that some butterflies **hide** in trees and plants. Butterflies don't have many ways to **defend** themselves. However, their coloring is one **adaptation** that keeps them **safe**.

We are already planning another trip to the Butterfly House. Next time, I want to bring my camera!

Sample Inference

"I read that Pablo went to the Butterfly House at the zoo.

I know that Pablo likes butterflies.

And so I can guess that Pablo has a great time."

◀ = A good place to make an inference

73

Read a Story

Genre

This story tells about things that could really happen. It is **realistic fiction**.

Plot

The events in a story are the plot.

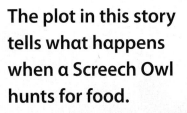

The plot in this story tells what happens when a Screech Owl hunts for food.

Twilight Hunt

A Seek-and-Find Story

written and illustrated
by Narelle Oliver

▶ **Set a Purpose**
A Screech Owl hunts for food. Will
it find what it needs to **survive**?

It is **twilight.** The babies **are hungry**.
The Screech Owl's **hunt** must begin.

◀ Screech Owl

In Other Words
twilight early night
are hungry need food
hunt search for food

On **silent** wings, the Screech Owl flies.

It watches for **movement**. It listens for tiny sounds.

At that moment a Bark Moth **flutters toward** a tree.

Bark Moth ▶

In Other Words
silent quiet
movement **animals** or **insects** that move
flutters toward flies to

Can the Screech Owl **snap it up**?
The moth **has disappeared**.

In Other Words

snap it up catch the moth
has disappeared has gone
where it cannot be seen

Nearby a Katydid **hops**.
The Screech Owl follows it.

Katydid ▶

In Other Words
Nearby Close by
hops jumps

▶ **Before You Move On**

1. **Sequence** What does the Screech Owl do at the beginning of the story? Why?
2. **Plot** What happens when the Screech Owl sees the Bark Moth and Katydid?

▶ **Predict**
What will the Katydid and the
other **insects** and **animals** do?

In a flash, the Katydid **has
vanished**.

In Other Words
In a flash Quickly
has vanished has gone away

80

Out from the leaves, a Treefrog
jumps.

Treefrog ▶

All of a sudden, it is **nowhere to be found**.

In Other Words

All of a sudden Just then; Suddenly

nowhere to be found gone

A Lizard **scuttles** up a speckled rock.
In the blink of an eye, there is **no
trace of it at all**.

Lizard ▶

▶ **Before You Move On**

1. **Plot** Was your prediction correct? How did
   the Katydid stay **safe**?
2. **Make Inferences** Why is it so hard
   for the Screech Owl to catch **insects**
   and **animals**?

▶ **Predict**
Will the Screech Owl ever
find food?

Finally, a **giant** Luna Moth **drifts** down.
There is no **escape**. The hunt is over.

◀ **Luna Moth**

84

Far away, a Great Horned Owl
is watching.

Great Horned Owl ▶

Sensing danger, the Screech Owl
swoops to land.

With feathers pulled tight, the
Screech Owl has disappeared.
So, the Great Horned Owl **flies on**.

The Screech Owl waits. It is silent and **still**.

Then **noiseless** wings take the **hunter** home. ❖

In Other Words
still not moving
noiseless quiet
hunter Screech Owl

▶ **Before You Move On**
1. **Plot** Does the Screech Owl find food? What happens?
2. **Make Inferences** Why do you think the Screech Owl hides from the Great Horned Owl?

Meet the Author

Narelle Oliver

As a girl growing up in Australia, Narelle Oliver enjoyed exploring the local countryside. Now, Ms. Oliver writes and illustrates children's books about nature. Before she wrote *Twilight Hunt,* Ms. Oliver explored the forests where owls live.

▲ Narelle Oliver writes books that help people learn about nature.

Writer's Craft

The writer uses precise words such as *flutters* and *swoops* to tell exactly how animals and insects move. Find more precise words. Say each word as you act out how something moves.

Talk About It

1. What is something from the story that a Screech Owl does in **real life**? Read it aloud.

   The Screech Owl _____ .

2. Choose an **animal** from the story. **Describe** what you know about its **color**, **shape**, and **size**.

   The _____ is _____ . It has _____ .

3. The Screech Owl hunts for food at twilight. Tell about another animal and how it finds its food.

   When the _____ hunts, it _____ .

Learn test-taking strategies.
⊘ NGReach.com

Write About It

Find your favorite picture in "Twilight Hunt." Write a caption to tell what is happening.

This picture shows _____ .

Plot

What happens at the beginning, middle, and end of "Twilight Hunt"?

Beginning-Middle-End Chart

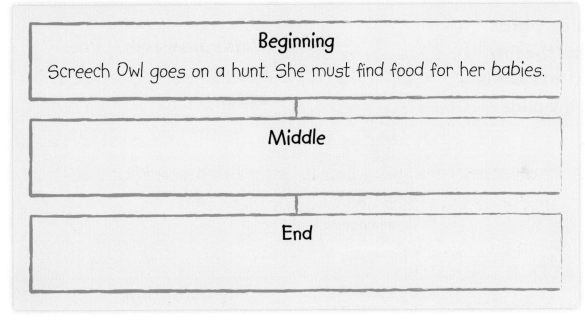

> **Beginning**
> Screech Owl goes on a hunt. She must find food for her babies.
>
> **Middle**
>
> **End**

Now use your chart. Tell your partner the plot, or what happens in "Twilight Hunt."

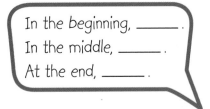

In the beginning, _____ .
In the middle, _____ .
At the end, _____ .

Fluency

Comprehension Coach

Use the Comprehension Coach to practice reading with the correct expression. Rate your reading.

Use a Dictionary

You can **look in a dictionary** for word meanings. Use alphabetical order to find the words. Find the word **adaptation** in the dictionary.

Guide words show the first and last words on the page.

Words are listed in **alphabetical order**.

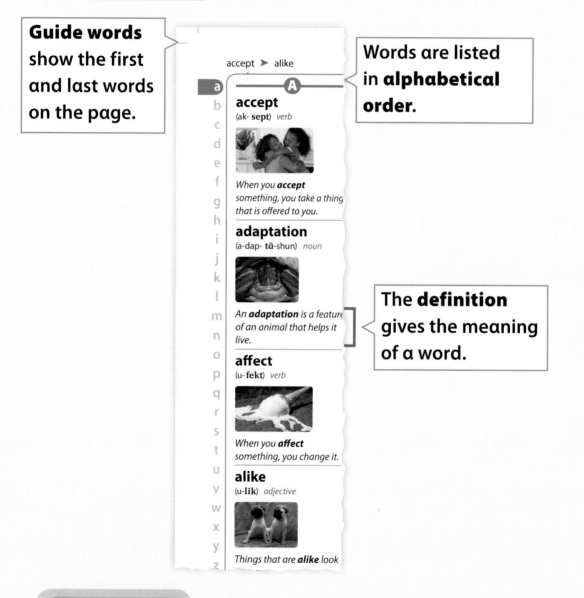

accept ➤ alike

accept
(ak- **sept**) *verb*

*When you **accept** something, you take a thing that is offered to you.*

adaptation
(a-dap- **tā**-shun) *noun*

*An **adaptation** is a feature of an animal that helps it live.*

affect
(u- **fekt**) *verb*

*When you **affect** something, you change it.*

alike
(u-līk) *adjective*

*Things that are **alike** look*

The **definition** gives the meaning of a word.

Try It Together

What words come after **adaptation** on this dictionary page? Where would you find the word **amaze**?

Connect Across Texts Find out how some living things **hide** in their **habitats**.

Genre A **science article** can give facts about living things.

Hide and Seek

From *Weekly Reader*

Habitats

Animals and insects live in different habitats. To stay safe, they use camouflage. This helps them blend into their environments. On the next pages, see if you can find the hidden creatures.

▲ There are many trees in a forest.

The waters of the ocean are filled with life. ▼

▲ A rain forest gets a lot of rain each year.

In Other Words

use camouflage hide by looking like the things around them

blend into their environments look like their **habitats**

In a forest, trees give **shelter** and food. Here, a mantis uses its **shape** to hide in leaves.

◀ A mantis is on this plant. Can you find it?

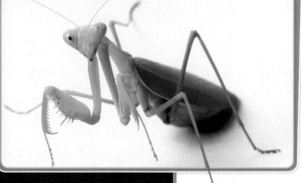

praying mantis

In Other Words
shelter safe places to live

▶ **Before You Move On**

1. **Make Inferences** How does camouflage help **animals** and **insects** stay **safe**?
2. **Predict** Look at the pictures on pages 96–97. What do you think you will learn on those pages?

Oceans

In the ocean, many animals use **color** to **match** their habitat. Do you see the goby fish?

goby fish

▲ **Where is the goby fish in this photo?**

In Other Words
match look like

Rain Forests

A rain forest is home to many plants, animals, and insects. Here, a leaf katydid uses its shape and color to look like a plant.

leaf katydid

▲ A leaf katydid is **hiding**. Can you find it?

▶ **Before You Move On**

1. **Confirm Prediction** What did you learn about **animals** and **insects** on pages 96 and 97? Was your prediction correct?

2. **Make Inferences** How does camouflage help a leaf katydid to **survive**?

Compare Genres

How are "Twilight Hunt" and "Hide and Seek" the same?
How are they different?

Realistic Fiction

Science Article

tells about things that could really happen

gives facts about living things

 **Talk Together**

What does it take to **survive**? Draw a picture of an **animal** in its **habitat**. Then tell the class how the animal survives there. Use **Key Words** as labels.

Action and Helping Verbs

An **action verb** tells what someone or something does.
Sometimes a **helping verb** works with an action verb.

Grammar Rules Action and Helping Verbs	
For Action Verbs	
• Use **-s** at the end of an action verb if the subject is **he**, **she**, or **it**. • Do not use **-s** for **I**, **you**, **we**, or **they**.	A Screech Owl **hunts**. She **hunts**. The mother owls **hunt**. They **hunt**.
For Action Verbs with Helping Verbs	
• A **helping verb** comes before the **main verb**.	A Katydid **can vanish**. Katydids **can vanish**. A tree frog **might jump**. Tree frogs **might jump**.

Read Action and Helping Verbs

Read these sentences. Find the action and helping verbs.

Lizards can scuttle up the rock.

The Great Horned Owl does not see the Screech Owl.

Write Action and Helping Verbs

Write two sentences that describe what the Screech Owl does. Use action and helping verbs. Share your sentences with a partner.

99

Explain

Listen and chant.

Chant (((MP3)))

Sea Creatures and Their Features

The firefly squid is tiny but bright.
Its tentacles light up the sea.
It **uses** blue light to catch its prey,
But it just looks pretty to me!

A hammerhead shark is twenty feet long.
It has teeth **in** its mouth to tear food.
It eats lots of prey, like shy stingray.
That hammerhead's one scary dude.

hammerhead
shark

firefly squid

stingray

Key Words

Look at the photos.

water

food

shelter to stay safe

What do animals need?

to catch **prey**

to hide from **predators**

features that help them adapt to their habitat

Talk Together

Look at the picture of the giraffe. What features does a giraffe use to survive?

Compare

A group is made up of things that are alike. You can use groups to **compare** things, or tell how they go together.

Comparison Chart

Features	Creatures
has tentacles  	
has sharp teeth  	
has fins 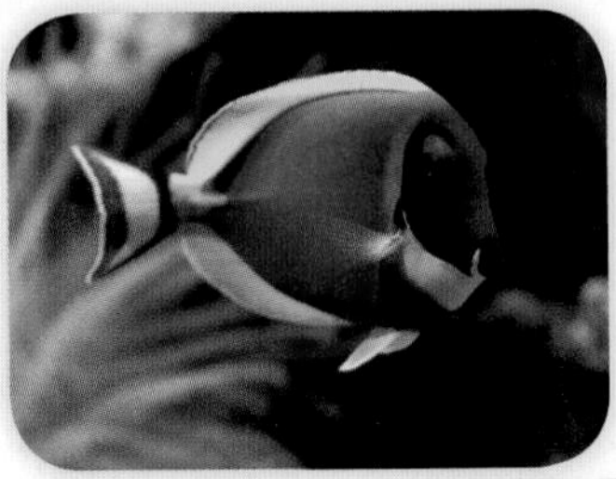 	

Write ways to group animals here.

Put like things together.

Talk Together

Choose picture cards of these and other animals. Find ways that animals are alike. Group them in a comparison chart.

More Key Words

attack
(u-**tak**) *verb*

Some animals **attack** other animals to say "go away"!

attract
(u-**trakt**) *verb*

The light from a bulb will **attract** a moth to it.

message
(**me**-sij) *noun*

You can send a **message** for a friend to read.

recognize
(**re**-kig-nīz) *verb*

It's easy to **recognize** people that you know.

seem
(**sēm**) *verb*

The game **seems** hard, but it is really easy to play.

Talk Together

Make a Vocabulary Example Chart for each **Key Word**. Then compare your chart with a partner's.

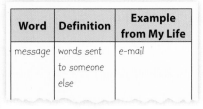

Word	Definition	Example from My Life
message	words sent to someone else	e-mail

Add words to My Vocabulary Notebook.
NGReach.com

Learn to Make Inferences

Look at the two photos. Read the text. Then think of what you know about animal adaptations. Put your ideas together to figure something out, or **make an inference**.

When it is in danger, the puffer fish gets big.

You can **make inferences** about things you read.

How to Make Inferences

👁	**1.** Look for details in the text.	I read _____ .
☁	**2.** Think about what you already know.	I know _____ .
🧩	**3.** Put your ideas together. What else can you figure out?	And so _____ .

Talk Together

Read Maryam's oral report. Read the sample inference. Then use **Language Frames** to tell a partner about your inferences.

Oral Report

Tropical Fish

Many people choose tropical fish as pets. Before buying any fish, you need to find out which fish make the best pets.

Betta fish are a popular choice. They **seem** pretty and cheerful. But male bettas are not cheerful at all! They **attack** all other fish. Bettas send out a clear **message**: "We need space!"

Pet owners are also **attracted** to angelfish. You may **recognize** them because of their long stripes. These shy fish are not like bettas. Wild angelfish use their stripes to hide in long plants. Big fish cannot catch them. It is a special **feature** that helps the little fish survive.

Sample Inference

"I read that betta fish attack other fish.

I know that people usually keep fish together in aquariums.

And so I know that pet owners should not put betta fish with other fish."

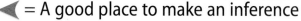

◀ = A good place to make an inference

Read a Science Article

Genre

A **science article** gives information. This one tells how some living things survive.

Text Features

Look for **headings**. They tell what the parts of the article are about.

heading [

Lights That Help Mushrooms

Mushrooms have spores. A spore is like a seed. The mushrooms spit their spores into the air. The wind carries the spores to new places where they grow into new mushrooms.

NATIONAL
GEOGRAPHIC

Living Lights

by **Dr. Dennis Desjardin**

Professor of Biology, San Francisco State University

Comprehension Coach

▶ **Set a Purpose**
Find out how some living things
use light to survive.

Lights at My Feet

I was in a forest in Brazil (bru-**zil**).
Strange lights were all around my
feet. They looked like stars on the
ground. They were mushrooms!

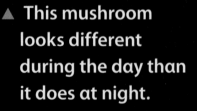

▲ This mushroom
looks different
during the day than
it does at night.

◀ These mushrooms
glow in the dark.

In Other Words
glow shine

108

The mushrooms were bioluminescent (bī-ō-lū-mu-**ne**-sunt). They could make light.

I am a **scientist**. I study mushrooms. I wanted to learn more about them and other living lights. Turn the pages to see what I learned.

▲ Here I am studying mushrooms.

◀ Bioluminescent mushrooms

▶ **Before You Move On**

1. **Use Text Features** Point to the heading. What does it tell you?
2. **Make Inferences** What do you think Dr. Desjardin wants to learn about this kind of mushroom?

Lights That Help Mushrooms

Mushrooms have spores. A spore is like **a seed**. The mushrooms spit their spores into the air. The wind carries the spores to new places where they grow into new mushrooms.

Sometimes insects carry spores to new places. Light **attracts** insects. When they land on the glowing mushrooms, some spores might stick to them. When the insects leave, so do the spores!

▲ Not too long ago, I discovered something new. It was a new kind of bioluminescent mushroom, shown here.

In Other Words

a seed the part of a plant that makes a new plant

This mushroom grows on the sides of trees. It is from Australia.

▶ Before You Move On

1. **Identify Details** Why do some insects like bioluminescent mushrooms?

2. **Make Inferences** What would happen to the mushrooms without the wind or insects?

Lights That Invite Insects

Some animals make light, too. A **glowworm** makes **sticky threads**, like a **spider web**. It hangs the threads from the tops of **caves**. The threads make a sticky trap.

cave

▲ A dark cave is a good place for a glowworm's trap.

In Other Words

◀ **glowworm** a kind of insect that makes light
sticky threads thin strings that hold on to things
spider web trap a spider makes
caves large holes in or above the ground

Then the glowworm shines its light. Other insects fly to the light and get stuck in the threads. Then the glowworm eats the insects.

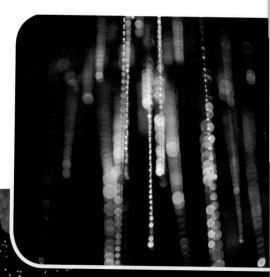

▲ Look closer at the glowworms' light!

▲ Glowworms light up this cave. They look like stars.

▶ Before You Move On

1. **Make Inferences** Why do glowworms hang their threads at the tops of caves instead of at the bottoms?

2. **Compare** How are glowworms different from other insects?

Lights That Send Messages

One kind of beetle called a firefly uses light to talk to other fireflies. The light in its tail blinks on and off.

▲ **Flashing lights help fireflies find other fireflies.**

Sometimes a firefly flashes its light to warn of danger. But most of the time, fireflies are just trying to find each other.

A **male** firefly **flashes** a light. A **female** firefly flashes back to answer. They keep flashing until they find each other.

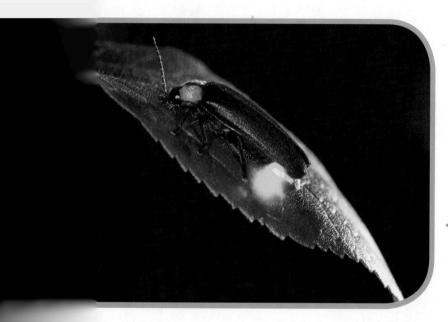

◀ A firefly uses its light to send a message to other fireflies.

▶ Before You Move On

1. **Details** How do fireflies send **messages** to each other?
2. **Compare** How is a glowworm like a firefly? How is it different?

rds

es

Lights in the Sea

Many living lights live in the deep sea. An anglerfish has a **rod** on its head. The end of the rod glows. It attracts small fish. When a fish swims to the light—SNAP! The anglerfish eats it.

rod

▲ **This anglerfish uses its light to catch fish.**

In Other Words
rod long, thin body part

Ocean **predators** often look up to the **surface**. They know a dark shape may be **food**.

▲ This shark looks for dark shapes in the water.

▶ **Before You Move On**

1. **Use Text Features** Look at the heading. What is this part of the article about?
2. **Predict** How does light help some ocean animals hide from **predators**?

Lights That Hide Animals

The anglerfish's light attracts **prey** . Other ocean animals use light to **escape** or hide from predators.

Bioluminescent animals are hard to see in the bright water. So the predator **moves on**.

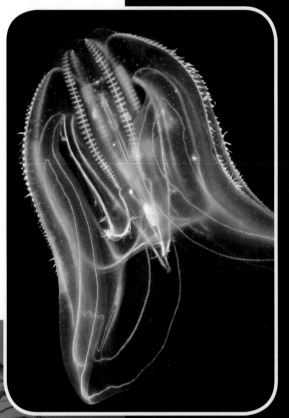

This comb jelly makes light to scare predators. ▶

▲ **Some jellyfish are hard to see in bright water.**

In Other Words
escape get away
moves on leaves

118

Many animals are bioluminescent. To me, **that's exciting**.

There are many questions left to answer. Trying to find the answers will be a **great adventure**. ❖

▲ Some squids are bioluminescent.

▲ Pinecone fish can also make light.

▶ **Before You Move On**

1. **Explain** How does light help ocean animals escape from some **predators**?
2. **Details** Name three ways some animals use light to survive in their environments.

Talk About It

1. What did you learn from the **science article**?
   Give an example.

   I learned _____ .

2. **Explain** how the anglerfish **attracts** its **prey**.

   The anglerfish _____ .

3. Fireflies use light to send **messages**. Tell how other
   animals send messages to each other.

   _____ also send messages. They _____ .

Learn test-taking strategies.
NGReach.com

Write About It

Animals use light in many different ways. Think of
an animal that uses light. What does the animal use
light to do? Write a sentence.

_____ use light to _____ .

Compare

How do different animals use light in "Living Lights"?

Comparison Chart

How It Uses Light	Animal
to attract prey	glowworm anglerfish
to send messages	

Now use your comparison chart. Tell a partner about the animals in "Living Lights."

> Some animals use light to _____ .
> These animals include: _____ .

Fluency  Comprehension Coach

Use the Comprehension Coach to practice reading with the correct phrasing. Rate your reading.

Use Context Clues

When you read a new word, look at all the words around it. These **context clues** can help you figure out the meaning of the new word.

A bright light can attract bugs at night.
The bugs **want to go near** the light.

context clues

The words "want to go near" give clues about what attract means.

Try It Together

Read these sentences. Look for context clues that tell what the word **prey** means.

Small fish can be **prey** for large fish. The large fish try to hunt and eat them.

Connect Across Texts Find out ways living things stand out to survive.

Genre Poems often use words to create pictures in your mind. Some poems use rhythm, words that repeat, or words that rhyme, or have the same ending sound.

Clever Creatures

written and illustrated by **Douglas Florian**

The Firefly

On August nights
The firefly lights
Blink
ON and OFF
Amongst the trees
But have no need
For **batteries.**

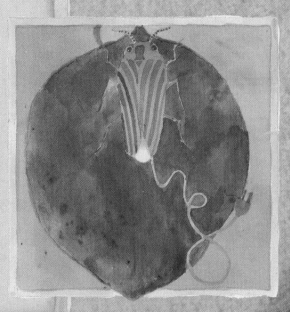

Fireflies use light to send **messages**, such as "Come here!" or "Look out!"

In Other Words
Clever Creatures Smart Animals
Amongst Around
batteries things that store electricity ▶

▶ **Before You Move On**

1. **Details** How do fireflies send **messages**?
2. **Poetry** Point to and say two words in the poem that rhyme. What picture do you see in your mind?

The Io Moth

The Io moth
Has **mam-moth** eyes
That are not real—
They're a disguise
To **ward off** birds
And other creatures,
Like garter snakes
And science teachers.

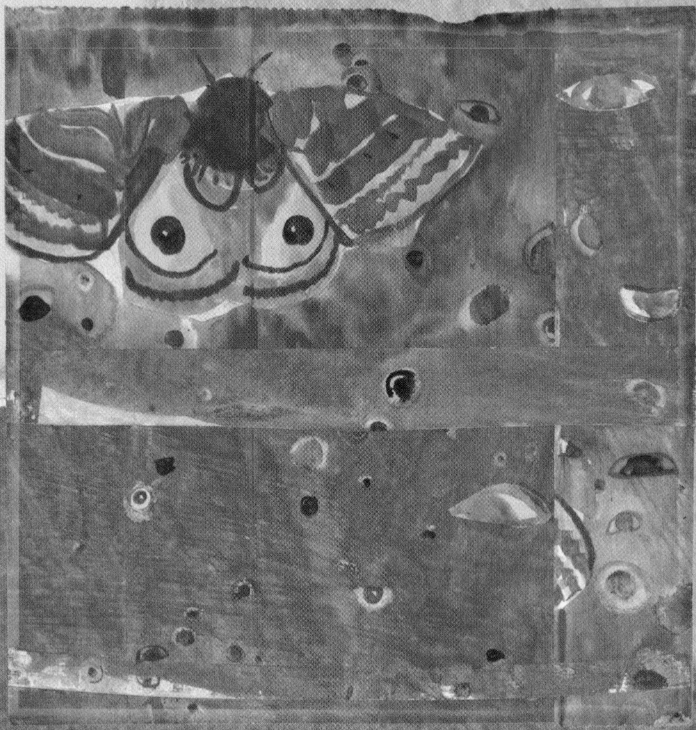

The Io moth's wings look like eyes. These markings scare away **predators**.

In Other Words

mam-moth very large

They're a disguise They are markings that help the moth look like something else

ward off scare away

The Diamondback Rattlesnake

Fork in front
Rattle behind.
The lump in the middle?
Don't pay any mind.

Scales up high,
Scales down low.
The lump in the middle?
You don't want to know.

Diamonds above,
Diamonds below.
The lump in the middle?
A rabbit too slow.

The sound of the snake's rattle tells other animals to stay away. ▼

▶ **Before You Move On**
1. **Make Inferences** Why do the Io moth's markings scare **predators** away?
2. **Clarify** What part of the snake is the "fork in front"?

Compare Genres

How are "Living Lights" and "Clever Creatures" different?
How are they the same?

Comparison Chart

Text Features	"Living Lights"	"Clever Creatures"
is about animals	✔	✔
includes words that rhyme		✔
has facts		
has photographs		
has illustrations		

Both selections have this feature.

Only one selection has this feature.

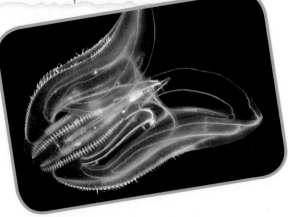

Talk Together

What does it take to survive? Talk with a partner. Ask your partner to name an animal or insect. Then use **Key Words** to tell your partner about **features** it uses to survive.

Verbs *be* and *have*

Forms of the verbs **be** and **have** can be used as helping verbs and as main verbs.

Grammar Rules Forms of *be* and *have*	be	have
• For yourself, use	am	have
• When you talk to one or more people, use	are	have
• For one other person or thing, use	is	has
• For yourself and others, use	are	have
• For other people and things, use	are	have

You can write a subject and a form of *be* or *have* in a short way.   I am = I'm   she is = she's   is not = isn't

Read Forms of *be* and *have*

Read these sentences. Find forms of *be* and *have*.

> Mushrooms have spores. A spore is like a seed.
> Many animals are bioluminescent. Others aren't.

Write Forms of *be* and *have*

Write two sentences about a plant or animal that makes light. Use forms of *be* and *have*.

Write Like a Scientist

Write an Article

Write an article that compares how two animals survive. Add your article to a class science magazine.

Study a Model

An article gives facts about a topic. Read Kate's article about what porcupines and sea urchins do to survive.

Bristly Beasts

by Kate Petrie

Do you know that some animals use spikes to protect themselves? Both porcupines and sea urchins use spikes to protect themselves.

The porcupine has sharp quills on its tail. When a hungry coyote comes by, the porcupine turns and slaps it in the face with its tail. The quills stick. The coyote leaves in a hurry!

In the oceans, sea urchins also use spikes. The spikes cover their bodies. When anything touches the urchin, it moves its spikes in that direction. Even hungry animals back off!

The topic sentence tells the **main idea** of the article.

The article compares two animals. The text gives **facts and details** for each animal.

Prewrite

1. **Choose a Topic** Talk with a partner. Think of interesting animals to write about. Choose two animals that fit into a group because of how they protect themselves.

My favorite animal is _____ .

_____ sounds interesting. Tell me why you like it.

2. **Get Organized** Porcupines and sea urchins fit into a group. They are both animals with spikes. Use a comparison chart to show how your animals fit into a group.

Comparison Chart

Animals with Spikes	Porcupines and Sea Urchins
How they use spikes	• move spikes toward other animals • scare away the animals
What the spikes are like	• sharp • can stick in other animals

Draft

Use your comparison chart to write a draft.

• Write a topic sentence that tells your main idea.

• Turn your details into sentences that explain how each animal protects itself.

Revise

1. **Read, Retell, Respond** Read your draft aloud to a partner. Your partner retells what you wrote about. Next, talk about ways to make your writing better.

The first animal survives by_____ .

I don't understand how _____ .

2. **Make Changes** Think about your partner's ideas. Then make your changes. Use the Revising Marks on page 563.

- Make sure your topic sentence clearly tells your main idea.

> Did you know that some animals use spikes to protect themselves?
> ∧ ~~Animals have to protect themselves.~~

- Add plenty of facts and details to develop the main idea.

>   hungry   turns and   with its tail
> When a coyote comes by, the porcupine slaps it in the face.
>   ∧   ∧   ∧

Edit and Proofread

Work with a partner to edit and proofread your article. Pay special attention to action and helping verbs.

Publish

On Your Own Make a final copy of your article. Read it to a friend.

Presentation Tips	
If you are the speaker…	**If you are the listener…**
Pronounce all important words clearly.	Take notes about what you hear.
Pause after each important detail.	Compare what you hear to what you already know.

With a Group Make a science magazine that has all of your articles. Include a picture of each animal. Use a computer to design a cover for your magazine.

How Animals Survive

What does it take to survive?

Talk Together

In this unit, you found lots of answers to the **Big Question**. Now, use your concept map to discuss the **Big Question** with the class.

Concept Map

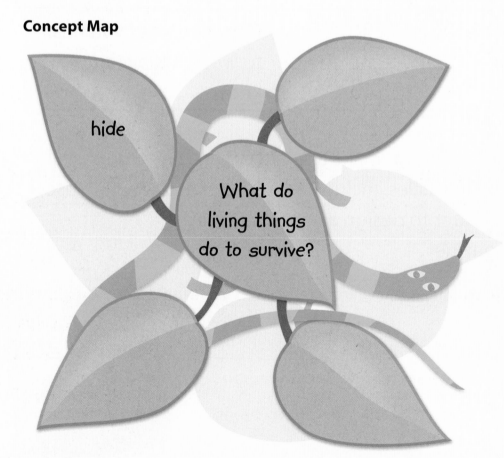

hide

What do living things do to survive?

Share Your Ideas

Choose one of these ways to share your ideas about the **Big Question**.

Do It!

Play Animal Concentration

Write ways animals survive on one set of cards. Write animals and insects on another set of cards. Mix the cards and turn them over. Match the animals to the ways they survive.

Talk About It!

Make a Riddle

Choose an animal from one of the selections. Tell your partner a riddle about it. See if your partner can guess the animal.

> I am bright and hang in caves. What am I?

> A glowworm!

Write It!

Write a Scientific Log

Pretend you are a scientist. You are studying an animal from one of the selections. Draw the animal. Describe what it does to survive.

October 12

Today, I studied the amazing Io moth.

Do It!

Make a Nature Show

Pretend to make a TV show. It is about amazing animals and how they survive. Choose the animals. Then plan the show and work with classmates to present it.

Water for Everyone

? **BIG** Question

Where does water come from?

Unit at a Glance
▸ **Language**: Ask for and Give Information, Define and Explain
▸ **Literacy**: Ask Questions
▸ **Content**: Water

Unit 3

Share What You Know

Do It!

❶ **Think** of ways that people use water.

❷ **Act out** one idea. Work with a group. Have the class guess what you are doing.

❸ **Make** a poster showing your group's idea of how people use water.

Build Background: Watch a video about water.
◎ NGReach.com

High Frequency
Words

are

that

they

those

Ask for and Give Information

Listen and sing.

Rain and Clouds

Song ((MP3))

There **are** clouds out, dear Rudi,
   dear Rudi, dear Rudi.
It may rain now, dear Rudi,
   and what is the rain?

It is water, dear Lupe,
   dear Lupe, dear Lupe.
It is water, dear Lupe,
   that water is rain.

But what are **those** clouds,
   dear Rudi, dear Rudi?
But what are those clouds,
   dear Rudi, those clouds?

They are water, dear Lupe,
   dear Lupe, dear Lupe.
Drops of water, dear Lupe,
   together make clouds.

Tune: "There's a Hole in the Bucket"

Key Words

Look at the diagram about water.

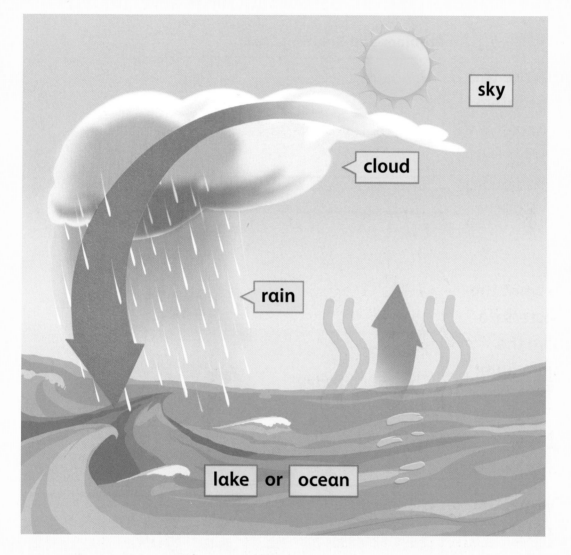

Water falls from the sky as rain. It rises into the sky as water vapor.

Look at the arrows on the diagram. Where does water come from? Where does it go?

Problem and Solution

A story's plot is built around a **problem**. The characters try to **solve** the problem. Use a chart to show how things work out.

Problem-and-Solution Chart

Write the problem here. >

Problem:
Rudi and Lupe cannot play outside.

Write what the characters do to solve the problem here. >

Event 1:
They run inside.

Event 2:
They find a game.

Write how the characters solve the problem here. >

Solution:
Rudi and Lupe play inside.

Talk Together

Tell your partner how you solved a problem. Together, fill out a problem-and-solution chart.

More Key Words

absorb
(ub-**zorb**) *verb*

The mop **absorbs** the water.

become
(bē-**kum**) *verb*

A caterpillar **becomes** a butterfly.

carry
(**kair**-ē) *verb*

The friends **carry** their boat to the water.

change
(**chānj**) *verb*

He **changes** the color of the wall from white to red.

rise
(**rīz**) *verb*

The tall buildings **rise** high up into the sky.

Talk Together

Work with a partner. Use **Key Words** to ask and answer questions.

What happens when a sponge **absorbs** water?

It **becomes** wet.

Add words to My Vocabulary Notebook.
NGReach.com

Ask Questions

As you read, **ask questions**. You can find the answers to some questions in the book. Read to find the answers. This will help you understand the story better.

This picture shows me writing a description. It is about how water gets from a little lake to the big ocean.

ONE TIME

Look at Lupe's picture. **Ask yourself questions** about it. Then read what she wrote. Find the answers to your questions.

How to Ask Questions

?	**1.** Ask a question.	I wonder _____ .
👁	**2.** Look for the answer. You might find the answer in the text. Or you might have to think and search.	I read _____ . So _____ .
💭	**3.** Think about the answer. Read on and ask more questions.	Now I wonder _____ .

Language Frames

?   I wonder _____ .

👁   I read _____ .

     So _____ .

☁   Now I wonder

      _____ .

Talk Together

Read Lupe's description. Read the sample question. Then use **Language Frames** to tell a partner your questions.

Description

The Little Lake and the Ocean

The little lake has lots of water. Miles away, there is a problem at the ocean. Its water level is falling. One day, it gets hot at the lake. The heat makes drops of water **change**. They turn into gas called water vapor.

Then warm air starts to carry the vapor. It **rises** high up in the sky. When the warm air meets cold air, it forms a cloud. Winds **carry** the cloud to the sea. The cloud **absorbs** more water from the air. It grows heavy with water droplets. What will the cloud do with all those droplets? It starts to rain! That is how the little lake brings water to the ocean.

Sample Question

"I wonder what's going to happen to the lake.

I read that it gets hot. So water turns to vapor.

Now I wonder where the vapor will go."

◀ = A good place to ask questions

141

Read a Story

Genre

A **traditional tale** is a very old story. It often tells how something in nature came to be. This tale is from the Diné, or Navajo, people in Arizona and New Mexico.

Setting

The setting is where and when a story happens.

This story happens when a fire starts and comes toward people's homes.

FROG BRINGS RAIN

by **Joseph Bruchac**

illustrated by **S.D. Nelson**

▶ **Set a Purpose**
Find out what this Diné tale
explains about nature.

Long ago Fire **escaped and spread** down the
mountain toward the homes of the First People.

In Other Words
escaped and spread
started and moved

144

Cardinal flew to First Woman.

"Look," he said. "Fire is coming. I flew too close.
It turned my feathers red."

"What can we do?" First Woman asked.

"Water will **put out** Fire," First Man said.

In Other Words

put out stop

146

First Woman made a bottle **of reeds and clay**.
She filled it with Water.
"Who will take this to Fire?" she asked.

In Other Words

of reeds and clay
   with plants and mud

▶ **Before You Move On**

1. **Setting** Where and when does this story happen? How do you know?

2. **Problem/Solution** What is the problem in this story? How does First Woman try to solve it?

▶ **Predict**
Who will First Woman find
to **carry** Water to Fire?

Mockingbird, Nighthawk, and Canary could not
do it. But Robin **carried** Water to Fire. She flew so
close, her chest turned red. Water **spilled from** the
bottle, but **not enough** to put out Fire.

In Other Words
spilled from fell out of
not enough she needed more Water

First Woman asked the **Hunting People**.
"Who will take Water to Fire?"
Bear and Bobcat, Wolf and Mountain Lion
would not help.

In Other Words
Hunting People
Land Animals

149

First Woman asked the **Water People**.
"Who will take Water to Fire?"
Snail in his **spring** said he was too slow.

Otter and Beaver, Muskrat and Mink said
their river needed Water. Without it, their
home would **go dry**. Then all would be **desert**.

▶ **Before You Move On**

1. **Character** The animals won't help First
   Woman. How does that make her feel?
2. **Ask Questions** Think about this part of
   the story. Ask a question about what you
   might find out in the next part.

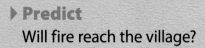

▶ Predict
Will fire reach the village?

Finally First Woman asked Frog in his **swamp**. Frog soaked up Water from the swamp **with his coat**. Then White Crane carried him over Fire.

In Other Words
swamp very wet land
with his coat by pulling the water up into his skin

152

Frog **shed** the water.

On the north side of the mountain, it fell as black **rain**. On the south side of the mountain, it was blue rain.

In Other Words
shed dropped

On the east side, it fell as white rain. On the west side, it was yellow rain.

Water put out Fire. Then Frog and Crane **returned** home.

In Other Words
returned went back

Clouds of four colors **hung** over the land. Black clouds hung over the north, white clouds over the east, blue clouds over the south, and yellow clouds over the west.

In Other Words
hung stayed

To this day, Frog **remains** in his swamp.
With his song, "Harrumph, Harrumph," he calls
those clouds to bring rain back to the land. ❖

▶ **Before You Move On**

1. **Confirm Prediction** Was your prediction correct? Explain.
2. **Problem/Solution** Do Frog and Crane help solve the problem in the story? How?

Meet the Author

JOSEPH BRUCHAC

AWARD WINNER

As a child, Joseph Bruchac lived with his grandparents in a small town. When the local farmers told tales, Mr. Bruchac loved to listen!

Today, Mr. Bruchac tells stories from his own Native American heritage. He knows that storytellers must also be good listeners. "We have two ears and only one mouth," he says. "We need to listen at least twice as much as we speak."

Joseph Bruchac still lives in his grandparents' house near the mountains.

Writer's Craft

Reread page 144 of *Frog Brings Rain*. It is a good beginning because it makes you want to read more. You want to know if the fire burns the homes. Think about a story you can tell. Write a good beginning. Surprise your readers or make them curious.

Talk About It

1. "Frog Brings **Rain**" is a **traditional tale**. It tells how something happened. What does it tell about?

   "Frog Brings Rain" tells how _____ happened.

2. Who would not **carry** Water to Fire? **Give information** about them.

   _____ would not carry Water to Fire because _____ .

3. **Ask a question** about one of the pictures in the story. Then reread the text to answer your question.

   My question is: _____ ? The text says _____ .

Learn test-taking strategies.
NGReach.com

Write About It

Write a question about the story. Have a partner write the answer. **Change** places and take turns writing questions and answers.

> **Question:** Why did _____ ?
>
> **Answer:** It _____ because _____ .

Problem and Solution

How do characters solve a problem in "Frog Brings Rain"?

Problem-and-Solution Chart

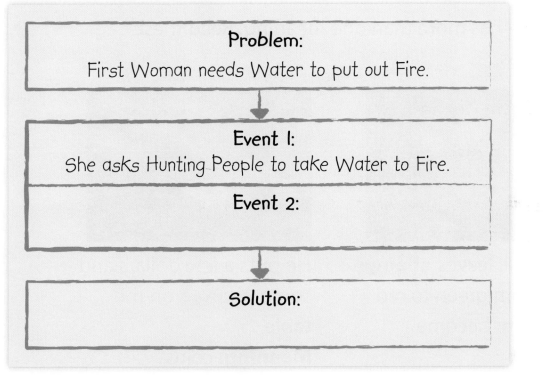

Problem:
First Woman needs Water to put out Fire.

Event 1:
She asks Hunting People to take Water to Fire.

Event 2:

Solution:

Now use your problem-and-solution chart. Tell a partner how First Woman and Frog solve the problem in "Frog Brings Rain."

The problem is _____ .
First Woman asks _____ .
Then she asks _____ .
_____ and _____ solve the problem by _____ .

Fluency  Comprehension Coach

Use the Comprehension Coach to practice reading with the correct expression. Rate your reading.

Multiple-Meaning Words

Some words have **more than one meaning**. You can use the words near the word to figure out the correct meaning.

Change has more than one meaning. Read these examples.

In the fall, leaves **change** color from green to red.
Meaning: become different

He puts a few dollars and some **change** on the table.
Meaning: coins

Try It Together

Read these sentences. Then follow the directions.

First Woman asks Snail in his **spring** to take Water to Fire. But Snail is too slow. Then, Frog **springs** up from his swamp. He will take Water to Fire.

1. Look at the first sentence. What does **spring** mean?

2. Look at the second sentence. What words help you understand the meaning of **springs**?

Make Rain

Connect Across Texts You read a tale about how rain came to be. Now read the scientific explanation.

Genre A **science experiment** gives steps to show how something happens in nature.

Do an experiment to see how **rain** forms. You will need: a glass jar, hot water, a plate, and ice cubes.

1 Have your teacher pour two inches of hot water into the jar.

2 Cover the jar with a plate. Wait five minutes.

▶ **Before You Move On**

1. **Details** What materials do you need for this experiment?
2. **Predict** What do you think you'll read about next? What will you find out?

161

 Put ice cubes on the plate. Wait 15 minutes.

4 Watch for drops of water to fall like rain!

What happens in the jar?

Hot water makes warm, wet air called steam. Steam **rises** up to the cold plate. The cold air changes the warm steam into water. Then heavy drops of water fall.

Water drops fall.

Steam rises up.

Hot water makes steam.

What happens in the sky?

The sun heats the water. The warm, wet air rises up into the **sky**. If the warm, wet air meets the cold air, rain **clouds** form. When the clouds have enough water, the drops fall to the ground as **rain**.

How Rain Forms

cloud

colder air

sun

cold air

rain

warm, wet air

▲ **Look at the illustration above. It shows what happens when warm air meets cold air.**

▶ **Before You Move On**

1. **Explain** Use your own words to tell how rain forms.
2. **Use Text Features** Look at the illustration. What do the arrows show?

Compare Explanations

An explanation helps you understand how things work. How are the explanations in "Frog Brings Rain" and "Make Rain" different?

Comparison Chart

How Is Rain Made?

Traditional Tale Explanation	Science Experiment Explanation
• Frog carries water. • •	• Warm, wet air rises. • •

Write the explanation from "Frog Brings Rain" here.

Write the explanation from "Make Rain" here.

Talk Together

Where does water come from? Choose one explanation of how **rain** is made. Draw a picture. Then use **Key Words** to label your picture.

Adjectives and Articles

Adjectives tell more about a noun. **Articles** come before a noun or an adjective.

Grammar Rules Adjectives and Articles

Adjectives can tell about	
• size	A **small** bird takes Water.
• shape	She carries the **round** bottle.
• color	Her feathers turn **red**.
• Use **a** if the next word starts with a **consonant**.	**A s**low snail will not help.
• Use **an** if the next word starts with a **vowel or silent h**.	**An o**tter in the river will not help.
• Use **the** to tell about something specific.	Frog is **the** animal that says he will help.

Read Articles and Adjectives

Read this passage. Find the articles and adjectives.

Frog soaked up Water from a small swamp. He looked big and round. Frog shed black rain on the tall mountain.

Use Articles and Adjectives

Pretend you are First Woman. Write two sentences that tell what Fire looks like. Use articles and adjectives.

Define and Explain

Listen and sing.

What Is a Pump?

Song (((MP3)))

A pump is a machine.
We keep it nice and clean.
With valves and pipes and other parts,
This pump is a machine.

It has a job to do.
It **does** it well for you.
It gets fresh water from the ground
And brings it up to you.

Water from the ground.
Yes, water from the ground.
Because this pump can do its job,
There's water all around!

Tune: "The Farmer in the Dell"

Key Words

How does water get from under the ground to the house in this picture?

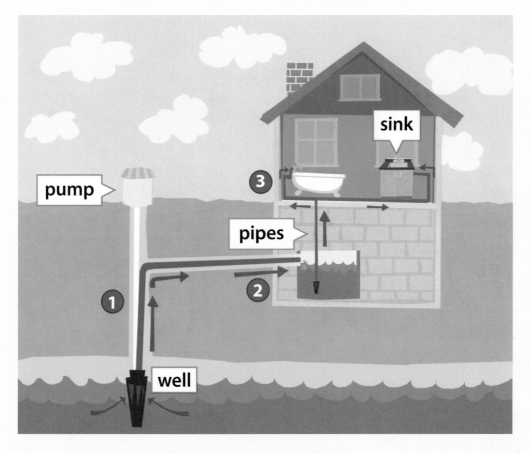

1. A **pump** is a **machine**. It **draws** water up from **wells**.

2. **Inventions** like a water filter clean the water. Now it is safe to drink.

3. **Pipes** carry water to places at home, like the sink.

Talk Together

Look at the diagram on this page. What happens to the water? Where does it go? How does it get there?

Cause and Effect

A **cause** is why something happens. An **effect** is what happens. Use a chart to show cause-and-effect relationships.

Cause-and-Effect Chart

Cause:

Ella puts up a poster.

> Write why something happens here.

Effect:

Kids stop wasting water.

> Write what happens here.

Talk Together

Tell a partner about what happened because of an action you took. Together, make a cause-and-effect chart.

More Key Words

clean
(klēn) *adjective*

The dog is **clean** after her bath.

healthy
(hel-thē) *adjective*

Eating fruit helps you stay **healthy**.

provide
(pru-vīd) *verb*

A water fountain **provides** water to drink.

require
(ri-kwī-ur) *verb*

This ride **requires** two people.

source
(sors) *noun*

The sun is a **source** of heat and light.

Talk Together

Tell a partner what a **Key Word** means. Then your partner uses the word in a sentence.

Require means to need something.

I require food and water.

Add words to My Vocabulary Notebook.
NGReach.com

Ask Questions

As you read, **ask questions**. You can find the answers to some questions in your head. Think to come up with answers. This will help you understand the text better.

> What's wrong, Will?

> Sadie might knock over Fluffy's water!

Ask yourself questions about the text. Use what you know to figure out the answers.

How to Ask Questions

?	**1.** Ask a question.
💭	**2.** Think about what you already know. Think about what the author tells you.
🧩	**3.** Think about the answer. Read on and ask more questions.

I wonder _____ .

I know _____ . The author tells me _____ .

So _____ . Now I wonder _____ .

Language Frames

? I wonder _____ .

☁ I know _____ .
The author tells
me _____ .

🧩 So _____ . Now
I wonder _____ .

Talk Together

Read Ella's essay. Read the sample question.
Then use **Language Frames** to tell a partner
your questions.

Essay

My Wonderful Waterer

My friend Will just got a kitten. Will wants his
kitten to have fresh, **clean** water because he
wants Fluffy to stay **healthy** . Will's sister crawls
on the floor. She might get into Fluffy's bowl or
knock it over!

Today I sketched my idea for an **invention** .
I **required** several things to make it. First, I
collected the things. Then, I asked my mother
to help.

Sample Question

"I wonder what will
happen if Sadie spills the
water.

I know that little kids get
into things they shouldn't.
The author tells me that
Sadie crawls on the floor.

So Will is worried that
Sadie will get into the
water. Now I wonder what
Will is going to do."

Mom and I decided to make this Wonderful Waterer! It
provides a **source** of water for the kitten. It should have a
good effect on Fluffy's health—and keep Sadie dry, too. I
hope that Will loves it. He says he already does!

◀ = A good place to ask questions

Read a Magazine Article

Genre

A **magazine article** is nonfiction. It can tell about real people, places, and events.

Text Features

A **diagram** can show how something works.

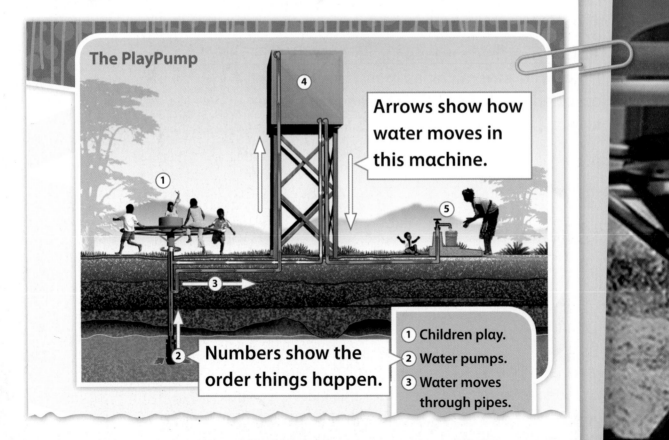

The PlayPump

Arrows show how water moves in this machine.

Numbers show the order things happen.

1 Children play.
2 Water pumps.
3 Water moves through pipes.

PlayPumps

Turning Work into Play

by Catherine Clarke Fox

Comprehension Coach

▶ **Set a Purpose**
Find out how a new **invention**
helps many people.

Our Water, Our Life

Everyone needs water. We use water to drink, cook, and clean.

People in some countries use a lot of water every day. Homes have sinks and **showers**.

sink ▷

▲ **This boy uses water to keep his pet clean.**

In Other Words

showers pipes that water comes through ▶

174

◀ **You can get a drink from a drinking fountain.**

Schools and parks have drinking fountains.

Some people even swim in pools full of water. It helps them **cool off** and have fun.

▼ **Water is fun to play in and keeps kids cool.**

In Other Words
cool off not be too hot

▶ **Before You Move On**

1. **Ask Questions** What do you know about water? What is the author saying about water on these pages?

2. **Compare** How are sinks, showers, and drinking fountains the same?

The World Needs Water

All people need water to survive. In some parts of the world, **clean** water can be hard to find.

In some rural parts of Africa, people must walk far to get water from **wells**. Then they have to carry the water home.

▼ **This man drinks water from a gourd.**

In Other Words
a gourd the hard shell of a fruit

176

▲ **These women carry clean water home.**

Luckily, a new **invention** is making a big change for many people. The PlayPump is bringing water to many of these rural communities.

AFRICA

▶ **Before You Move On**

1. **Details** How do some people in Africa get their water home?
2. **Cause/Effect** Why do you think someone invented the PlayPump?

A Wonderful Invention

For some kids, the PlayPump is the first **merry-go-round** they've ever seen. They give a push. Then they jump on. They go for their first ride. Soon, smiles **break out** on their faces.

▼ **Children in South Africa play on the PlayPump.**

In Other Words

merry-go-round playground ride

break out show

▲ The PlayPump is like a merry-go-round. It is great fun.

The fun of **whirling** in a circle is just part of what makes the PlayPump special. This **incredible** **invention** changes kids' playtime. It also changes people's lives.

▶ **Before You Move On**

1. **Ask Questions** The author says this merry-go-round changes people's lives. What questions do you want to ask her about it?

2. **Predict** How do you think the new **invention** works?

Work Is Play

The PlayPump turns work into play. As the merry-go-round **spins**, it **pumps** clean water. The water comes up from deep underground. It goes into a huge **water tank**.

◄ **The children help pump up water as they play.**

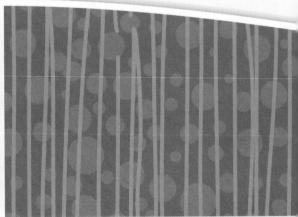

In Other Words
spins turns
pumps brings up
water tank something that holds water ▶

The PlayPump

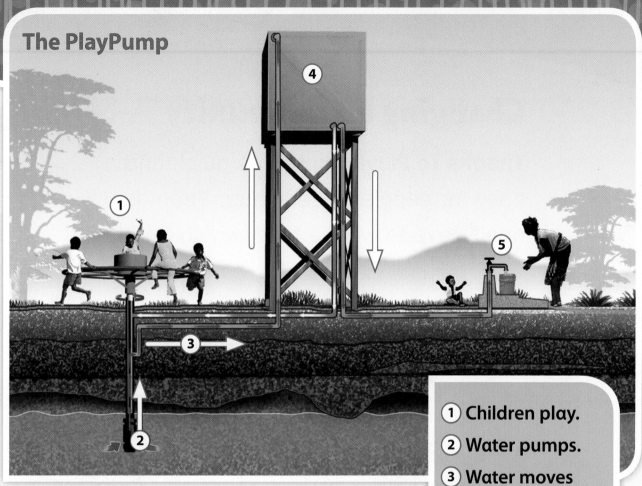

1. Children play.
2. Water pumps.
3. Water moves through pipes.
4. Water goes to the tank.
5. People get water from a faucet.

The tank holds **a supply of** water for everyone in the community. When people need water, they can just **turn on a faucet**.

In Other Words

a supply of some

turn on a faucet get water from a **pipe**

▶ **Before You Move On**

1. **Confirm Prediction** Was your prediction about the PlayPump correct?
2. **Use Text Features** Look at the diagram. Where does the water go after it is pumped out of the ground?

181

Changing a Community

Thanks to PlayPumps, it is quick and easy for people to get water. People don't have to walk a long way to find it.

▼ These boys wash their hands at a faucet.

In Other Words

Thanks to Because of

▲ **Children get ready for class at this school in Africa.**

The **pumps** are also places where kids and **adults** like to **visit**. PlayPumps are often **set up** near schools. This makes it easy for kids to play on them before and after class.

In Other Words
adults men and women
visit spend time together
set up put

▶ **Before You Move On**
1. **Cause/Effect** Why do PlayPumps make people happy?
2. **Ask Questions** Ask a question about the heading for this section. As you reread the text, look for the answer to your question.

Water for Millions

PlayPumps are made in South Africa. Today, there are more than 1,200 PlayPumps in five African countries. They bring water to almost **two million** people.

PlayPump Locations
PlayPumps can be found in five African countries.

AFRICA

Zambia

Mozambique

Swaziland

Lesotho

South Africa

In Other Words
Millions
Many, Many People
two million
2,000,000

184

▲ Clean water makes everyone smile.

The idea is clever, but simple.

Kids play. Water pumps. ❖

In Other Words

The idea is clever, but simple. It is a smart plan that is easy to understand.

▶**Before You Move On**

1. **Details** Where are PlayPumps located?
2. **Use Text Features** How does the map on page 184 help you understand the text?

Talk About It 💬

1. What **invention** does the **magazine article** tell about? Tell the name of the **machine** and one thing you learned about it.

   The name of the machine is _____ . I learned _____ .

2. **Define** the word <u>invention</u>. **Explain** what the invention in the article does.

   <u>Invention</u> means _____ . In the article, the invention _____ .

3. **Ask a question** about the **pump** . Find sentences that tell the answer.

   My question about the pump is _____ . I found the answer _____ .

Learn test-taking strategies.
⊘ NGReach.com

Write About It ✏️

Write sentences telling how the PlayPump helps **provide** people with water. Tell why this is an important invention.

The pumps _____ .

This is important because _____ .

Cause and Effect

What causes things to happen in "PlayPumps"?

Cause-and-Effect Chart

Cause:

Kids ride on the PlayPump and turn the wheel.

Effect:

Now use your cause-and-effect chart. Tell a partner about more causes and effects in "PlayPumps."

_____ . So _____ .

Fluency 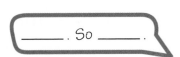 Comprehension Coach

Use the Comprehension Coach to practice reading with the correct intonation. Rate your reading.

Suffixes

A **suffix** is a word part that you add to the end of a word. This can change the word's meaning.

The suffix **-y** can change a noun to an adjective.

| health | + | **y** | = | **healthy** |

Drinking water is good for your health. It is a **healthy** thing to do.

The suffix **-ion** can change a verb to a noun.

| invent | + | **ion** | = | **invention** |

People invent many things. The PlayPump is one **invention**.

Try It Together

Read these sentences. Then follow the directions.

> This water is not safe to drink. It is full of **dirt**. How do people **act** when it rains?

1. Add **-y** to the word **dirt**. What new word does it make?

2. Add **-ion** to the word **act**. What new word does it make?

Connect Across Texts Now read about someone who cares about an important water source in the United States.

Genre A **profile** briefly describes a person. It tells what the person does and cares about.

The Mighty
Colorado

BY MIMI MORTEZAI

Where do you get your water? You may get it from the Colorado River. The Colorado **provides** water to **thirty million** people in the United States. It gives them water to drink. It helps them stay **clean**. It even helps them grow **crops**.

In Other Words
thirty million very many
crops food

▶ **Before You Move On**

1. **Ask Questions** What is one question you have about the Colorado River? How will you find the answer?
2. **Details** Name things that people do with the water **provided** by the river.

Jon Waterman knows a lot about the Colorado River. He is a National Geographic Explorer. He rode down the entire river. Sometimes, though, he had to stop and walk. Why? Parts of the river **had dried up**. One reason was **droughts** and warmer temperatures on Earth. Another reason was that people had used too much of the river's water.

▲ **Jon Waterman explores the Colorado River.**

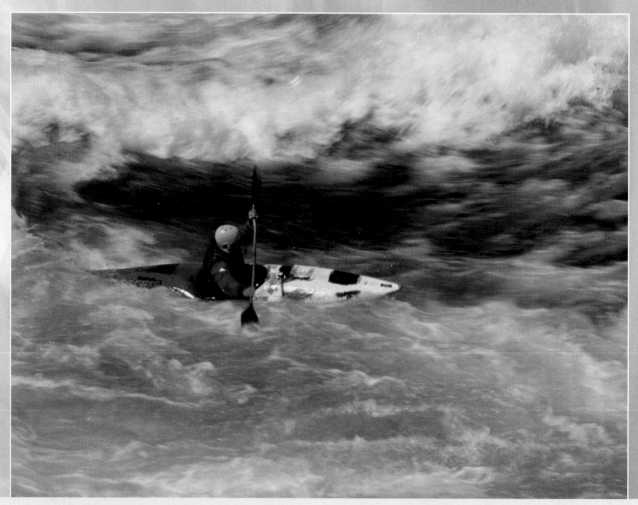

▲ **Sometimes Mr. Waterman rides down the river.**

In Other Words

had dried up were without water

droughts months or years without rain

The Colorado River is 1,450 miles long. ▶

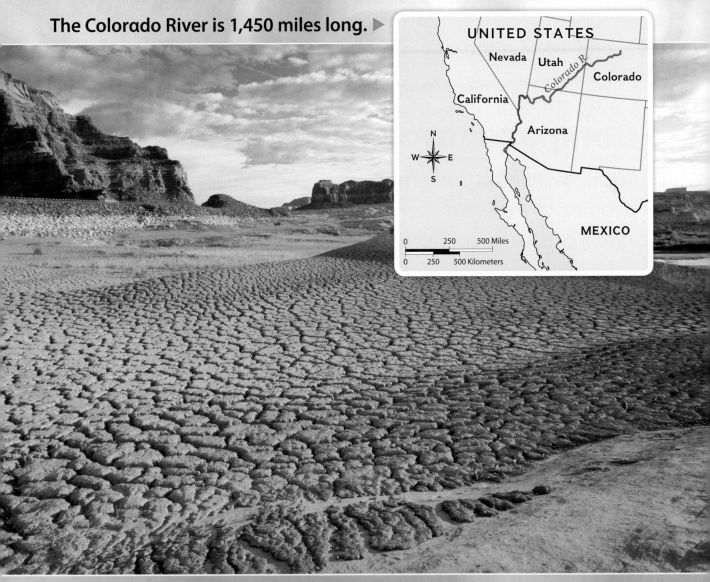

UNITED STATES

Nevada Utah

Colorado R.

Colorado

California

Arizona

N
W — E
S

0   250   500 Miles
0   250   500 Kilometers

MEXICO

▲ **Without rain, rivers dry up.**

Mr. Waterman says the Colorado River needs our help. We must change the way we use water. **Otherwise**, there will be less water every year. We need the river so we can survive. The river needs us, too! ❖

In Other Words
Otherwise If we don't

▶ **Before You Move On**
1. **Cause/Effect** Why did parts of the river dry up?
2. **Explain** Tell a partner why you think the Colorado River is important.

Compare Information

Both "PlayPumps" and "The Mighty Colorado" tell how people get water. How are these ways different? Work with a partner to complete the chart.

Comparison Chart

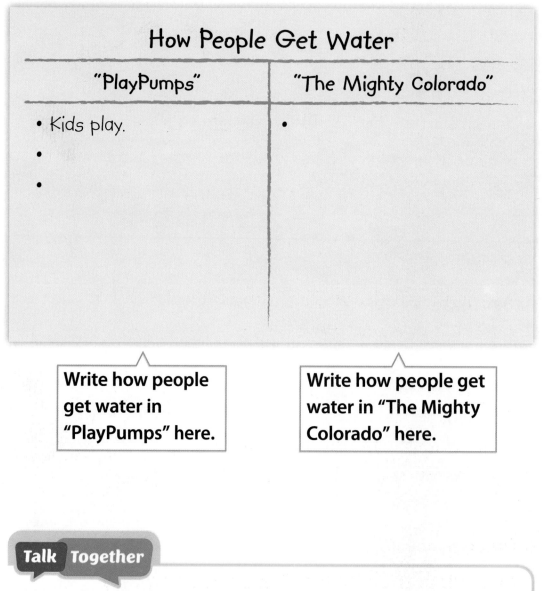

How People Get Water	
"PlayPumps"	"The Mighty Colorado"
• Kids play.	•
•	
•	

Write how people get water in "PlayPumps" here.

Write how people get water in "The Mighty Colorado" here.

Talk Together

Where does water come from? Look at the pictures in "Playpumps" and "The Mighty Colorado." Then use **Key Words** to tell a partner how people get **clean** water.

Adverbs

Adverbs tell about actions. An adverb can tell **how** or **when**.

> ## Grammar Rules **Adverbs**
>
> | | |
> |---|---|
> | • Many **adverbs** tell how something happens. These adverbs usually end in -**ly**. | Kids play **happily** on the PlayPump.
Water moves **quickly** from the well to the tank. |
> | • Some **adverbs** tell when something happens. | **Soon** the tank is full.
People have clean water **now**. |

Read Adverbs

Read these sentences from "PlayPumps." Find the adverbs that tell how and when.

Luckily, a new invention is making a big change for many people.

Today, there are more than 1,200 PlayPumps in five African counties.

Use Adverbs

Write two sentences about PlayPumps. Tell how they work. Use adverbs that tell how and when. Then share your sentences with a partner.

Write as a Storyteller

Write a Folk Tale

Where do rivers come from? What can stop the rain? Write a folk tale about water. Turn your folk tale into a picture book.

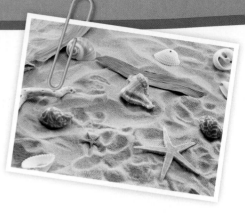

Study a Model

A folk tale is an old story that people have told for many years. Some folk tales tell how something came to be.

The Lonely Ocean
by Latisha Grant

Ocean was very lonely. People said her waves were too strong. So no one came near her.

One day, Ocean had a great idea! That night, she pushed pretty shells and rocks up onto the sand. The next morning, a girl saw the gifts. "Look!" she shouted. Soon, everyone came to see what Ocean had left!

Soon Ocean had a lot of visitors. She wasn't lonely anymore!

The **problem** gets the story started.

Latisha uses **words that sound like her**.

The **events** tell what happens.

The **solution** tells how the problem is solved.

Prewrite

1. **Choose a Topic** Talk with a partner. Write questions you have about water. Choose a story idea.

Why is water _____?

_____ sounds interesting. Tell me more.

2. **Get Organized** Use a problem-and-solution chart to organize your ideas.

Problem-and-Solution Chart

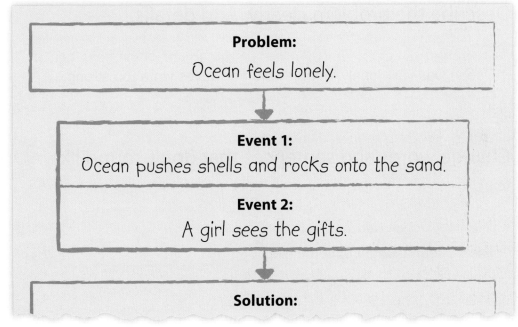

Problem:
Ocean feels lonely.

Event 1:
Ocean pushes shells and rocks onto the sand.

Event 2:
A girl sees the gifts.

Solution:

Draft

Use your chart to write a draft of your folk tale.

- Describe the problem.

- Write a sentence about each event.

- Tell what the solution is.

Revise

1. **Read, Retell, Respond** Read your draft aloud to a partner. Your partner retells your story. Next, talk about ways to make your writing better.

> Your folk tale is about _____ .

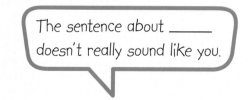

> The sentence about _____ doesn't really sound like you.

2. **Make Changes** Think about your partner's ideas. Then make changes. Use the Revising Marks on page 563.

   • Describe the problem clearly. Add details.

   > So no one came near her.
   > Ocean was very lonely. People said her waves were too strong. ∧

   • Change words and sentences that don't sound like you.

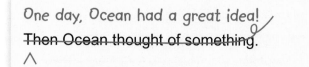

   > One day, Ocean had a great idea!
   > ~~Then Ocean thought of something.~~
   > ∧

Edit and Proofread

Work with a partner to edit and proofread your folk tale. Use adjectives when you need them. Also check that you use articles correctly.

<table>
<tr><td>

Spelling Tip

✔ Adding **-ly** turns many adjectives into adverbs. They tell how something happens.

soft + ly = softly

</td></tr>
</table>

Publish

On Your Own Turn your folk tale into a picture book! Put a few sentences on each page. Add pictures. Then read your story to your classmates.

Presentation Tips	
If you are the speaker…	**If you are the listener…**
Change your voice to match the actions in the story.	Picture the events that the reader describes.
Point to pictures in your book as you tell what is going on in the story.	Does the story sound like a folk tale to you? Why or why not?

With a Group Take turns reading your picture books to younger students. Make sure they all can see your pictures as you read!

Where does water
come from?

Talk Together

In this unit, you found lots of answers to the **Big Question**.
Now, use your concept map to discuss the **Big Question** with
the class.

Concept Map

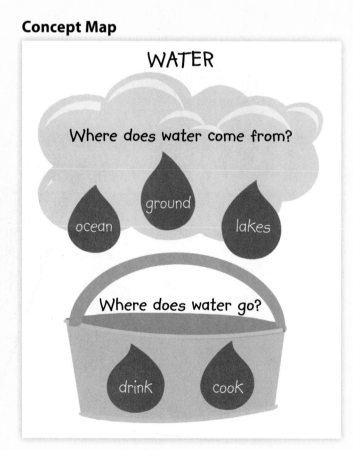

WATER

Where does water come from?

ocean

ground

lakes

Where does water go?

drink

cook

Share Your Ideas

Choose one of these ways to share your ideas about the **Big Question**.

Write It!

Keep a Water Log

Think about how you used water today. When did you use it? How did you use it? Write about each time.

> This morning: I used water to brush my teeth.
>
> At lunch: I washed my hands.

Talk About It!

Give an Interview

What ways do people get water? Think of questions to ask. Ask a partner your questions. Be sure to listen carefully to the answers. Then switch roles.

Do It!

Act Out the Water Cycle

Make up movements to show how rain is made in clouds. Use sounds and props. Perform the mime for the class.

Write It!

Write a Letter

Write a short letter to a rain cloud. Tell the cloud why it is important. Tell how it helps you. Be sure to include the date, a greeting, and a closing. Share your letter with a classmate.

Lend a Hand

BIG
Question

What are our
responsibilities
to each other?

Unit
4

Share What You Know

1. **Think** about a good deed you did or that someone did for you.

2. **Make** a gift box. Draw or make something that shows the deed. Put it in the box.

3. **Share** the deed with the class by telling about it.

Do It!

Build Background: Watch a video about good citizenship.
🔵 NGReach.com

High Frequency
Words
feel
know
think

Express Feelings and Ideas

Listen and sing.

Doing Good

Song ((MP3))

I **think** that we all should
Try to do something good.
I **know** that we all care.
We have a lot to share.

I want to do what's right.
I think we really could
Show respect, not neglect.
We'll **feel** good!

Tune: "This Little Light of Mine"

Key Words

What is good **citizenship**? What is not good citizenship?

People show good citizenship when they

- are **thoughtful**.

- show **respect** for others.

- are **responsible**.
- are **grateful**.

People do not show good citizenship when they

- are **mean**.
- are rude.

- are irresponsible.
- are ungrateful.

Talk Together

Look at the words and the pictures. How can good citizenship make a difference?

Character Traits

Write about character **traits**. Tell what the characters do and what they are like.

Character Map

Character	What the Character Does	What the Character Is Like
Isabel	She picks up a book for her mother.	She is kind.

Here, Mamá, let me get that.

Think about what the character does. How would you describe the character? Write it here.

Write the character's name here.

Write the character's actions here.

Talk Together

Tell your partner about two characters from your favorite stories. Use a character map to tell about them.

More Key Words

character
(**kair**-ik-tur) *noun*

She helps her brother. This shows good **character**.

choice
(**chois**) *noun*

He will make a **choice** between the apple and the hotdog.

courage
(**kur**-ij) *noun*

She jumps into the pool. She has **courage**!

right
(**rīt**) *adjective*

It is not wrong to help others. It is **right**.

save
(**sāv**) *verb*

He **saves** the boy from falling.

Talk Together

Make a Study Card for each **Key Word**. Compare your cards with a partner's.

save

What it means: Keep something safe

Example: when I knocked over the lamp but caught it before it broke

Not an example: when I dropped the bowl and it broke

Add words to My Vocabulary Notebook.
NGReach.com

Learn to Make Connections

Look at the cartoon. Does it make you think of something in your life? If it does, then you have **made a connection**.

Abuelito, you look cold. Can I get you a blanket?

Thank you, hija. You are very thoughtful !

When you read, you can **make connections** to your life. You can also connect to other things you have read.

How to Make Connections

👁	**1.** Read the text. Think about what it is about.	I read about _____ .
💭	**2.** Think about things you have read or seen. How are they the same as the text? How are they different?	It makes me think of _____ .
🧩	**3.** Ask yourself: *How does this help me understand what I read?*	Now I understand _____ .

Talk Together

Read Isabel's journal and the sample connection. Then use **Language Frames** to tell a partner about the connections you make.

Journal

September 7, 2010

    Starting now, I am going to write about kindness. I think that kind acts show a person's character . For example, yesterday my friend Eileen forgot her lunch. Jose gave her half of his sandwich and a piece of cake that he had planned to save for later.

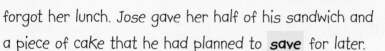

Sample Connection

"**I read about** Eileen. She forgot her lunch.

It makes me think of when I left my lunch on the school bus.

Now I understand why sharing your lunch is very thoughtful."

    Sometimes, it takes courage to do what is right . Today on the playground, kids started teasing a girl in my class named Lisa. She was afraid. Eileen made a hard choice . She could have ignored them, but she told them to stop it right now! I know it was hard for her to go against a crowd. The other kids listened, though, and stopped being mean . I think that Jose and Eileen both have excellent characters.

◀ = A good place to make a connection

207

Read a Fable

Genre

A **fable** is a story that teaches a lesson.

Moral

In a fable, the moral tells what you can learn from the story.

> fable

The girl ran down the path carrying a basket of eggs. "When the eggs hatch," she thought, "I'll sell the chickens and be rich!"

Suddenly, the girl tripped over a rock. She fell and smashed all the eggs—along with all her dreams!

—————

moral > **Moral:** *Do not count your chickens before they hatch.*

—————

Aesop's Fables

retold by **Shirleyann Costigan**

illustrated by **Janie Bynum**

These famous fables are over two thousand years old. Are their lessons about helping others still true today?

Set a Purpose

This fable teaches a lesson about kindness. Find out what the lesson is.

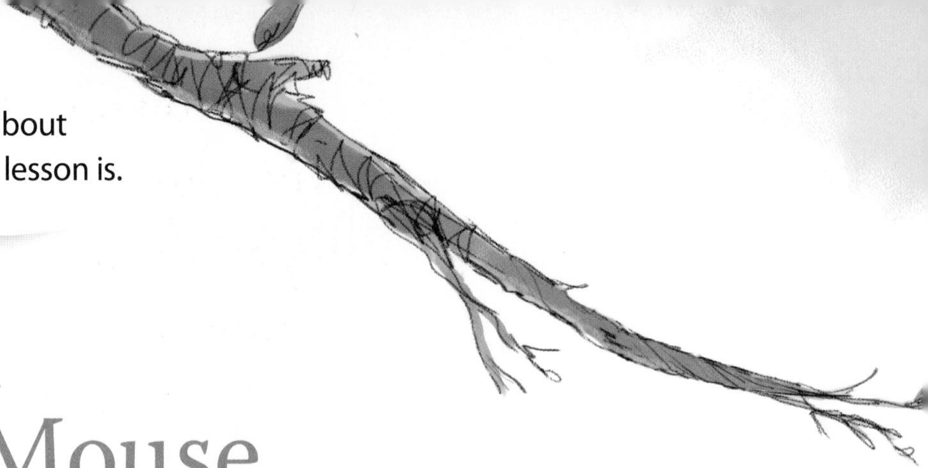

The Lion and the Mouse

One morning, a mouse **came upon** a sleeping lion. She was hurrying to get home to her babies, so she quickly **scampered** around him. But that was a mistake! The lion heard her **rustling** through the leaves.

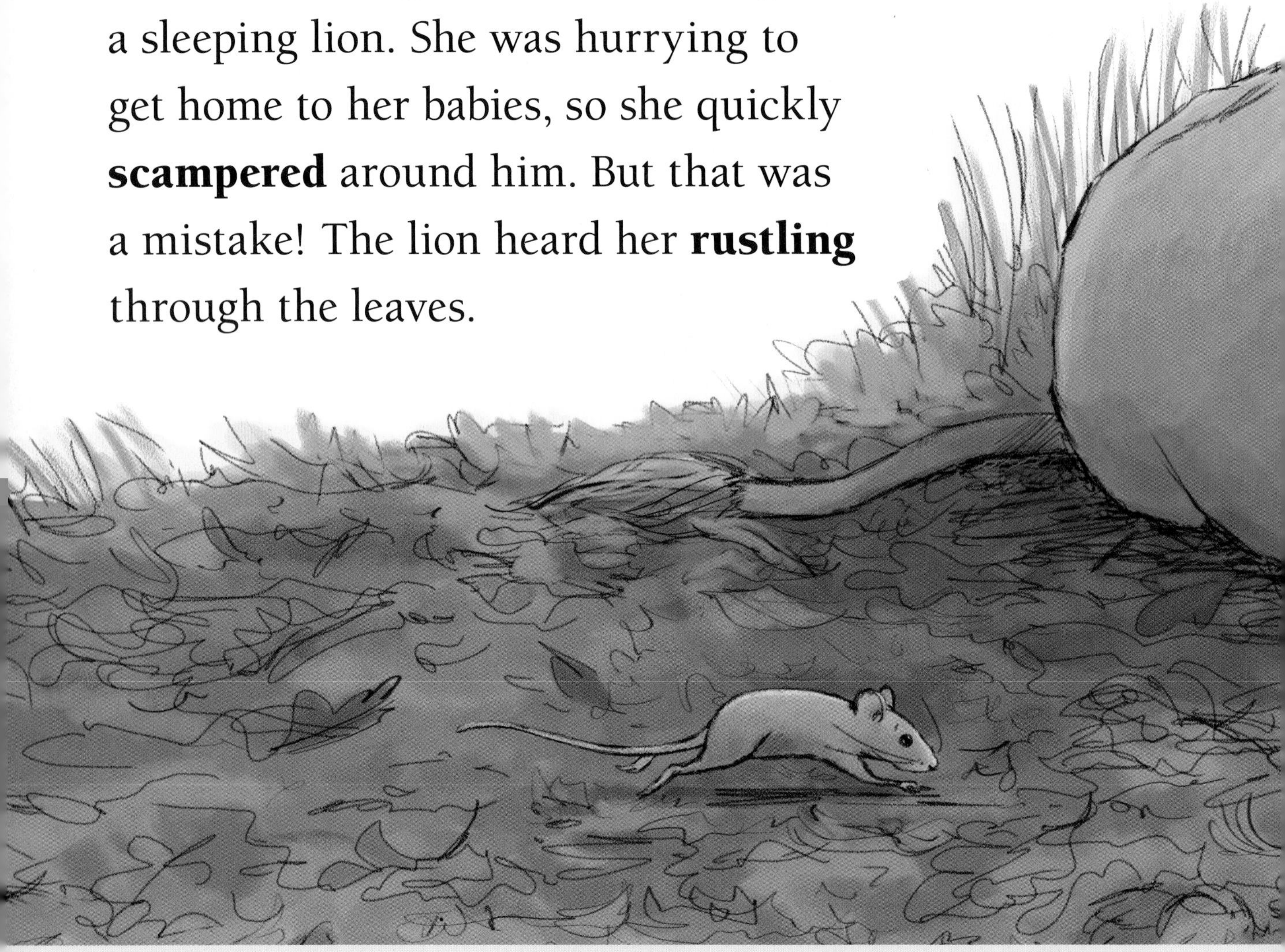

In Other Words

came upon found
scampered ran
rustling moving

The lion opened one eye and yawned, then . . . *Whump!* He **trapped** the mouse under his **paw**.

"Don't eat me!" the mouse cried **fearfully**. "You are so large. You need a much bigger meal than me!"

"Ah!" said the lion. "But you will **make a tasty snack**."

"No, no!" the mouse **pleaded**. "What will my babies do if you eat me?"

"You have babies?" asked the lion.

"Yes!" said the **terrified** mouse. "And they are always hungry. **Spare me**, and maybe I could help you someday."

The lion laughed at such a **ridiculous** idea, but he put her down. "Go home, little mother," he said **generously**.

▶ **Before You Move On**

1. **Character Traits** What does the lion do? What does this tell you about him?

2. **Make Connections** Have you ever felt like the mouse in this fable? Have you ever acted like the lion? Explain.

▶ **Predict**

One day hunters trap the lion. Will
the mouse help him? How?

The next day, hunters trapped the lion in a net.
The lion **struggled to escape**, but he could not.

Suddenly a tiny voice whispered, "**Don't worry**,
lion. I will help you."

In Other Words

struggled to escape tried to get away

Don't worry Do not be afraid

Quickly, the tiny mouse **chewed** a hole in the net. The **amazed** lion was **free**.

"Thank you, my little friend," said the **grateful** lion. Then they hurried away.

———————

Moral: *Great help can come from small friends.*

———————

In Other Words
chewed used her teeth to make
amazed surprised
free out of the net

▶ **Before You Move On**

1. **Confirm Prediction** How does the mouse help the lion? Was your prediction correct?
2. **Theme** Tell the lesson of the story in your own words.

▶ **Set a Purpose**
A farmer finds an eagle caught in a trap. Find out what happens next.

SCREE

The Farmer and the Eagle

One spring morning, Farmer Bean went into his barn. All the animals greeted him with their calls. Then he heard a strange cry.

Screeeech! It came from the place where the mice liked to **nest** in the hay.

In Other Words
nest make homes

216

Farmer Bean followed the sound and found an eagle caught in a **mousetrap**.

"Well, well," said the farmer **gently**. "You tried to catch a mouse, but you caught yourself instead."

The eagle **glared angrily** until the farmer set it free.

In Other Words
mousetrap trap to catch mice ▶
gently with kindness
glared angrily looked mad

▶ **Before You Move On**

1. **Character Traits** What does the farmer do for the eagle? Why?
2. **Make Connections** How is the farmer like the lion in "The Lion and the Mouse"?

217

▶ **Predict**
Do you think the eagle and the farmer
will meet again? What will happen?

That afternoon, Farmer Bean sat down to eat his lunch **beside** a rock wall. Suddenly he heard the same loud cry.

Screeeech! He looked up just as the eagle **swooped** down and grabbed his hat. Farmer Bean jumped up.

In Other Words
beside next to
swooped flew quickly

218

"Come back!" he cried. Then he **raced after** the eagle. On they went, over field and hill, until the eagle dropped the hat. Farmer Bean angrily picked up his hat and walked back to the wall.

In Other Words
raced after ran to try to catch

But the wall was not there! It had **tumbled down and crushed** his lunch.

Farmer Bean **searched the sky** for the eagle. "You **saved** my life!" he called, but the eagle was gone.

Moral: *Help can come from unexpected places.*

▶ **Before You Move On**

1. **Confirm Prediction** Was your prediction correct? Explain.
2. **Character** Do you think the farmer was surprised when the eagle helped him? Why or why not?

Meet the Legend

Aesop

"Aesop's Fables" are a collection of very famous, very old stories. They are called "Aesop's Fables" because many people believe they were written by a man from ancient Greece named Aesop. Aesop told wise stories that used animals to teach lessons about people. People say that Aesop was a slave, but he was such a wonderful storyteller that his master set him free.

Today, "Aesop's Fables" are some of the most famous stories in the world.

▲ This is the way one artist pictured Aesop.

Writer's Craft ✏️

Words like *scampered*, *screech*, and *crushed* are vivid words. They make a story interesting. Write your own interesting sentence. Make sure to include vivid words!

Talk About It

1. What is the moral of the **fable** "The Lion and the Mouse"? What lesson did you learn?

   The moral is _____. I learned _____.

2. Imagine you are Farmer Bean. What do you **think** about the eagle? How do you **feel** about the eagle's **choice** to **save** your life?

   I think _____. I feel _____.

3. **Compare the settings** of the two fables. How are they alike? How are they different?

   The settings are alike because _____.

   The settings are different because _____.

Learn test-taking strategies.
NGReach.com

Write About It

What is your favorite fable? Tell why you like it. Explain what you learned from it.

I like _____ because _____. I learned about _____.

Character Traits

What do the characters in "Aesop's Fables" do? What are they like?

Character Map

Character	What the Character Does	What the Character Is Like
the lion	lets the mouse leave	generous
Farmer Bean		

Now use your character map. Tell a partner about the other characters in "Aesop's Fables."

> My favorite character is _____ .
> This character _____ .
> This character is _____ .

Fluency   Comprehension Coach

Use the Comprehension Coach to practice reading with the correct expression. Rate your reading.

Suffixes

A **suffix** is a word part. You can add a suffix to the end of a word.

You can use word parts to figure out what a new word means.

The suffix **-ful** means "full of."

| thought | + | **ful** | = | **thoughtful** |

The **thoughtful** farmer frees the eagle.

The suffix **-ship** means "the state or quality of."

| citizen | + | **ship** | = | **citizenship** |

Helping others shows good **citizenship**.

Try It Together

Read the sentences. Then answer the questions.

My little brother could not tie his shoes. It was a real hardship, until I showed him how. I was happy to be so helpful.

1. Name the words that include the suffixes <u>-ful</u> and <u>-ship</u>.

2. What does each word mean?

224

Connect Across Texts Read what people from around the world have to say about helping others.

Genre A **proverb** is a short saying that gives good ideas about how to live.

Wisdom of the Ages

Proverbs can help us remember to do our very best. What do these proverbs say about helping others?

If the heart is good, the **deeds** will be good.
            —*Japanese proverb*

Today is my turn, and tomorrow is your turn.
            —*Samoan proverb*

In Other Words
Wisdom of the Ages Good Ideas People Have Learned
deeds things you do

▶ **Before You Move On**
1. **Make Connections** In "The Lion and the Mouse," the **grateful** mouse frees the lion. How is this like the first proverb?
2. **Clarify** What do you think it means to have a "good heart"? Explain.

Someone who gives
to me, teaches me to give.
—*Danish proverb*

Do good deeds and
don't worry about who
deserves them.
—*Mexican proverb*

To give quickly is a
great virtue.
—*Hindu proverb*

In Other Words
deserves should get
great virtue good thing to do

Good **actions** are
not **lost**.

—*Turkish proverb*

Do a good deed
and then do it again.

—*Welsh proverb*

In Other Words

actions things you do

lost forgotten

▶ **Before You Move On**

1. **Describe** Look at the photos. Which good deeds can be done again and again?
2. **Make Connections** Tell about a time someone did a good deed for you. Which proverb would you use to describe it?

Compare Settings and Plots

Compare the plots and settings of the two fables by Aesop. How are they the same? How are they different? Work with a partner to complete the comparison chart.

Comparison Chart

Title	Setting	Plot
"The Lion and the Mouse"	takes place in the forest	
"The Farmer and the Eagle"		

Tell about the setting of each fable here.

Tell about the plot of each fable here.

Talk Together

Why should people do good deeds? Pantomime doing a good deed with a partner. Then perform your skit for the class.

Complete Sentences

A sentence is a group of words that tells a complete thought. A **complete sentence** has two parts.

Grammar Rules Complete Sentences

• A sentence has a naming <u>part</u>. • A sentence has a <u>telling</u> <u>part</u>.	<u>The lion frees</u> <u>the mouse</u>.
• A sentence begins with a capital letter.	The mouse helps the lion. **capital letter**
• A sentence ends with a punctuation mark.	The lion is grateful. **period**

Read Complete Sentences

Read this passage. Tell the parts of each sentence. Point out the capital letters and periods.

Farmer Bean went into his barn. All the animals greeted him with their calls. Then he heard a strange cry.

Write Complete Sentences

Write two complete sentences that tell what happens after Farmer Bean frees the eagle. Read them to a partner.

Express Opinions

Listen and chant.

Heroes and Leaders

Chant

A hero can be anyone.
I think they're all around.

I disagree! They're hard to find!
Real heroes can't be found!

You believe that heroes
  are the people on T.V.
Real heroes **help** serve others.
That can start **with** you and me!

I agree!

Key Words

What are the people doing in these pictures?

Leaders . . .

share their **ideas**.

Heroes . . .

aid people in need.

How do people make a difference?

Grown-ups . . .

act as an **example**.

Kids . . .

help **serve** others.

What do you think about the sentences above?
Tell why you agree or disagree.

Sequence

Show **how things happen in order**. This is the **sequence** of events.

Sequence Chain

| First | Next | Then | Finally |

Show what happens first here.

Add more events from left to right. Use time-order words like "then."

Show what happens last here.

Talk Together

Use the picture cards. Work with a partner. Make a sequence chain to show the events in order.

More Key Words

chance
(chans) *noun*

She takes care of the plant so it has a **chance** to grow.

cost
(cawst) *noun*

The **cost** of the shirt is $20.00.

decide
(di-sīd) *verb*

She and her mom **decide** what to get at the store.

generous
(je-nu-rus) *adjective*

She is **generous** when she shares with her friends.

support
(su-port) *verb*

Friends **support** each other by listening.

Talk Together

Write a sentence for each **Key Word**. Compare your sentences with a partner's.

generous

Scott is generous because he shares his lunch with me.

Add words to My Vocabulary Notebook.
NGReach.com

Learn to Make Connections

Look at the photo and the text. Do you think of something from the world around you? If so, then you have **made a connection**.

Too much paper can be a big problem.

When you read, **make connections** to the world around you.

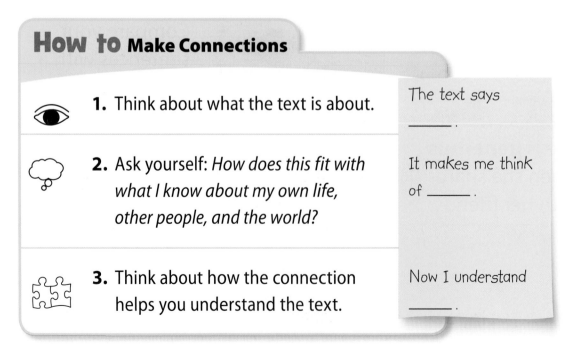

How to Make Connections

👁	**1.** Think about what the text is about.	The text says _____ .
💭	**2.** Ask yourself: *How does this fit with what I know about my own life, other people, and the world?*	It makes me think of _____ .
🧩	**3.** Think about how the connection helps you understand the text.	Now I understand _____ .

Talk Together

Read Javier's opinion essay. Read the sample connection. Then use **Language Frames** to tell a partner about your connections.

Opinion Essay

Reduce, Reuse, and Recycle

Do you agree that we should save trees and make less litter? I believe that you can do both of these things by using less paper!

First, think about whether you really need to use paper. For example, you can use a sponge instead of a paper towel. In that way, you save paper and the **cost** of a paper towel!

Next, when you **decide** to use paper, save it to use again. Some people think you always have to use a clean sheet of paper. I think we can use both sides. That would save loads of paper, too!

Finally, **support** the earth by recycling paper. This is your **chance** to save trees and make less litter. Show Earth that you care!

Sample Connection

"**The text says** that we can save trees if we cut down on the paper we use.

It makes me think of recycling programs that we have in our town.

Now I understand how to make less litter."

◄ = A good place to make a connection

Read a Human-Interest Feature

Genre

A **human interest feature** tells about real people and events.

Text Feature

A **map** can show you where things are.

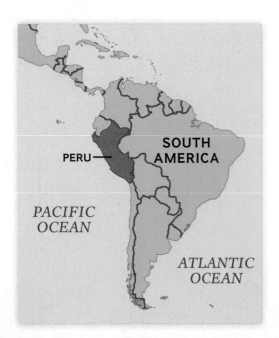

Giving Back

by **William Albert Allard**

▶ **Set a Purpose**
Find out how a picture can
make a difference.

William Albert Allard is a photographer. His
pictures are in many books and magazines. As
Mr. Allard **travels** around the world, he looks
for good photos and stories to share.

▲ **William Albert Allard**

▲ **Mr. Allard takes pictures of places all over the world.**

All of Mr. Allard's pictures show interesting people and places. But one photograph of a young **shepherd** in Peru changed people's lives. Read what Mr. Allard has to say about the photograph that made him want to give something back.

In Other Words
shepherd person who takes care of sheep

▶ **Before You Move On**

1. **Use Text Features** Look at the map. What does it show?
2. **Make Connections** What does it mean to "give something back"? How do people give back to others?

239

One spring afternoon, I was driving down the road. A boy was standing by the edge of the road, and he was crying. A driver had come down the road and **smashed through** his **band** of a dozen sheep. About half of them were dead.

The driver never stopped. But we did.

Mr. Allard took this photo of the shepherd boy. ▶

In Other Words
smashed through hit
band group

▶ **Before You Move On**

1. **Sequence** What happened before Mr. Allard came down the road in Peru?
2. **Use Text Features** Look at the photo. How does it make you feel?

241

The boy was nine or ten years old. I learned that his name was Eduardo. Eduardo's family **depended on** those sheep to earn money. Eduardo was responsible for them. Now he must go home and tell his family that half of their sheep were dead.

▲ In Peru, many young boys work to help their families.

In Other Words
depended on needed

As Eduardo looked up at me, I took just a few pictures. He was **shattered**. Then after a few minutes, we left. We didn't give the boy anything. I probably should have. But I didn't.

Mr. Allard took this picture of the roads in Peru.

▶ **Before You Move On**

1. **Sequence** What does Mr. Allard do after he takes the picture of Eduardo?
2. **Make Comparisons** This selection and "Aesop's Fables" both tell about helping others. Tell how they are different.

When I got back to my **hotel**, I thought a lot about Eduardo. I thought about his broken sheep and his tears. I thought about his family. I **realized** what it meant to lose that many sheep. The mountains of Peru can be a hard place to live and work.

▲ **Peru can be a difficult place to live.**

In Other Words
hotel place where I was staying
realized started to understand

Later, *National Geographic* magazine printed the picture of Eduardo. But I **didn't expect** what happened next. Children and other readers from all over the world **responded to** that photograph. They were very **generous** . They sent in more than $6,000.

▲ Allard enjoys sharing his pictures with others.

In Other Words
didn't expect was surprised at
responded to **decided** to act because of

▶ **Before You Move On**

1. **Make Inferences** How do you think William Allard feels about Eduardo and his family?

2. **Sequence** What happens after the picture of Eduardo is printed in the magazine?

An **organization** that **aids** people found Eduardo's family. They had a big **celebration**. They **replaced** the boy's sheep. They built a water pump for the village. The rest of the money went to help children in Peru go to school.

▼ **Eduardo holds one of his new sheep.**

In Other Words
An organization A group
celebration party
replaced bought new sheep
    to take the place of

▲ Eduardo's village in Peru.

Over the years, my pictures have **entertained** people. They have **brought people pleasure.** But this picture changed someone's life for the better. It made a real difference in Eduardo's life.

In this case, I was no longer taking, but helping to give.

In Other Words
entertained interested
brought people pleasure made people smile

▶ **Before You Move On**

1. **Explain** How did the organization help Eduardo's village?
2. **Make Connections** How can other photos make a difference in the world? Compare one you know about to William Allard's photo.

Talk About It 🗨

1. Tell one thing about the author that you learned from the **human-interest feature**.

   I learned that the author _____ .

2. Is William Allard a **hero** ? Tell your **opinion**.

   I think _____ because _____ .

3. Think about Eduardo and his village. **Make a connection** to something you know about. How does this help you understand Eduardo's problem?

   I think about _____ . I know that _____ .

   Now I understand _____ .

Learn test-taking strategies.
🔗 **NGReach.com**

Write About It ✏

With a partner, write a letter to William Allard. Tell him your **ideas** and thoughts about his story.

Dear Mr. Allard,
I think _____ . I agree that _____ . I disagree that _____ .
Yours truly,

Sequence

What happens in "Giving Back"? Make a sequence chain.
Show the events in order.

Sequence Chain

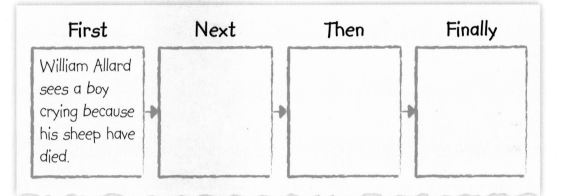

First	Next	Then	Finally
William Allard sees a boy crying because his sheep have died.			

Now use your sequence chain to retell
the events in "Going Back" to a partner.

First, _____ .
Next, _____ .
Then, _____ .
Finally, _____ .

Fluency Comprehension Coach

Use the Comprehension Coach to practice reading with
the correct phrasing. Rate your reading.

Synonyms

Synonyms are words with the same or almost the same meaning. Look at the examples. Compare the meanings of each word.

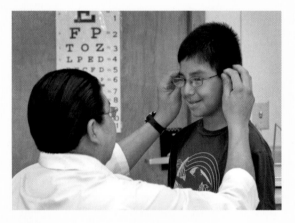

aid : to help someone

The doctor **aids** children with eye problems. He gives them glasses.

support : to help someone by giving money, food, or other things they need

This program **supports** children in other countries.

Try It Together

Read this passage. Then answer the questions.

This program **helps** children who need eyeglasses. Without eyeglasses, the children had a **hard** time seeing. Now, they do not think it is difficult to see the world around them. The program serves others by giving things they need.

1. Find a synonym for **helps** in the passage.

2. Find a synonym for **hard** in the passage.

IRAQ

Connect Across Texts Find out how another caring group is making a difference in Iraq.

Genre A **web-based news article** is posted on the Internet. It tells about events that really happened.

http://ngreach.com

Iraqi Children Get Wheelchairs—and Big Smiles

by Carol Jordan and Arwa Damon

HOME · **WORLD** · U.S. · POLITICS · ENTERTAINMENT · HEALTH · TECH · TRAVEL · BUSINESS · SPORTS

Search ▶

| NEXT ≫

MAIN

Iraqi Children Get Wheelchairs— and Big Smiles

Brad Blauser

BAGHDAD, Iraq (CNN)—

Mothers and fathers hold their **helpless children** in their arms. Other parents carry their teenage kids everywhere. Some parents in Iraq do this every day. It's because their children cannot walk.

In Other Words

helpless children children who cannot move without help

▶ **Before You Move On**

1. **Make Connections** What do the sentences tell you about families?
2. **Make Inferences** Why do the parents treat the children so gently?

251

HOME · **WORLD** · U.S. · POLITICS · ENTERTAINMENT · HEALTH · TECH · TRAVEL · BUSINESS · SPORTS

Search ▶

《 PREV | NEXT 》

MAIN

Iraqi
Children Get
Wheelchairs—
and Big Smiles

Brad Blauser

Iraqi Children Get Wheelchairs—and Big Smiles
PAGE [2] OF 3

Brad Blauser **decided** to help these families. He started a special **program**. It gives free **wheelchairs** to Iraqi children.

Blauser said, "The parents **realize** the gift that is being given to their children. They reach out to hug you."

▲ **This child has a disease called polio. She gets a new wheelchair.**

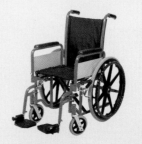

In Other Words
program plan to help others
◀ **wheelchairs** chairs with wheels
realize understand

252

The children also say thank you. Blauser **remembers** one boy. "He **couldn't** move his legs or his arms. But when we sat him in his chair, he gave us the thumbs up."

▼ **An Iraqi boy gives the thumbs up sign. He is thanking Brad Blauser (center).**

‹‹ PREV | NEXT ››

In Other Words
remembers thinks about
couldn't could not

▶ **Before You Move On**

1. **Details** How does Brad Blauser **support** families in Iraq?

2. **Make Connections** How does it feel when someone says "thank you"? How do you think Brad Blauser feels?

HOME · **WORLD** · U.S. · POLITICS · ENTERTAINMENT · HEALTH · TECH · TRAVEL · BUSINESS · SPORTS   Search ▶

Iraqi Children Get Wheelchairs—and Big Smiles
PAGE [3] OF 3

One father had carried his son 6 miles to get a wheelchair. "People **rushed over** to take the boy from his arms," Blauser remembers. "And he said, 'No. I've been carrying this child all his life. I can carry him the last 100 yards to **receive** his wheelchair.'"

▲ A father carries his son. They are going to get a wheelchair.

In Other Words
rushed over moved quickly
receive get

254

Brad Blauser works to help Iraqi parents to improve their children's lives. Since 2005, his program has given out nearly 750 free wheelchairs to families **in need**. ❖

▲ **Blauser holds a boy who will receive a wheelchair.**

‹‹ PREV |END

In Other Words
in need who need them

▶ **Before You Move On**

1. **Clarify** Why does the father on page 254 want to carry his son all the way?

2. **Make Connections** Think about a **hero** like Brad Blauser. Tell how the person makes a difference.

Compare Author's Purpose

Compare each author's purpose for writing "Giving Back" and "Iraqi Children Get Wheelchairs—and Big Smiles." Work with a partner to fill in the chart.

Comparison Chart

Author's Purpose	William Allard	Carol Jordan and Arwa Damon
to persuade		
to inform		✔
to entertain		
to share experiences	✔	
to tell about other part of the world		

> Put a check next to the author's purpose for each selection. Remember that an author can have more than one purpose.

Talk Together

How do people make a difference? Draw a picture that shows people making a difference. Use **Key Words** to explain your drawing to a partner.

Subject-Verb Agreement

A **subject** tells who or what a sentence is about. A **verb** tells what the subject is, does, or has. In a complete sentence, the subject and the verb must agree.

Grammar Rules Subject-Verb Agreement

	Subject	Verb
• When the subject is only **one person or thing**, the verb ends in **-s**.	The **boy**	wait**s**.
• When the subject is **more than one person or thing**, the verb does not end in **-s**.	**Parents**	smile.

Read Sentences

Read these sentences. Name the subject and verb of each sentence. Tell why they agree.

> The parents reach out to hug Blauser. The children also say thank you. Blauser remembers one boy.

Write Sentences 🖉

Write two sentences about Brad Blauser's wheelchair program. Make sure the verbs agree with the subjects. Share your sentences with a partner.

Write as a Reporter

Write an Interview ✏

Interview a person who has done a good deed. Publish your interview for classmates to read.

Study a Model

To do an interview, you ask someone questions. Then you write the questions and answers. Read Loana's interview.

Elliot Cantor

by Loana Huynh

Elliot Cantor started a Baseball Buddy team for kids with special needs.

Why did you start this group? My little brother loves baseball, but he wears leg braces. I wanted to give kids like him a chance to play.

How did you get started? I called friends I thought might want to be a Buddy. Almost everyone agreed!

What do the Buddies do? Each Buddy is matched with a player. They play together for the whole game. Everyone has fun!

The title and first sentence **introduce** the person being interviewed.

Loana asks questions that **focus** on what Elliot did. She uses question words like *Why, How,* and *What.*

The questions are presented in an **order** that makes sense.

Prewrite

1. **Choose a Topic** Talk with a partner. Brainstorm a list of people you know who have done good deeds. Choose one to interview. Write the questions you will ask.

_____ did a good deed when he/she _____ .

_____ sounds interesting. What questions will you ask?

2. **Get Organized** Interview the person you chose. Record the answers. Use a sequence chain to organize what you've learned.

Sequence Chain

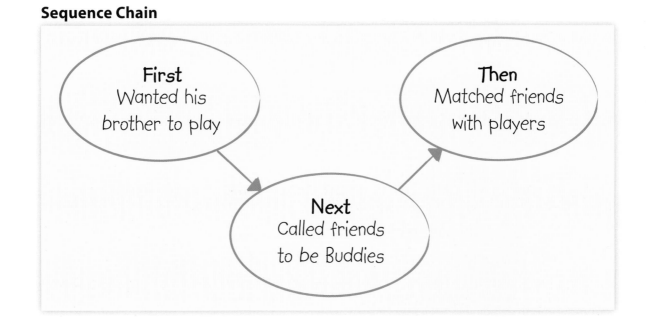

First
Wanted his
brother to play

Next
Called friends
to be Buddies

Then
Matched friends
with players

Draft

Use your chart to write a draft of your interview.

- Begin by introducing the person you interviewed.

- Include your best questions and answers.

- Use the person's exact words in the answers.

Revise

1. **Read, Retell, Respond** Read your interview aloud to a partner. Your partner retells the most important details. Next, talk about ways to make your writing better.

> You interviewed _____ about _____.

> The question about _____ doesn't really fit the topic.

2. **Make Changes** Think about your partner's ideas. Then make changes. Use the Revising Marks on page 563.

   - Are all of the questions about the topic? Remove any that aren't.

     > Why did you start this group?
     > ~~Do you like baseball?~~
     > ∧

   - Put your questions in an order that makes sense.

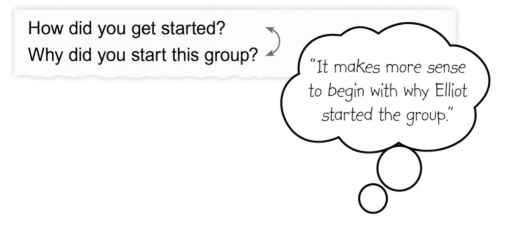

> How did you get started?
> Why did you start this group?

> "It makes more sense to begin with why Elliot started the group."

Edit and Proofread

Work with a partner to edit and proofread your interview. Use complete sentences unless the other person's exact words include a sentence fragment.

Publish

On Your Own Share your interview with your class. Choose a partner to read the answers as you read the questions.

Presentation Tips	
If you are the speaker…	**If you are the listener…**
Make eye contact with your listeners.	Think about what you want to learn from this interview.
Keep your voice natural, as though you were asking the questions for the first time.	Listen to see if you think the writer asked good questions.

With a Group Put your interviews together. Make a Good Deeds Newsletter. Print copies to share with others.

Headlines

HIGH SCHOOL   September Issue, Vol. III

Good Deeds Newsletter
Elliot Cantor
by Loana Huynh

Elliot Cantor started a Baseball Buddy team for kids with special needs.

Why did you start this group?

My little brother loves baseball, but he wears leg braces. I wanted to give kids like him a chance to play.

BIG

Question

What are our
responsibilities
to each other?

Talk Together

In this unit, you found lots of answers to the **Big Question**.
Now, use your concept map to discuss the **Big Question** with
the class.

Concept Map

to be kind

Why Should We Lend
a Hand to Others?

Share Your Ideas

Choose one of these ways to share your ideas about the **Big Question**.

Write It! ✏️

Write a Proverb

Write your own proverb about helping others. Draw a picture to illustrate it. Share your proverb with the class.

Doing good makes you feel good!

Talk About It! 💬

Give an Opinion

Think about the different people and characters you have read about. What makes them kind? How are they heroes? Tell a partner your feelings and opinions. Then switch roles.

Do It! ✋

Perform a Play

Work with three or more classmates. Make a short play using one of the fables. Include dialogue. Perform the play for the class.

Write It! ✏️

Write a Chant or Song

Write a short chant or song about helping others. Include repetition and rhyme. Share your chant or song with the class.

Helping others is the thing to do.

Everything Changes

BIG Question

Why is nature always changing?

Unit at a Glance
▶ **Language**: Engage in Discussion, Make Comparisons
▶ **Literacy**: Visualize
▶ **Content**: Changes in Nature

Unit
5

Share What You Know

① **Draw** a picture of your favorite time of year. Work with a partner.

Do It!

② **Share** your picture with the class.

③ **Place** all of the pictures in order of the seasons. Work with the whole class.

Build Background: Use this interactive resource to learn about cycles in nature.
NGReach.com

Engage in Discussion

Listen and read along.

Dialogue ((MP3))

Day and Night

 I think day is better than night.

 Why do you think so?

 Because it is bright.

 I think night is better than day.

 Why do you think so?

It's hard to say!
I like planet Mars—
I love all the stars!

 And I love the Milky Way!
I guess I like **both** night and day.

Key Words

The **moon** and **stars** come out at night.

Day **begins**.

The sun moves high in the sky. **Shadows** get short.

What changes happen on Earth every day?

The sun moves lower in the sky. Shadows get long.

The sun sets.

Day **ends**. **Night** begins.

Talk Together

What do you see during the day? How is it different from what you can see at night?

267

Theme

The **theme** of a story is its main message. Look for clues about the theme of the story below.

A Night Under the Stars

Theme Chart

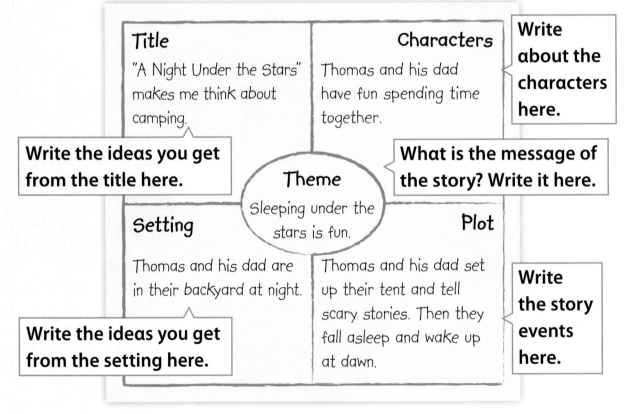

Title

"A Night Under the Stars" makes me think about camping.

Write the ideas you get from the title here.

Characters

Thomas and his dad have fun spending time together.

Write about the characters here.

Theme

Sleeping under the stars is fun.

What is the message of the story? Write it here.

Setting

Thomas and his dad are in their backyard at night.

Write the ideas you get from the setting here.

Plot

Thomas and his dad set up their tent and tell scary stories. Then they fall asleep and wake up at dawn.

Write the story events here.

Talk Together

Tell your partner about your favorite story. Write the details in a theme chart. Work together to find the theme of the story.

More Key Words

appear
(u-**pēr**) *verb*

The whale **appears** above the water.

motion
(**mō**-shun) *noun*

The man is in **motion**.

observe
(ub-**zurv**) *verb*

She **observes** the insect.

pattern
(**pa**-turn) *noun*

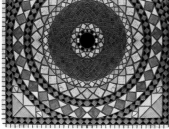

Orange, gray, and blue tiles make a **pattern** on this floor.

repeat
(ri-**pēt**) *verb*

She has to **repeat** what she said because her friend did not hear her.

Talk Together

Make an Expanded Meaning Map for each **Key Word**. Compare your maps with a partner's.

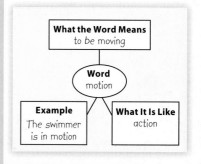

Add words to My Vocabulary Notebook.
NGReach.com

Learn to Visualize

As you read, try to **visualize**, or form pictures in your mind. Look for words that tell how things look, taste, smell, feel, and sound.

I wake up. The warm sun shines through my window.

It's breakfast. I hear the bacon as it sizzles. I smell the frybread.

After school, I play in the park. The wind whistles as I play on the swing.

Try to **visualize** what Thomas does.

How to Visualize

👁	**1.** As you read, look for words that describe how things look, taste, smell, feel, and sound.	I read _____ .
☁	**2.** Use the words to create pictures in your mind.	I think it _____ like _____ .
✏	**3.** Draw the picture. Show how you see things in your mind.	I draw _____ .

Talk Together

Read Carmen's story. Read the sample visualization.
Then use **Language Frames** to tell a partner how
you visualized things in the story.

Story

Playtime in the Park

My friend Thomas likes to play in the park every
day after school. He loves to play on the swings.
The **motion** of his legs and body make him go
really high.

Thomas always notices things. He **observes**
how the park changes from spring to summer. As
time goes on, he notices a **pattern**.

In spring, tulips **appear** in the green grass.
Thomas calls me and asks, "Why are you inside?
Don't you want to come out and play?" I run outside.
We play tag and hide-and-seek.

In summer, the grass is still green, but the tulips
are gone. We try to **repeat** the games we play in
spring, but we get too hot. Then we lie in the shade.

"Is there anything else we
can do?" he asks.

"I know," I say. "Let's run
through the sprinklers!" Then we
play until it is almost night.

Sample Visualization

"I read about Thomas
playing on a swing in
the park.

I think it feels like the
wind is rushing past him
as he swings through
the air.

I draw a boy smiling as
he swings on the swing."

◀ = A good place to visualize

271

Read a Story

Genre

Realistic fiction is a made-up story that seems like it could really happen.

Characters

Characters are the people in a story.

mother

boy

When the Wind Stops

by **Charlotte Zolotow**

illustrated by **Stefano Vitale**

▶ **Set a Purpose**
A boy **wonders** why the **day**
must **end**. Find out what he learns.

The bright sun had shone all **day**, and now the day was **coming to an end**. The sun **sank lower** into the **glowing** pink clouds. The little boy was sorry to see the day end.

In Other Words
wonders thinks about
coming to an end almost over
sank lower went down
glowing bright

Later, his mother came to say good **night** .

"Why does the day have to end?" he asked her.

"So night can **begin** ," she said, "look."

Through the window, the little boy could see **a pale sliver of moon** in the **darkening sky** behind the branches of the pear tree.

In Other Words
a pale sliver of moon some of the **moon**
darkening sky sky that was getting darker

"But where does the sun go when the day ends?" the little boy asked.

"The day **doesn't** end," said his mother. "It begins **somewhere else**. The sun will be shining there, when night begins here. Nothing ends."

"Nothing?" the little boy asked.

"Nothing," his mother said. "It begins in another place or in a different way."

In Other Words
doesn't does not
somewhere else in another place

276

▶ **Before You Move On**

1. **Explain** What does the boy learn about **day** and **night**?
2. **Visualize** Picture the boy and his mother talking about the end of the day. Where are they? What do you see?

▶ **Predict**
Look at the pictures. What questions
will the little boy ask next?

The little boy lay in bed, and his mother sat beside him.

"Where does the wind go when it stops?" he asked.

"It **blows away** to make the trees **dance** somewhere else."

In Other Words
blows away goes to another place
dance move and shake

"Where does the **dandelion fluff** go when it blows away?"

"It carries the seeds of new dandelions to someone's **lawn**."

"Where does the mountain go after the top?"

"It goes down to where it becomes the **valley**."

"Where does the rain go when a storm **is over**?"
"It goes into clouds to make other storms."

"Where do clouds go when they move across the sky?"

"They go to **make shade** somewhere else."

▶ **Before You Move On**

1. **Confirm Prediction** What did the boy ask? Was your prediction correct?
2. **Visualize** Think about trees "dancing." What else do you see, hear, and feel when the wind blows?

▶ **Predict**

Look at the pictures. What part of nature will the boy learn about next?

"**W**hat about the leaves when they **turn color and fall**?"

"They go into the ground to become part of new trees with new leaves."

In Other Words

turn color and fall change colors and fall off the trees

282

"But when the leaves fall, that is the end of something!" the little boy said. "It is the end of autumn."

"Yes," his mother said. "The end of autumn is when the winter begins."

"And the end of winter . . . ?" the little boy asked.

"The end of winter, when the snow **melts** and birds come back, is the beginning of spring," his mother said.

The little boy smiled.

In Other Words
melts turns into water

"It really does go on and on," he said. "Nothing ends."

He looked out at the sky. The sun was gone completely and the **lovely** pink clouds had **disappeared**. The sky was dark and purple-black, and high above the branches of the pear tree shone a thin moon.

In Other Words
lovely pretty
disappeared gone; left

"Today is over," his mother said, "and it's time for sleep. Tomorrow morning, when you wake, the moon will be beginning a night far away, and the sun will be here to begin a new day." ❖

▶ **Before You Move On**

1. **Confirm Prediction** What does the boy learn about nature?
2. **Character** How does the boy feel about what he has learned? How can you tell?

Meet the Author
Charlotte Zolotow

AWARD WINNER

From the time Charlotte Zolotow was a child, she always had a big imagination. Ms. Zolotow is in her 90s now, but she still remembers how it felt to be young. Her many stories show that her imagination has only grown bigger and better over the years.

▲ Charlotte Zolotow's friends sometimes call her "CZ."

Writer's Craft

Charlotte Zolotow uses details such as "lovely pink clouds" and "purple-black" sky to help you see and feel what is happening in the story. Write your own sentence about nature. Be sure to use a lot of details!

Talk About It

1. Name one thing in the story that is **realistic**. Read it aloud.

   _____ could happen in real life.

2. The boy's mother says, "Nothing **ends**." What does she mean? **Discuss** your ideas with a partner.

   I think _____ because _____ .
   I don't think _____ because _____ .

3. What do you see from your window before you go to bed? Find words in the story that describe the **night** sky. Then create a picture in your mind. Tell a partner what you see, hear, and smell.

   I see _____ .
   I hear _____ .
   I smell _____ .

Learn test-taking strategies.
🅝 NGReach.com

Write About It ✏️

Find your favorite part of the story. Write a sentence telling why you like the part. Tell how it makes you feel.

Today we read _____ .
I like _____ because _____ .
It makes me feel _____ .

Theme

What is the theme of "When the Wind Stops"?

Theme Chart

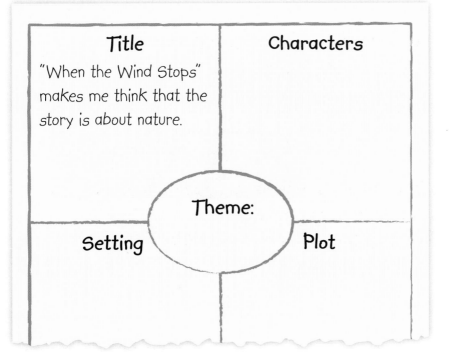

Title

"When the Wind Stops" makes me think that the story is about nature.

Characters

Theme:

Setting

Plot

Now use your theme chart. Tell your partner about the theme of "When the Wind Stops."

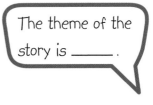

The theme of the story is _____ .

Fluency  Comprehension Coach

Use the Comprehension Coach to practice reading with the correct expression. Rate your reading.

Antonyms

Antonyms are words with opposite meanings. Look at the pictures below. Read the antonyms. Then compare their meanings.

begin : When something starts, it **begins** .

Day begins at sunrise.

end : When something stops, it **ends** .

Day ends at sunset.

> **Try It Together**

Read the passage from "When the Wind Stops." Then answer the questions.

> Later, his mother came to say good night. "Why does the **day** have to **end**?" he asked her. "So night can begin," she said, "look."

1. Find an antonym for **day**. Use it in a sentence.

2. Find an antonym for **end**. Use it in a sentence.

Connect Across Texts Now read this article to find out why some changes in nature happen.

Genre A **science article** is nonfiction. It can tell how something in nature works. It might also have an **experiment** you can try to see how things work.

Day and Night

by Glen Phelan

Earth

axis

▲ Earth spins on an imaginary line. It is called an axis. This diagram shows how.

Around and Around

The **planet** we live on seems to **stand still**, yet Earth is always moving. It rotates, or spins, around and around. You cannot feel Earth rotate because you are moving along with it.

In Other Words
planet world
stand still not move
imaginary pretend

▶ **Before You Move On**

1. **Use Text Features** How does the diagram help you understand the way **Earth** spins?
2. **Predict** How do you think the way **Earth** spins is connected to **day** and **night**?

Because Earth spins, only one part can **face** the sun at a time. When the sun reaches the part facing it, it makes day. The other part of Earth **doesn't** get any sun at that time, so it is night.

This part of Earth faces the sun. It is day on this part.

This part of Earth faces away from the sun. It is night on this part.

sun

Earth

▲ In some parts of the world right now, it is day. In other parts, it is night.

In Other Words
face turn toward
doesn't does not

Sunrise and Sunset

From Earth, it looks like the sun moves across the sky. But the sun does not move. Earth moves. When Earth starts to face the sun, the sun looks like it **rises** into the sky. When Earth starts to turn away from the sun, the sun looks like it goes down.

It looks like the sun comes up in the morning.

At **night**, it looks like the sun goes down.

12:00 p.m.

7:00 a.m.

7:00 p.m.

▲ As **Earth** spins, it looks like the sun moves across the sky.

In Other Words
Sunrise When the Sun Comes Up
Sunset When the Sun Goes Down
rises goes up

▶ **Before You Move On**

1. **Visualize** Point to a spot on land in the diagram. Move your finger up. Describe how the sky looks at that time.

2. **Explain** Why does it look like the sun is moving down in the sky at sunset?

Try this experiment to see how day turns to night.
You will need:

- a partner • a flashlight • a ball

1. PARTNER 1 holds the ball.

2. PARTNER 2 shines the flashlight on the ball.

3. PARTNER 2 asks someone to turn off the classroom lights.

4. PARTNER 1 slowly rotates the ball as PARTNER 2 shines the light on it.

flashlight

ball

PARTNER 1

PARTNER 2

What Happens?

Light shines on different parts of the ball as it turns. Now pretend the ball is Earth and the flashlight is the sun. When one part of Earth faces the sun, it is daytime. When it turns away from the sun, it is night. So when day begins on your side of the world, night begins for someone on the other side!

night

CHINA

UNITED STATES

day

In China, it is **night**. But in the United States, it is **day**.

▶ **Before You Move On**

1. **Clarify** How does the experiment help you understand **day** and **night**?
2. **Use Text Features** What helps you know what to do in the experiment?

Compare Author's Purpose

The authors of "When the Wind Stops" and "Day and Night" both had more than one reason for writing. **Compare and explain their purposes** to complete the chart.

Comparison Chart

Charlotte Zolotow	Glen Phelan
• to tell about how nature changes	• to tell about changes in nature
•	•
•	•

Write more reasons for writing from "When the Wind Stops" here.

Write more reasons for writing from "Night and Day" here.

Talk Together

Why is nature always changing? Draw a series of pictures to show one of the cycles in nature. Explain your pictures to the class. Use **Key Words**.

Kinds of Sentences

A group of words that tells a complete thought is a sentence.
There are four **different kinds of sentences**.

Grammar Rules Kinds of Sentences

• A **statement** tells something. It ends with a **period**.	It is morning. The day is just beginning.
• A **question** asks something. It ends with a **question mark**.	Where did the moon and stars go?
• An **exclamation** shows strong feeling. It ends with an **exclamation mark**.	What a great day!
• A **command** tells someone to do something. It ends with a **period**.	Make your bed, please.

Read Kinds of Sentences

Read this passage. Find two different kinds of sentences. Then make up your own sentence.

> The little boy lay in bed, and his mother sat beside him. "Where does the wind go when it stops?" he asked. "It blows away to make the trees dance somewhere else."

Write Kinds of Sentences

Pretend you are looking out a window at the world. Write two different kinds of sentences about what you see. Read your sentences to a partner.

High Frequency **Words**

and

but

different

have

Make Comparisons

Listen and sing.

Autumn and Winter

Song (((MP3)))

Both autumn **and** winter **have** weather that's colder
Than summer and spring, when warm days are long.
In autumn it's chilly, **but** in winter it's snowy.
In fall, leaves are falling. In winter, they're gone.

I love fall and winter because they are **different**.
In winter we sled, but in autumn, we run.
Both autumn and winter have one thing in common:
Both seasons are favorites for all kinds of fun.

Tune: "Cockles and Mussels"

Key Words

Weather and temperature change with the **seasons**.

spring

summer

winter

fall or autumn

Talk Together

Look at the photos. What happens in each season? What changes with each season?

Compare and Contrast

To **compare**, look for how things are alike. To **contrast**, look for how things are different. Compare and contrast the animals below.

Comparison Chart

	Summer	Winter
Brown Bears		
Wolves		

Write or show facts about the animals here.

Look for how the animals are alike and different.

Talk Together

With your partner, choose two picture cards. Talk about what is the same and what is different. Together, fill in a comparison chart.

More Key Words

affect
(u-**fekt**) *verb*

The hot sun **affects** ice cream. It makes ice cream melt.

explain
(ik-**splān**) *verb*

She **explains** the math problem to her student.

happen
(**ha**-pun) *verb*

They watch what **happens** in the game. They see a homerun.

measure
(**me**-zhur) *verb*

He **measures** the doorway to see how big it is.

reason
(**rē**-zun) *noun*

Hard work and practice are the **reasons** she is a good dancer.

Talk Together

Make a Word Web of Examples for each **Key Word**. Compare your webs with a partner's.

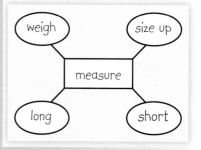

weigh — size up — measure — long — short

Add words to My Vocabulary Notebook.
NGReach.com

Learn to Visualize

As you read, try to **visualize**, or form pictures in your mind.

I love autumn. I hike in the woods. I *see* red, yellow, and orange leaves on the trees.

I love summer. We swim at a white sandy beach. The ocean is green and blue.

Try to **visualize** what Abby and Leon are talking about.

How to Visualize

👁	**1.** As you read, look for words that describe how things look, sound, smell, taste, and feel.	I read _____.
💭	**2.** Use the words to create pictures in your mind.	I see _____.
✏️	**3.** Draw the picture. Ask yourself: *How does this help me understand what I read?*	I draw _____. Now I understand _____.

Talk Together

Read the letter that Leon writes to Abby. Read the
sample visualization. Then use **Language Frames**
to tell a partner how you visualized things in the letter.

Letter

July 15, 2010

Dear Abby,

The **reason** I am writing is to tell you about my vacation.
We are staying in the same beach town we stayed in last
winter, but it is very different in summer. Let me **explain**.
On summer mornings, crowds of people flock to the beach
to swim. When that **happens**, it's hard to find room to put
down a towel!

In winter, clouds often block the sun. The sky is not blue. It
is gray. This **affects** the number of tourists who come to the
beach. I think the beach looks prettier when there are just a
few people.

The two seasons at the beach are alike in one way. During
both seasons, we buy food at the local market and have fresh
fish to cook and eat.
I like both seasons at
the beach. I wish you
were here in summer!

Your friend,

Leon

Sample Visualization

"I read about Leon's
vacation at the beach.

I see a sunny, crowded
beach.

I draw a white beach
crowded with swimmers.
Now I understand why
it is hard for Leon to
find a place to put his
towel."

◀ =A good place to visualize

Read a Poem

Genre

A **poem** uses words in a special way to tell about ideas. This poem gives facts about the seasons.

Text Features

A **diagram** uses pictures, arrows, and labels to show how something works.

Earth's Orbit

picture

label Sun

Earth

arrow

What Makes the Seasons?

written and illustrated by
Megan Montague Cash

The day began with sprinkling rain

tapping at the windowpane.

Rain has turned the sky to gray.

Our snowman friend has gone away.

Fresh green leaves are peeking out.

What makes this their time to sprout?

In Other Words
tapping at the windowpane hitting against
   the window
sprout begin to grow

Spring's mild weather wakes the seeds,

bringing showers each seed needs.

Spring was here but couldn't stay.

Spring left on a summer day.

In Other Words

mild warm and wet

wakes the seeds gets the seeds ready to grow

showers rain

Plants that once were hardly there

now have flowers everywhere.

Each tree and weed and lima bean

shows its favorite shade of green.

Why is this a growing season?

Plants grow tall, but what's the reason?

Plants grow best in summer light,

when days are long and warm and bright.

▶ **Before You Move On**

1. **Details** What **happens** in **spring**? What **happens** in **summer**?

2. **Visualize** Look at the pictures. Tell how **summer** feels, looks, and smells.

▶ **Predict**
What will **happen** when the
summer is over?

But when the summer days are done,

the autumn days have just begun.

The sun grows dim, the wind blows cold.

Green leaves turn to red and gold.

The colored leaves dance all around.

But why do leaves fall to the ground?

In Other Words
grows dim is not as bright
dance all around move in
the wind

In all the leaves on all the trees

are teeny tree food factories.

Leaves use sun to make the food.

When there's less sun, leaves come unglued.

In Other Words

teeny tree food factories small parts that
    make food for the tree

come unglued fall from the tree

The weather brought a change last night.

Winter turned the world to white.

Puffy flakes swirled high and low.

Snow makes flurries. What makes snow?

In chilly clouds the raindrops freeze.

It's one of winter's recipes.

In Other Words
flurries snowflakes that blow around in the wind
freeze turn cold and hard
It's one of winter's recipes. It is something
   that **happens** in **winter**.

Winter is a time for sleep.

Trees are resting. Seeds will keep.

Many creatures sleep and wait.

Winter's time to hibernate.

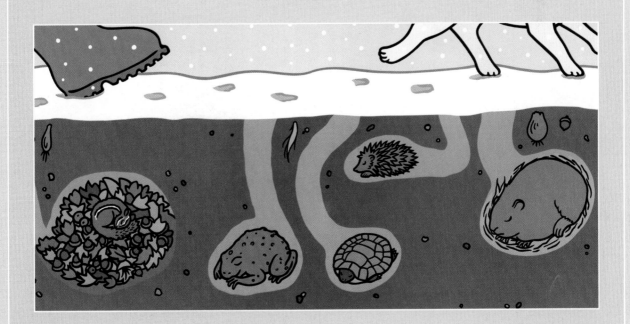

In Other Words
creatures animals and insects
Winter's **Winter** is
hibernate sleep until spring comes again

▶ **Before You Move On**

1. **Confirm Prediction** What **happens** when **summer** is over? Was your prediction correct?

2. **Visualize** What do snowflakes look like? How do you think they feel?

▶ **Predict**
Look at the diagram below. What
causes the **seasons** to change?

But what controls the season's change?

And what makes weather rearrange?

Earth's yearly trip around the sun

affects the seasons one by one.

Earth's Orbit

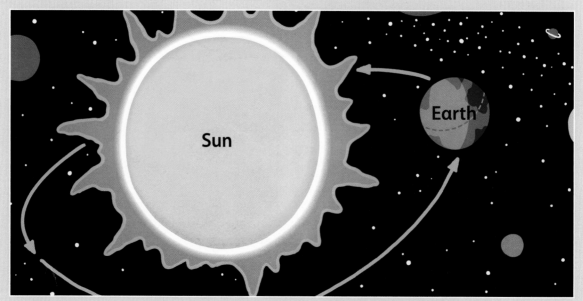

▲ Earth takes a whole year to move around the sun.

In Other Words
controls makes; causes
rearrange change from **season** to **season**
Orbit Path Around the Sun

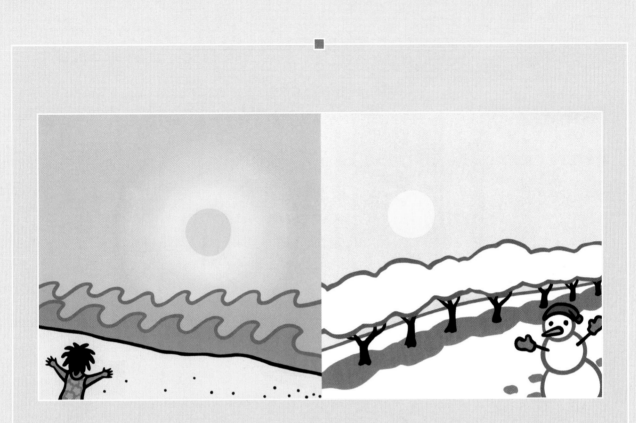

In summer when the days are long

the sun shines down both hot and strong.

While winter has the shortest days —

less time for Earth to get warm rays.

Earth's Hemispheres

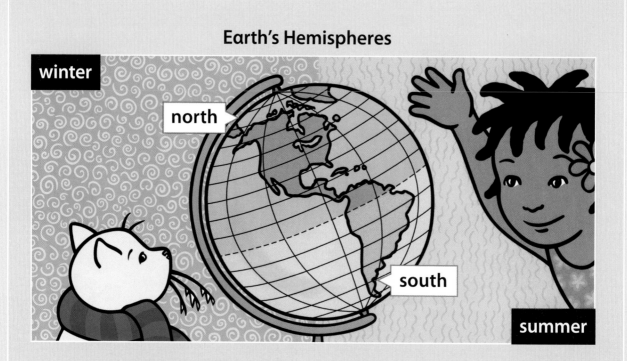

But when you have a summer day,

it's winter half the world away.

If summer blossoms open wide,

it's winter on Earth's other side.

In Other Words

Earth's Hemispheres The Two Main
   Parts of Earth

half the world away on the other side
   of Earth

blossoms flowers

Seasons change four times a year.

When each one ends, the next one's here.

Enjoying changes one by one

makes the seasons so much fun.

In Other Words

the next one's here another **season** begins

▶ **Before You Move On**

1. **Confirm Prediction** What causes the **seasons** to change?
2. **Make Comparisons** Find words in the poem about how **summer** and **winter** are different. Describe each season to a partner.

317

Talk About It

1. **Poems** use words in an interesting way. Find your favorite lines in the poem. What do you find interesting about them?

   I like it when the author says, "_____."
   It is interesting because _____ .

2. **Compare** the **weather** in **spring** and **summer**. How is it alike? How is it different? Give examples from the text.

   Spring and summer are alike because _____ .
   They are different because spring weather is _____, but summer weather is _____ .

3. What season is it? What **season** will follow? Describe what you will see, hear, smell, and taste when the season changes.

   I will see _____ .   I will smell _____ .
   I will hear _____ .   I will taste _____ .

   Learn test-taking strategies.
   NGReach.com

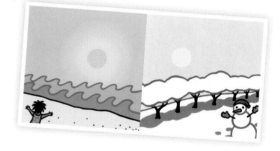

Write About It

Work with a partner to write a poem about your favorite season. Tell how the season looks, sounds, feels, smells, and tastes.

   Spring looks _____ .
   It sounds _____ .
   It smells _____ .

Compare and Contrast

Think about the ideas in "What Makes the Seasons?" How are the seasons alike? How are they different?

Comparison Chart

	Spring	Summer	Fall	Winter
Leaves	sprout			
Raindrops	fall			
Snow	melts			
Days	get longer			

Now use your comparison chart. Tell your partner how the seasons are alike and different in "What Makes the Seasons?".

> Spring and summer are alike because _____.
> Winter and spring are different because _____.

Fluency  Comprehension Coach

Use the Comprehension Coach to practice reading with the correct intonation. Rate your reading.

319

Multiple-Meaning Words

Some words have **more than one meaning**. You can use other words near the word to figure out the right meaning.

Fall is a multiple-meaning word. Look at these examples.

In the **fall**, the leaves change colors.
Meaning: the season before winter

Be careful not to **fall**!

Meaning: to trip or slip

Try It Together

Read this passage. Then answer the questions.

In the **spring**, my family always plants a garden. First, we put the seeds in the ground. After a while, new plants **spring** up from the dirt!

1. What does **spring** mean in the first sentence?

2. What does **spring** mean in the third sentence: "a season" or "grow quickly"?

Connect Across Texts Read about an amazing change that **happens** to some frogs each **winter**.

Genre A **science article** is nonfiction. It can explain something about nature.

A Winter Wonder

by *Tyrone Hayes, PhD*

Hi! My name is Dr. Tyrone Hayes. I **study** frogs and toads. I work in a **lab** and sometimes in muddy ponds.

Dr. Tyrone Hayes studies frogs and toads. ▶

In Other Words
study learn about
lab special room where scientists work ▶

▶ **Before You Move On**

1. **Visualize** What do you think Dr. Hayes feels, smells, and hears when he is at work?
2. **Make Inferences** How do you think Dr. Hayes feels about his work? Explain.

321

We know that **weather** changes with each **season** .
Did you know that some frogs change with the
seasons, too?

Winter can be a hard season for frogs. It's so cold
that many ponds **freeze**. Insects that frogs eat can
be hard to find, too.

But winter is no problem for the North American
wood frog! It has **an unusual** way to survive the
harsh winter. Each winter, the wood frog lets its
body freeze. Then it sleeps all winter long.

In the cold winter, many ponds freeze.

▲ **A North American wood
frog freezes each winter.**

In Other Words
freeze turn to hard ice
an unusual a very different
harsh long and cold

Soon the warm **spring** comes. That's when the frog wakes up! **Its body thaws.** Then it hops away until winter comes again.

This **unique** frog is **truly amazing**! ❖

In the spring, the wood frog wakes up again. ▶

In the warm spring, ponds are filled with life.

▶ **Before You Move On**

1. **Make Comparisons** Look at the photos on pages 322–323. Tell how the pictures are the same and how they are different.

2. **Main Idea** What is so unusual about the wood frog?

Compare Genres

"What Makes the Seasons?" is a poem. "Winter Wonders" is a science article. How are the two texts the same? How are they different? Work with a partner to complete the Venn diagram.

Venn Diagram

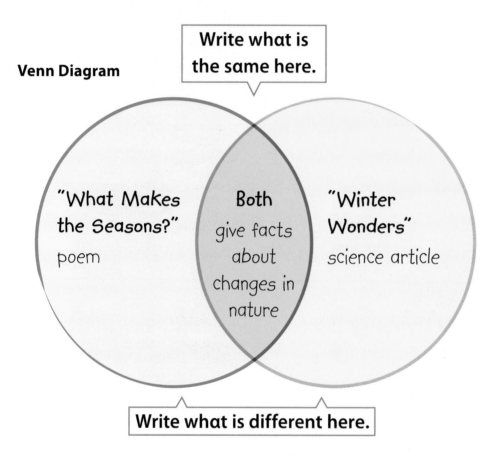

Write what is the same here.

"What Makes the Seasons?" poem

Both give facts about changes in nature

"Winter Wonders" science article

Write what is different here.

Talk Together

Why is nature always changing? Take turns choosing picture cards with a partner. Use **Key Words** to explain what happens during the season on the card you picked.

Grammar and Spelling

Questions

You can ask **questions** to get information. All questions begin with a capital letter and end with a question mark.

Grammar Rules Questions

	Question	Answer
• Some questions ask for a "yes" or "no" answer.	**I**s it spring yet**?**	Yes, it is.
	Is the plant growing**?**	Yes.
• Some questions ask for more information. • A question can start with **who**, **when**, **where**, **what**, or **how**.	**Who** can tell me about the seasons**?**	The teacher can tell you about the seasons.
	When will autumn end**?**	Autumn will end in November.
	Where can we go this summer**?**	We can go to the beach this summer.

Read Questions

Read these sentences. Name the sentences that ask questions. How do you know?

> Why is this a growing season?
>
> Plants grow tall, but what's the reason?
>
> Plants grow best in summer light,
>
> when days are long and warm and bright.

Write Questions ✏️

Write two questions about seasons. Ask a partner your questions.

Write as an Observer

Write a Comparison ✏

What are the seasons like where you live? Write a few paragraphs to compare or contrast two seasons. Work with your classmates to create a book of seasons.

Study a Model

When you compare, you tell how two things are the same. When you contrast, you tell how they are different. Read Andy's comparison of his two favorite seasons.

My Favorite Seasons

By Andy Halliday

I live near Dallas, Texas. My favorite seasons here are **fall and spring**.

The temperature during **both** seasons is great. It's usually in the 70s. That's not too hot and not too cold. It's perfect!

The weather during spring is a little **different** from the weather in fall. In spring, we get storms, with lots of wind, thunder and lightning. Once in a while, there's even a tornado!

In the fall, we don't get storms or tornadoes. We get football, **though**. That's just as exciting!

The **topic sentence** tells the two things you are comparing or contrasting.

Details are **organized** to show how the seasons are the same and different.

Special words help you signal what is the same or different.

326

Prewrite

1. **Choose a Topic** Which seasons will you write about? Talk with a partner to make your choice.

<table>
<tr><th colspan="2">Language Frames</th></tr>
<tr><td>Tell Your Ideas</td><td>Respond to Ideas</td></tr>
<tr><td>My favorite _____ are _____ .

The two _____ are alike because they both _____ .

The _____ are different because _____ .</td><td>Why are _____ and _____ your favorite _____ ?

What other things are alike?

You said _____ and _____ are alike, but I think they're different because _____ .</td></tr>
</table>

2. **Gather Information** Think of all the ways the two seasons are alike and different. Make notes to gather details.

3. **Get Organized** Put your ideas in a comparison chart.

Comparison Chart

	Fall	Spring
Temperature	in the 70s	in the 70s
Weather	thunderstorms	sunny weather
Sports	football	baseball

Draft

Use your comparison chart to write your draft.

- Write a topic sentence that tells the two things you are comparing.

- Arrange your details so that the comparison is clear. You can tell about one season first, and then the other. You can also put details about the same things together, like Andy did.

Revise

1. **Read, Retell, Respond** Read your draft aloud to a partner. Your partner listens and then retells the main details. Next, talk about ways to make your writing better.

Language Frames	
Retell	**Make Suggestions**
The _____ you compared are _____ and _____ .	I'm still not sure why you say _____ and _____ are alike. Can you add more details?
The _____ are alike because _____ .	The order you put the details in doesn't seem to make sense. Try moving _____ to _____ .
The _____ are different because _____ .	

2. **Make Changes** Think about your draft and your partner's ideas. Then use the Revising Marks on page 563 to mark your changes.

- Do you include enough details? Add more if you need them.

  > In spring, we get storms. with lots of wind, thunder and lightning.
  > ∧

- Make sure the comparison is clear. Check the order of your details.

  > The temperature during both seasons is great. It's usually in the 70s. ⟨We get tornadoes in the spring, though.⟩
  >
  > Move this to next paragraph.

Edit and Proofread

Work with a partner to edit and proofread your comparison. Be sure you use the correct end marks for different kinds of sentences. Use the marks on page 563 to show your changes.

Punctuation Tip

✓ When you write about temperature, do not use an apostrophe.

70s, not 70's

Publish

On Your Own Make a final copy of your comparison. Read it aloud to your class. See if they agree with how you described the seasons.

Presentation Tips	
If you are the speaker...	**If you are the listener...**
Stress comparison words such as *both*, *alike*, and *also*.	Summarize how the two subjects are alike and different.
If your listeners don't agree with your comparison, give more details or examples.	Is it clear how the subjects are alike or different? If not, ask questions.

With a Group Collect names of friends and family who live in other cities or states. Send them your comparisons. Ask them to write back and tell you how similar or different their own seasons are to yours. Share what you find out.

To: Rosal@ngreach.com
From: Andy@ngreach.com
Subject: Seasons
Attachment:

Hi Rosa!

I wrote this article about fall and spring in Dallas. What are those seasons like where you live? Write soon!

Andy

?
BIG
Question

Why is nature always changing?

In this unit, you found lots of answers to the **Big Question**. Now, use your concept map to discuss the **Big Question** with the class.

Concept Map

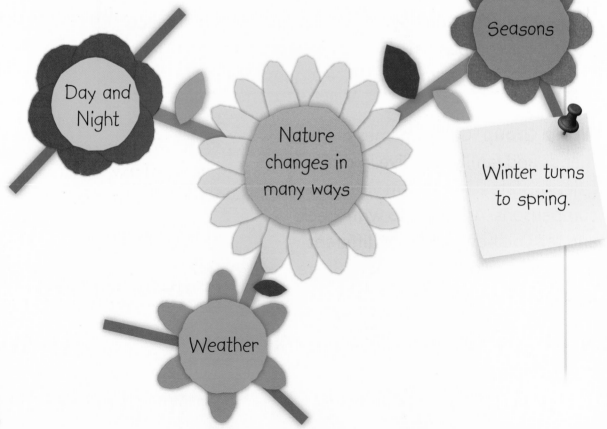

Seasons

Day and Night

Nature changes in many ways

Winter turns to spring.

Weather

330

Share Your Ideas

Choose one of these ways to share your ideas about the **Big Question**.

Write It!

Draw a Cartoon

Show what happens during the four seasons. Use one box for each season. Write what happens in each box. Share your cartoon with the class.

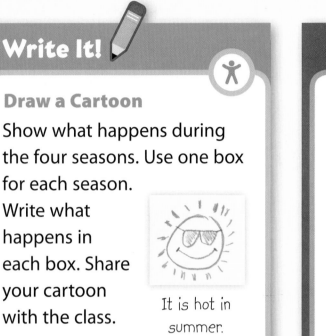

It is hot in summer.

Talk About It!

Discuss Nature Topics

On scraps of paper, write ways that nature changes. Put the topics in a box or hat. Take turns choosing topics and discussing them with a partner. Be sure to listen to your partner and speak clearly.

Do It!

Perform a Mime

Work with classmates to create a mime about a way that nature changes. Perform your skit for the class. Have classmates guess what you are miming.

Write It!

Write a Nature Log

Write about changes in nature that you see in the morning, in the middle of day, and at night. Write them in your log. Share with the class.

331

Better Together

BIG Question

Why do people work together?

Unit at a Glance
▶ **Language**: Give and Carry Out
  Commands, Express Needs and Wants
▶ **Literacy**: Determine Importance
▶ **Content**: Working Together

Unit
6

Share What You Know

Do It!

1. **Stand** back to back with a partner. Link arms.

2. **Work** together to pick up classroom items like books, chairs, even desks.

3. **Say** what you learned. What does it mean to work together on a task?

Build Background: Watch a video about cooperation.
NGReach.com

High Frequency Words

find

take

turn

Give and Carry Out Commands

Listen and read along.

Poem ((MP3))

Teamwork

Find a trash bag, maybe two.

One for me and one for you.

Take some gloves and put them on.

Pick up trash until it's gone!

Turn and look beneath each tree

And all around until you see

That teamwork helps to get things done

And helps make worktime lots of fun!

Key Words

How does teamwork help our community and **society**?

Team members work **together**.   Sometimes, we work **alone**.

We use **teamwork** to get the job done.

Talk in a group about a class project. When do people choose to work together? When is it good to work alone?

Story Elements

Use a story map to tell about the **characters**, **setting**, and **plot** of a story.

Story Map

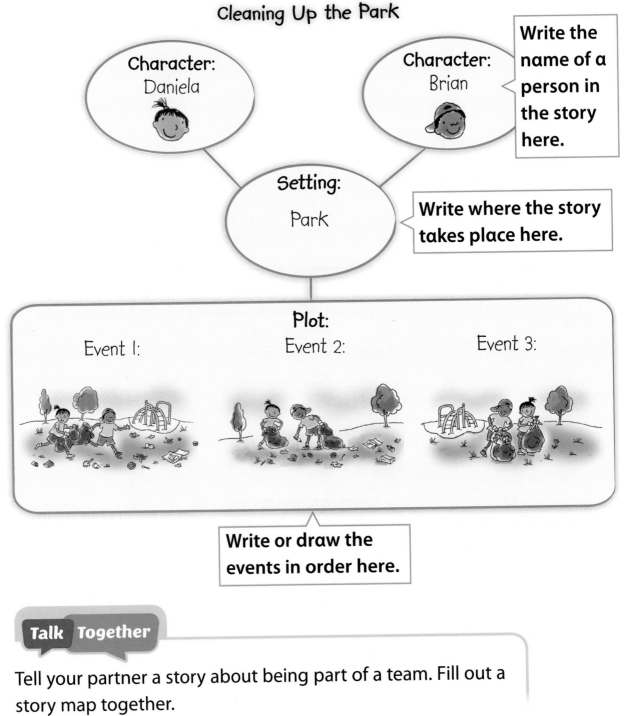

Cleaning Up the Park

Character: Daniela

Character: Brian

Write the name of a person in the story here.

Setting: Park

Write where the story takes place here.

Plot:

Event 1:   Event 2:   Event 3:

Write or draw the events in order here.

Talk Together

Tell your partner a story about being part of a team. Fill out a story map together.

More Key Words

add
(ad) *verb*

When you **add** things to a group, you make the group bigger.

cooperate
(kō-ah-pu-rāt) *verb*

Two girls **cooperate** with each other to plant trees.

enough
(ē-nuf) *adjective*

There is just **enough** milk to fill the glass.

possible
(pah-su-bul) *adjective*

Airplanes make it **possible** for people to fly. They are able to do it.

share
(shair) *verb*

It is nice to **share** food with others. The boy and girl each get some ice cream.

Talk Together

Make a drawing that shows the meaning for each **Key Word**. Then share your drawings with a partner.

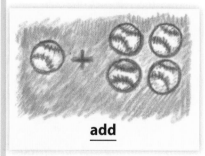

add

Add words to My Vocabulary Notebook.
🌐 NGReach.com

Learn to Determine Importance

How can you remember important ideas? A good way to do this is to **summarize** information.

Helping People Is Easy

Daniela and Brian see that the woman needs help.

Daniela and Brian help her and have fun.

When you **summarize**, you retell the important ideas. Use your own words.

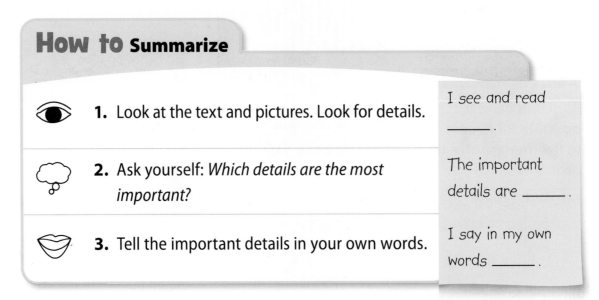

How to Summarize

👁 **1.** Look at the text and pictures. Look for details.

💭 **2.** Ask yourself: *Which details are the most important?*

👄 **3.** Tell the important details in your own words.

I see and read _____ .

The important details are _____ .

I say in my own words _____ .

Language Frames

👁 I see and read
　———— .

☁ The important
　details are
　———— .

👄 I say in my own
　words ———— .

Talk **Together**

Read Daniela's description and the sample summary. Then summarize the next part of the text. Use **Language Frames** to tell your partner your summary.

Description

Helping Is Fun

Yesterday morning, Brian and I were on our way to clean up the park. We saw a woman pushing a crying baby in a stroller. It hardly seemed **possible**, but she was holding two grocery bags, too.

Brian said, "Let's try to help."

We walked over to her. "I don't think you have **enough** arms for all that. I'll take the grocery bags," Brian said, laughing. "But why don't you rest first?"

"Here are some crackers you can **share** with the baby," the woman said.

I opened the box and offered one to the baby.

"Have some more," I said. The baby began to smile.

We started to walk. "I have to turn here at the corner," said the woman.

"Don't worry," I said. "We can help you bring your groceries home."

The baby began to laugh. "I think the baby will **cooperate** now," I **added**, laughing.

Sample Summary

"I see and read that the woman needs help.

The important details are she carries a lot, the baby cries, and Daniela and Brian want to help.

I say in my own words that Daniela and Brian stop to help the woman. Brian takes the bags and Daniela amuses the baby."

◀ = A good place to summarize

Read a Play

Genre

A **play** is a story that can be acted out.
A **script** is the written form of a play.

Parts of a Play

The script shows the **dialogue**, or the words
the characters say. **Stage directions** tell
them what to do.

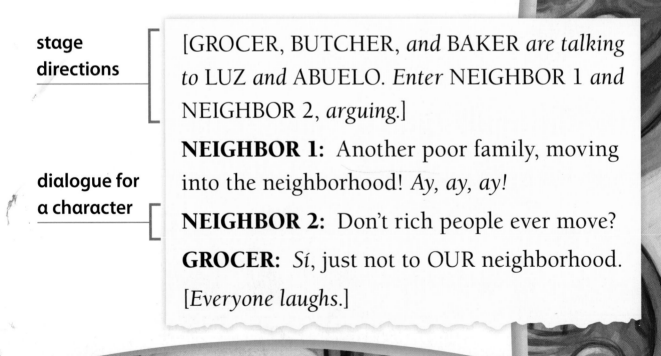

stage directions

[GROCER, BUTCHER, *and* BAKER *are talking
to* LUZ *and* ABUELO. *Enter* NEIGHBOR 1 *and*
NEIGHBOR 2, *arguing.*]

dialogue for a character

NEIGHBOR 1: Another poor family, moving
into the neighborhood! *Ay, ay, ay!*

NEIGHBOR 2: Don't rich people ever move?

GROCER: *Sí*, just not to OUR neighborhood.

[*Everyone laughs.*]

Domino Soup

a play by **Carmen Agra Deedy** · illustrated by **Dani Jones**

CHARACTERS:

ABUELO (Grandfather)

CRANKY OLD MAN
  (Unhappy Domino Player)

LUZ

NEIGHBOR 1

NEIGHBOR 2

GROCER (food seller)

BUTCHER (meat seller)

BAKER (bread seller)

NEW NEIGHBORS

Comprehension Coach

▶ **Set a Purpose**
Abuelo always wins a game of
dominoes. Find out how he does it.

ACT ONE

[**SETTING:** *A street corner in* **Miami's**
Little Havana: ABUELO *and* CRANKY
OLD MAN *are seated at a table, playing*
dominoes.]

ABUELO: I win the game!
CRANKY OLD MAN: Again? You
always win at dominoes!
ABUELO: I know. [*smiling*] **It's a gift.**
CRANKY OLD MAN: Bah! [*exits*]

Little Havana

Miami

In Other Words
◀ **Miami's Little Havana** a neighborhood in Miami, Florida
It's a gift. I am just lucky.
exits leaves

LUZ: How DO you do it, Abuelo?

ABUELO: I just get the other guys to play the dominoes I need.

LUZ: But how?

ABUELO: [*chuckles*] I just **make a little suggestion** or two. The trick is to have them think it was THEIR IDEA.

In Other Words
chuckles laughs
make a little suggestion give them an idea

▶ **Before You Move On**

1. **Character** How does Abuelo always win? What does this tell you about his character?
2. **Setting** Where does Act One take place? Describe the setting.

▶ **Predict**
What do the neighbors do
when a new family moves to the
neighborhood?

[GROCER, BUTCHER, *and* BAKER *are talking
to* LUZ *and* ABUELO. *Enter* NEIGHBOR 1 *and*
NEIGHBOR 2, **arguing**.]

NEIGHBOR 1: Another poor family, moving
into the neighborhood! ***Ay, ay, ay!***

NEIGHBOR 2: Don't rich people ever move?

GROCER: *Sí*, just not to OUR neighborhood.

[*Everyone laughs.*]

In Other Words
arguing talking angrily
Ay, ay, ay! Oh no! (in Spanish)
Sí Yes (in Spanish)

LUZ: [*clapping hands*] I know! We could all **share** what we have and make a **welcome dinner**!

[*Laughter stops.*]

BAKER: Me? I sell **barely enough** bread to buy more flour!

In Other Words
welcome dinner meal to greet the new family
barely only

345

BUTCHER: You should be a butcher! No one buys meat anymore. **Humph!** I dream of being a grocer!

GROCER: That's not a dream, my friend . . . **it's a nightmare**! I **make pennies on a plantain** and **break even** on a tomato.

NEIGHBOR 2: You see, Luz? We are all poor! Someone should make US dinner!

In Other Words
Humph! Ha!
it's a nightmare it is like a bad dream
make pennies on a plantain don't make much money by selling bananas
break even don't make any money

LUZ: But if we all—hmmm. [*rubs chin*] Abuelo, could you **spare** a domino . . . for Domino Soup?

ABUELO: Only one, *mi cielo*?

LUZ: Two would make the soup too strong!

ABUELO: [*hands over one domino*] *Claro*, of course.

[*Everyone follows LUZ as she hurries* ***offstage***.]

In Other Words
spare give me
mi cielo my dear (in Spanish)
offstage off of the stage

▶ **Before You Move On**

1. **Confirm Prediction** What was your prediction? Was it correct? Explain.
2. **Drama** Find the stage directions on page 345. What happens after Luz tells her idea?

▶ **Predict**

Luz wants to make Domino Soup.
How will she get everyone to work
together?

ACT TWO

[**SETTING:** *Abuelo's kitchen.*]

BUTCHER: What is Domino Soup?

LUZ: [*drops domino into a pot*] It's a food my
family has made for many years.

EVERYONE: Ahhhhh!

LUZ: [*sniffs*] Mmmm!

NEIGHBOR 1: I don't smell a thing!

NEIGHBOR 2: Me neither!

ABUELO: [***tapping heart***] You must have
a big heart to smell Domino Soup.

In Other Words
Me neither! I think the same thing.
tapping heart touching his chest

348

LUZ: Of course, an onion helps.

GROCER: [*coughs*] I might have an onion. [*exits*]

LUZ: And garlic would **be lovely**—

NEIGHBOR 1: I have garlic! And some potatoes—[*exits*]

NEIGHBOR 2: —and I have carrots! [*exits*]

In Other Words
be lovely make the soup taste good

LUZ: The smell is getting stronger, **no**?

BUTCHER: I smell **nada**, nothing. [*rolls eyes*] But **perhaps** with a bit of chicken . . . [*exits*]

BAKER: [*laughs*] I know, I know. **What's soup without bread?** [*exits*]

In Other Words
no isn't it
perhaps maybe
What's soup without bread? Soup tastes better with bread.

[ABUELO *and* LUZ *are* **alone** .]

ABUELO: You are a **clever** girl, granddaughter.

LUZ: I have a clever grandfather.

In Other Words
clever smart

▶ **Before You Move On**

1. **Summarize** How does Luz get everyone to **cooperate**?

2. **Drama** On page 348, Neighbors 1 and 2 say they can't smell the soup. Who speaks next? What does the person say?

▶ **Predict**
The soup is done. What do you
think will happen next?

ACT THREE

[**SETTING:** *Abuelo's busy kitchen.*]

[*Others return and* **add** *to the pot.*]

BAKER: [*bringing bread*] That
Domino Soup smells **deliciosa**!

[*Everyone agrees.*]

BUTCHER: [*with wonder*] And to
think it was made from a domino!

BAKER: You know, this **reminds
me of** my favorite soup that my
mama used to make. But she called
it Thimble Soup . . .

[*A knock at the door* **interrupts them.**]

In Other Words
deliciosa really good (in Spanish)
reminds me of makes me think about
interrupts them stops everyone from
talking

352

NEW NEIGHBOR: *Hola!* We—um, just moved in, and we smelled something . . . wonderful.

[*Everyone invites them in.*]

NEW NEIGHBOR: What a **big-hearted** neighborhood!

BUTCHER: [*laughing*] We are, aren't we? Who knew?

In Other Words
Hola! Hello! (in Spanish)
big-hearted friendly

BAKER: I hear there's a new family moving in next week.

NEIGHBOR 1: I have a great idea! We should welcome them to the neighborhood with a big **feast**.

NEIGHBOR 2: I'll bring the domino!

[ABUELO *hugs* LUZ *as* LUZ *winks at the **audience**.*] ❖

In Other Words
feast meal
audience people watching the play

▶ **Before You Move On**

1. **Confirm Prediction** Tell a partner what you predicted. Explain why it was or was not correct.

2. **Summarize** Use your own words to tell what happens in the final scene.

Meet the Author

Carmen Agra Deedy

When Carmen Agra Deedy was a young girl, she loved listening to her family's old stories from Cuba. Now she tells many of those stories.

Soon after learning how to read Ms. Agra Deedy discovered the town library. The librarian gave her many books to read, and her love of reading began. "No book was safe," she said. "I gobbled them up like potato chips."

▲ Ms. Agra Deedy says a good book is like a friend.

Writer's Craft

Carmen Agra Deedy knows that good dialogue shows how characters think and feel. Write words for Luz and her *abuelo* to say next. Remember to show their thoughts and feelings!

Talk About It

1. How does the **play** show **dialogue**, or words that the characters say? Give examples.

    The play shows dialogue with _____ . One example is _____ .

2. Pretend you are Luz. **Give commands** that tell how to make "Domino Soup."

    Please bring me the _____ . Then take _____ and _____ .
    Last, **add** _____ .

3. What does Abuelo mean when he says you need a big heart to smell Domino Soup? Explain why you think so.

    Abuelo means _____ . I think so because _____ .

Learn test-taking strategies.
NGReach.com

Write About It

Imagine you are one of the characters in the play. Write a sentence that tells why you think it is important for people to **share** their food. Use **Key Words** in your response.

We should share our food because _____ .

Story Elements

Make a story map for "Domino Soup."

Story Map

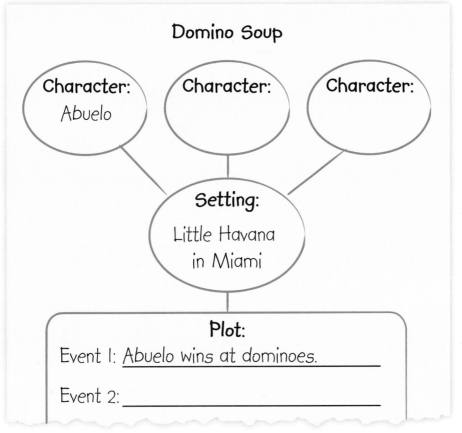

Domino Soup

Character: Abuelo

Character:

Character:

Setting: Little Havana in Miami

Plot:
Event 1: Abuelo wins at dominoes.

Event 2: _____

Now use your story map. Tell a partner about the characters, setting, and plot in "Domino Soup."

The play takes place in _____.
The characters are _____.
First _____. Next _____.
Then _____. Finally _____.

Fluency  Comprehension Coach

Use the Comprehension Coach to practice reading with the correct expression. Rate your reading.

Prefixes

A **prefix** is a word part. You can add a prefix to the beginning of a word. This can change the word's meaning.

The prefix **im-** means "not."

| **im** | + | **possible** | = | impossible |

It is **impossible** to make soup without a pot.

The prefix **co-** means "together."

| **co** | + | operate | = | **cooperate** |

We can **cooperate** to make soup.

Try It Together

Read the sentences. Then answer the questions.

> The **coworkers** wanted to try the soup right away. But they did not want to be **impolite**. So they waited until the soup was ready.

1. What is a **coworker**? Use the word in a sentence.

2. Polite means "acting in a nice way." What does **impolite** mean?

Connect Across Texts Now read a songwriter's version of the old folk tale "Stone Soup."

Genre A song is like a poem set to music. The words in a song are called **song lyrics**.

Stone Soup

by **John Forster and Tom Chapin**

illustrated by **Sonja Lamut**

In a threadbare town at the end of the war

A hungry soldier knocked on a door:

"Pardon me, Madam, I need some food . . .

Rum dum diddle-ii food!"

"I'm sorry, sir, but we are hungry, too.

There's no food left

In the whole hungry village."

In Other Words
threadbare poor
Pardon me Excuse me
village town

▶ **Before You Move On**

1. **Setting** How is the song's setting different from the setting in "Domino Soup"?
2. **Explain** Read the first four lines of the song aloud. Tell why the words sound musical.

359

So the soldier marched to the center of town,

"Hear ye! Hear ye! Gather 'round!"

He picked up a stone and gave it a kiss.

"Let's make soup out of this!"

"What? Soup from a stone?"

"Sure . . .

All you need is what you've got,

A tasty stone and water in a pot.

Takes some time but feeds a lot.

Stone soup tonight."

"Stone soup? Stone soup?

What is this fellow, a nincompoop?"

But the kids brought stones,

Which he put in the pot.

Boiled the whole thing piping hot.

Then he hushed the crowd and, solemn-faced,

Took a rum dum diddle-ii taste.

"Oh, this is gonna be good!"

"Please, Sir, please, can we have some?"

"No, not yet. It's not quite done.

It needs a soup bone . . . for flavor."

In Other Words

hushed the crowd and, solemn-faced
 told the people to be quiet, and calmly

gonna going to

for flavor to make it taste good

▶ **Before You Move On**

1. **Plot** How are the events in this song like the events in "Domino Soup"?
2. **Summarize** Use your own words to tell what happens on pages 360–361.

A little girl who'd brought a stone

Said, "We've been saving a big hambone.

Shall I get it?"

"That'd be nice."

She was back in a trice!

The soldier smiled.

"All you need is what you've got."

He took that bone and threw it in the pot.

Some grown-ups started to see the light.

"Stone soup tonight."

In Other Words
who'd who had
That'd That would
in a trice quickly
Some grown-ups started to see the light. Some adults began to understand what was happening.

362

Then he took a taste, took a taste:

"Oh, this is gonna be great!"

"Now, Sir, now, can we have some?"

"Not just yet. It's still not done.

It needs . . . a potato and . . . an onion."

The kids jumped up and off they tore

And brought the things that he'd asked for,

Not to mention turnip greens,

A carrot and some beans!

In Other Words
off they tore ran away
Not to mention They also brought

▶ **Before You Move On**

1. **Character** How are the soldier's actions like Luz's actions in "Domino Soup"? How are they different?

2. **Details** What do the kids bring to put in the soup?

The smell of soup began to float
Into every nose and throat,
Calling people like a drum,
"Rum dum diddle-ii yum!"

"Stone soup. Stone soup.
We want some of that tasty goop."

"No. Not yet. I'm still not through.
It needs one thing from each of you . . .
Whatever you can spare."

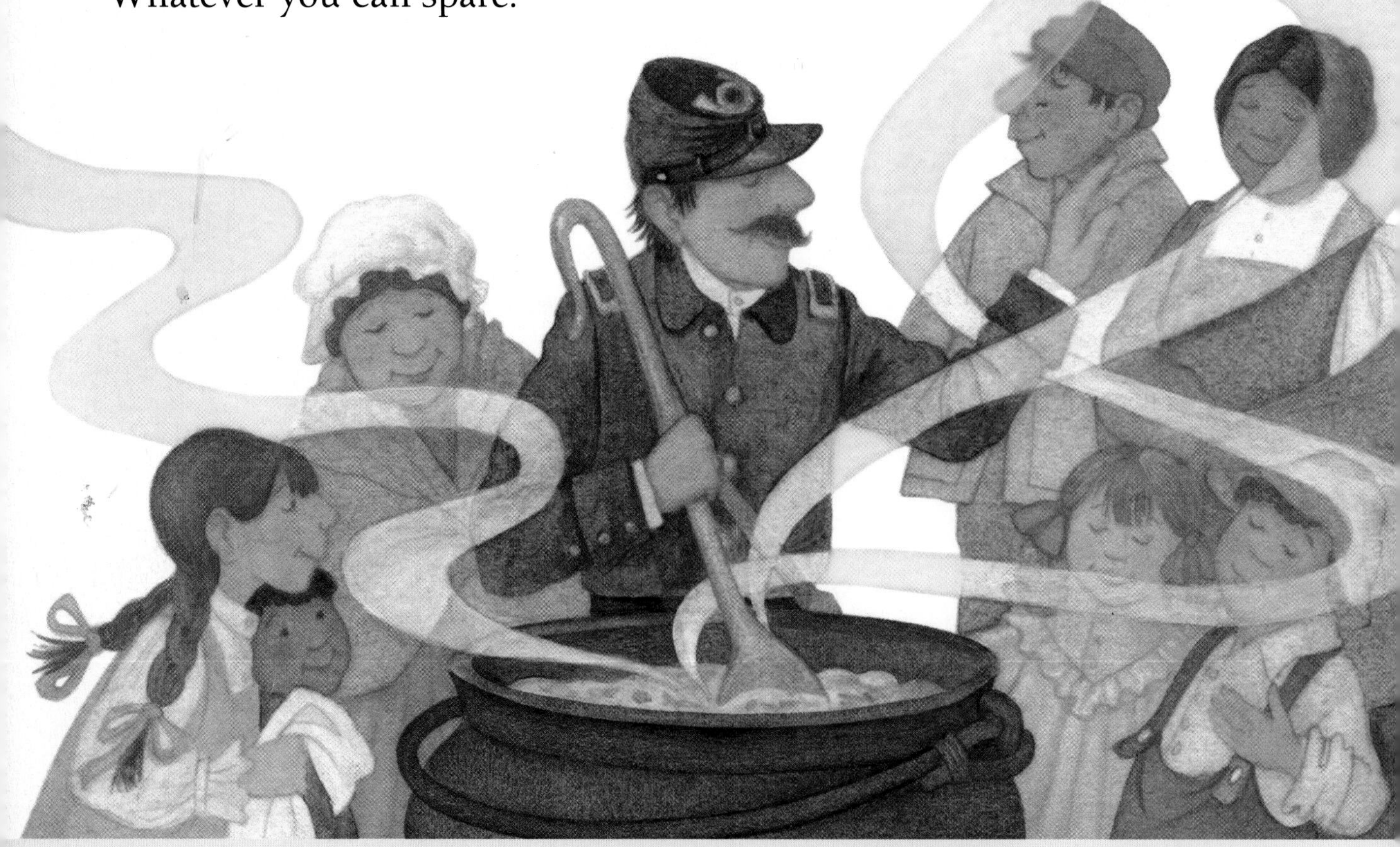

In Other Words

to float Into every nose and throat to smell wonderful to everyone

goop thick soup

spare **share** with us

So the villagers scattered to their root cellars,

Corn cribs and secret nooks

And brought back everything

From an eggplant to a pepperoni.

And that night the whole hungry village

Feasted on soup made out of a stone!

All we need is what we've got,

A tasty stone and water in a pot.

Little things become a lot.

Tiny gifts can fill the pot

When they're shared and served up hot.

Stone soup. Stone soup.

Stone soup tonight!

In Other Words

scattered to their root cellars, corn cribs and secret nooks ran to get food they had hidden

Feasted on Ate

▶ **Before You Move On**

1. **Clarify** The song says "Little things become a lot." What does this mean?
2. **Plot** How do the people in this song **cooperate** to make the soup? How is this like the events in "Domino Soup"?

365

Compare Two Versions of the Same Story

How are "Domino Soup" and "Stone Soup" alike? How are they different?

Comparison Chart

	"Domino Soup"	"Stone Soup"
Type of Story	play	song
Characters		
Setting		
Plot		

> Write the names of the characters here.

> Write details about the setting here.

> Write events from the plot here.

Talk Together

Work with two classmates. Write a short play about working **together**. Use **Key Words** in the dialogue. Perform your play for the class.

Pronouns

A **pronoun** is a word that can take the place of a noun. When you use a pronoun in a sentence, be sure to use the right one.

Grammar Rules Pronouns

• For yourself, use **I**.	My name is **Laura**. **I** am eight years old.
• For one man or boy, use **he** or **him**.	**Jorge** is my brother. I sit with **him**.
• For one woman or girl, use **she** or **her**.	My **grandmother** reads. **She** sits on the chair.
• For one place or object, use **it**.	I will give Jack this **book**. Jack wants to read **it**.
• For yourself and another person, use **we** or **us**.	**Jack and I** are best friends. **We** like to play at the park.
• For two or more people, places, or things, use **they** or **them**.	Our **neighbors** are at the park, too. Jack and I wave to **them**.

Read Pronouns

Read these sentences. Find four pronouns. Tell them to a partner.

> The boys work on a mural. First they draw a sketch. Then one boy colors it in. He uses bright colors. It is beautiful!

Use Pronouns

Write two sentences about how people in your neighborhood work together. Use at least one pronoun. Share with a partner.

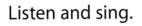

Express Needs and Wants

High Frequency
Words

good

need

some

want

Listen and sing.

Bake Sale

 Song

 I **want** a **good** project to work on.

 I think that I have a good plan.

Our library needs **some** more money.

Let's organize help if we can.

Chorus:

 Bake sale, bake sale—

We **need** more books for our library.

 Bake sale, bake sale—

We'll raise lots of money, you'll see.

Tune: "My Bonnie Lies Over the Ocean"

Key Words

How do you complete a **project**?

❶ **Organize** ideas.

❷ Make a **plan**.

❸ **Join** in.

❹ Use your **skills**.

❺ Work together.

Tell a partner about a project you worked on with other people.

Main Idea

The **main idea** is the most important idea in the text. **Details** tell more about this very important idea. Show how the information fits together. Use a main idea diagram.

Main Idea Diagram

Write details from the text here.

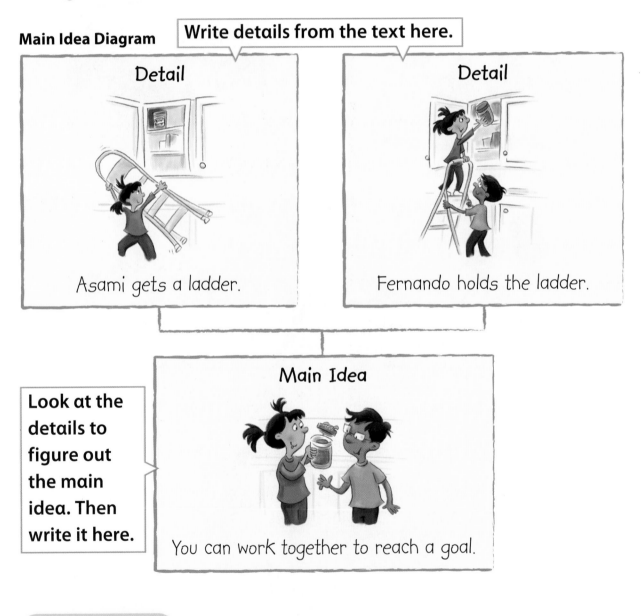

Detail

Asami gets a ladder.

Detail

Fernando holds the ladder.

Look at the details to figure out the main idea. Then write it here.

Main Idea

You can work together to reach a goal.

Talk Together

Tell your partner about a time when you worked with someone to reach a goal. Then make a main idea diagram.

More Key Words

dream
(drēm) *noun*

His **dream** is to win a medal at the track meet.

education
(e-ju-**kā**-shun) *noun*

You go to school to get an **education**.

opportunity
(ah-pur-**tü**-ni-tē) *noun*

She has an **opportunity** to kick the ball.

result
(rē-**zult**) *noun*

If you trip and drop a cup, the **result** is broken pieces.

success
(suk-**ses**) *noun*

They win the game. It is a big **success**!

Talk Together

Work with a partner. Use **Key Words** to ask and answer questions.

What opportunity does he have?

He has the opportunity to go to sports camp.

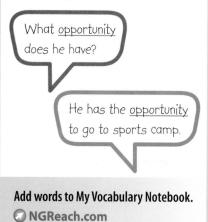

Add words to My Vocabulary Notebook.
NGReach.com

Learn to Determine Importance

When you want to understand something, look for what is important about it. Look for important **details**. Put these together to find the most important or **main idea** of the text.

Working Together Gets the Job Done

Carrying a Heavy Load

More Hands to Help

The Job Is Done

Look for clues as you read to find the **details** and the **main idea**.

How to Identify Main Idea and Details

👁	**1.** Read the text and look at the pictures.	I read about _____.
☁	**2.** Look for details that seem important.	The important details are _____.
🧩	**3.** Put the details together. Figure out the most important idea.	The main idea is _____.

Read Asami and Fernando's report and the sample. Then use **Language Frames** to state the details and the main idea. Tell your partner about them.

Report

Helping Others

Making a Plan

Our teacher, Ms. Cienfuegos, told us about a homeless shelter nearby. She explained that some families lose their homes. As a **result**, they have to live at the shelter. These people need furniture, and their children want toys. Our class saw an **opportunity** to do some good. We decided to give furniture and toys to the shelter. First, we needed our parents' help.

Putting the Plan into Action

We explained the project to our parents, and many decided to help. Planning the project gave us a real **education**. Some people had extra chairs and toys to give away. Other people helped load the truck. At the end of the day, we all helped unload the truck at the shelter. Our project was a bigger **success** than we dreamed it would be!

> **Sample Main Idea and Details**
>
> "I read about the families that live at the shelter.
>
> The important details are that these families need furniture and toys.
>
> The main idea is that the class decides to help these families."

◀ = A good place to identify details and a main idea

Read a Human Interest Feature

Genre

A **human interest feature** is nonfiction. It gives facts about people and events of today.

Text Feature

A **map** can show you where things are.

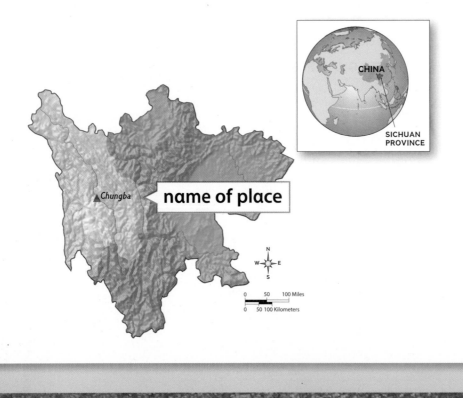

CHINA

SICHUAN PROVINCE

▲Chungba

name of place

N
W E
S

0   50   100 Miles
0   50 100 Kilometers

IN A MOUNTAIN COMMUNITY

by S. Michele McFadden

▶ **Set a Purpose**
Find out how people in one village
work together to build a school.

THE PEOPLE OF CHUNGBA

The Chungba community is high in the mountains on the Tibetan Plateau. It is far away from cities.

Many families in Chungba are **herders**. They move their animals from place to place. That way the animals can always find grass to eat.

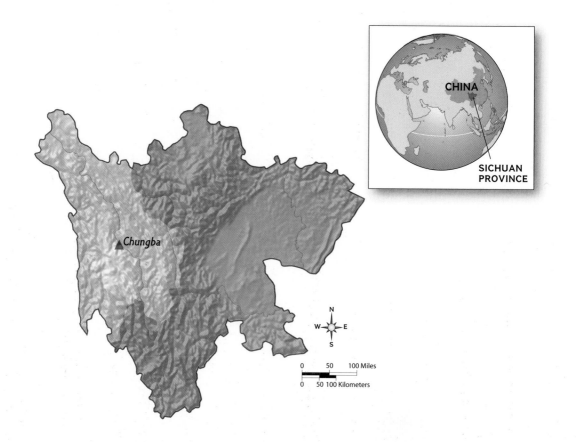

In Other Words

herders people who make groups of animals move

Most people in Chungba are farmers. Very **few** of the farmers have telephones, **electricity**, or **running water**.

Before 2002, only a few boys and very few girls from Chungba went to school.

◀ Herders take care of their dri and dzo. Dri are female yaks. Dzo are a cross between a yak and a cow.

The mountain community of Chungba

In Other Words

few Not many

electricity power

running water water that comes inside homes for drinking, cooking, or cleaning

▶ **Before You Move On**

1. **Use Text Features** Look at the map. Where is Chungba located?

2. **Summarize** What have you learned so far about Chungba?

A School for Chungba

The Chungba community wanted a school for their children. They asked the Rabgey family to help.

The Rabgey family agreed to help build a school to teach Tibetan and Chinese.

Machik is now a large organization. It helps many communities like Chungba.

At first, Pencho and Tsering Rabgey gave money to start the school. Then the Rabgeys started **an organization** to help **raise** money.

The organization is called Machik, which means "one mother." Two sisters, Tashi and Losang Rabgey, run Machik.

In Other Words
an organization a group
raise money find money to use for the school

▶ **Before You Move On**

1. **Main Idea** What was the Rabgeys' **dream**?
2. **Make Connections** Machik raises money for a school. What are two things you would try to raise money for?

Help from the Community

The people of Chungba wanted to help, too. They helped **clear the land**. They put up walls. They built classrooms and a kitchen. They built a library. The children live at the school most of the year, so they built rooms to sleep in.

▼ **People in the community helped get ready for the new school.**

In Other Words

clear the land make the land flat so they could build the school

▲ **The children are proud of learning Tibetan.**

AT THE NEW SCHOOL

At school, the girls and boys of Chungba learn in **Tibetan and Chinese**. They study science and math. They learn about Tibetan art, **stories**, and even **local dances**. And they use computers!

In Other Words
Tibetan and Chinese different languages
local dances dances from their community

▶ **Before You Move On**
1. **Explain** How did people **join** together to build the school?
2. **Make Comparisons** How is your own school like the Chungba school? Explain.

▲ the school before it was finished

▲ solar panels

▲ the community greenhouse

CARING FOR EARTH

The Rabgeys want people to learn to care for Earth. So the builders of the school used **local materials**.

In Other Words

local materials things made in or near the village

Machik put up solar panels. The solar panels turn the sun's heat into electricity for the school. They built a **greenhouse**, too. In the greenhouse, the community can grow vegetables even when it's cold out. The children eat vegetables from the greenhouse.

▼ Half the students at Chungba Primary School are girls.

In Other Words
greenhouse a warm place for growing plants inside

▶ **Before You Move On**
1. **Make Inferences** Why is a greenhouse good for the school?
2. **Use Text Features** Look at the photos on pages 382–383. How do they help you understand the text?

STUDENTS SHOW THEY CARE

Students at the new Chungba school want to care for Earth, too. They plant trees and help in the greenhouse. Many students are part of the "Clean Sweep" **project**. They work together to keep Chungba clean.

◄ Students and teachers pick up trash in the community.

Vegetables can grow all year in the greenhouse.

ANOTHER NEW SCHOOL FOR CHUNGBA

In 2008, Chungba Middle School opened. Now the children have a new school to go to when they get older.

This school has stores on the bottom floor. The money the stores make helps to pay for the new school. It also has a place where students in both schools can eat.

Chungba students make a movie.

▶ **Before You Move On**

1. **Details** What do the children do in the "Clean Sweep" **project**?
2. **Determine Importance** Do you think it is important to have stores at the school? Explain.

COMMUNITY PRIDE

Parents believe in the schools. Some parents walk for two days to meet with teachers. Some parents bring **yak butter** to share.

The teachers are proud, too. Most children in Chungba had never gone to school before.

▲ **Parents are proud of what their children have learned.**

In Other Words
yak butter butter made from yak milk

A Bright Future

The Rabgeys and Machik worked with many others to build the schools. **Volunteers** from Chungba and around the world helped. They all worked hard to make the Chungba people's **dream** come true.

▲ **The first class to complete Chungba Primary School.**

In Other Words

create make

Volunteers People who work without getting paid

▶ **Before You Move On**

1. **Make Connections** Think about a child's first day of school in Chungba. How was it like your first day at school?

2. **Summarize** Use one sentence to tell what you learned on pages 386–387.

Talk About It

1. What makes this selection a **human interest feature**?

   It is a human interest feature because _____ .

2. Describe the main reason why the Chungba school **project** is a **success**. Tell how you know.

   The main reason is _____ . I know because _____ .

3. Why do the people of Chungba feel such pride in their community?

   The people of Chungba are proud of _____ . They worked together to _____ .

Learn test-taking strategies.
⊘ NGReach.com

Write About It

Losang Rabgey helped her community **organize** to build the school. Write a sentence. Tell what you think about the Chungba School. Use at least one **Key Word**.

I think the school in Chungba
is _____ because _____ .

Main Idea

Make a main idea diagram for "In a Mountain Community." Look for important details in the text. Put them together to figure out the main idea.

Main Idea Diagram

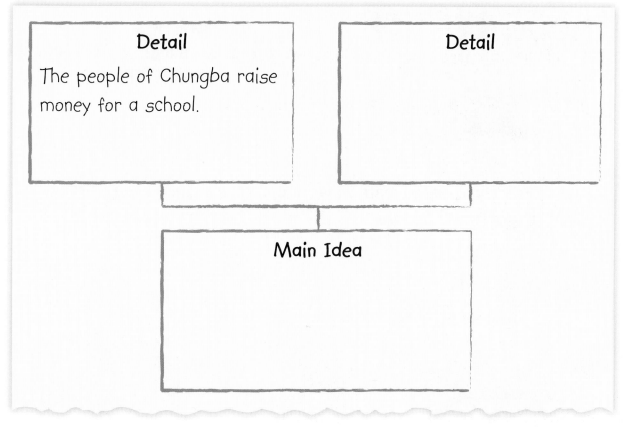

Detail	Detail
The people of Chungba raise money for a school.	

Main Idea

Now use your main idea diagram. Tell your partner about the main idea and details from "In a Mountain Community."

One detail is _____.
Another detail is _____.
The main idea is _____.

Fluency  Comprehension Coach

Use the Comprehension Coach to practice reading with the correct phrasing. Rate your reading.

389

Use Context Clues

If you read a word that you do not know, look at the words around it. These clues from the text, or **context clues**, can help you figure out the meaning of the word.

Before, the children did not have **a chance to learn new things**. Now, they have the **opportunity** to go to school.

> context clue

The words "a chance to learn new things" give a clue about what **opportunity** means.

Try It Together

Read the sentences. Then answer the questions.

My friends and I wanted to start a neighborhood garden. Our neighbors helped us buy the seeds. Everyone joined together to make the garden. Soon, we got the results we wanted: vegetables. Our project was a big **success**!

1. What does **success** mean?

2. What words help you understand the meaning?

Brooklyn, New York

PUERTO RICO

Mi Barrio

by George Ancona

Hi, I'm Marc Anthony. I live in Brooklyn, in a neighborhood called Bushwick. My parents came from Puerto Rico, but I was born here. Most of the people who live here speak Spanish. I go to **P.S.116**.

In Other Words

Mi Barrio My Neighborhood (in Spanish)

P.S.116 Public School 116

▶ **Before You Move On**

1. **Main Idea** What will this photo-essay be mostly about?
2. **Use Text Features** Look at the map of Earth. Point to the place Marc's parents came from.

There are many murals painted on the walls of the neighborhood. This one was painted by some of the kids in my school.

▼ Some of Marc's classmates painted this mural on cement walls.

We like to **get together** after school. Some days we go to the community center to draw pictures.

▲ Marc and his friend draw at the community center.

Marc helped to make the mural in this park.

In the summer we help artists paint murals. One of the **projects** we did is a little park with a mural.

Our murals help make our neighborhood beautiful. They make people think about **their culture**. ❖

In Other Words

their culture where they came from and who they are

▶ **Before You Move On**

1. **Clarify** What is a mural?
2. **Main Idea/Details** Name two details that support the idea that Marc and his friends like to paint.

More About Murals

- Artists create murals in communities all around the world. They use murals to help them share ideas and tell stories.

- Many murals show characters, and places that remind people of their **heritage**.

In Other Words

heritage who they are and where they
came from

▲ Diego Rivera, *Dream of a Sunday Afternoon in the Alameda*, 1947-48.

- Painting murals is nothing new. Artists have painted on walls for **centuries**.

- Murals can be on the inside of buildings or on the outside. When murals are on outside walls, artists must use special paints. Then even if it rains or snows, or if the sun is very hot, the mural will last a long time.

In Other Words

centuries hundreds of years

▶ **Before You Move On**

1. **Main Idea** Why are community murals important?

2. **Make Connections** Marc and his friends paint murals. How can you and your friends make your neighborhood a better place?

Compare Texts

"In a Mountain Community" is a human-interest feature. "Mi Barrio" is a photo-essay. How are the two selections alike and different?

Comparison Chart

	"In a Mountain Community"	"Mi Barrio"
It is in an urban community.		✔
It is in a rural community.	✔	
The community members help each other.		
The children help their community, too.		
The selection is illustrated with photographs.		
It is a true story.		

Put a check if the statement is true for the selection.

Talk Together

Look at a photograph from one of the selections. Describe it to your partner. Then have your partner describe a photograph to you. Use **Key Words** to talk about how people work together on **projects**.

Possessive Pronouns

A **pronoun** is a word that can take the place of a noun. Some pronouns **tell who owns something**. When you use a pronoun in a sentence, be sure to use the right one.

Grammar Rules **Possessive Pronouns**

• For yourself, use **mine**.	This paintbrush is **mine**.
• For yourself and one or more people, use **ours**.	The bright blue paint is **ours**.
• When you speak to one or more people, use **yours**.	The yellow paint is **yours**.
• For one man or boy, use **his**.	Teresa's painting looks different from **his**.
• For one woman or girl, use **hers**.	Rob's painting uses the same colors as **hers**.
• For two or more people, places, or things, use **theirs**.	Our class's paintings are more unusual than **theirs**.

Read Pronouns

Read the passage below. Find the possessive pronouns.

"This is what I painted," said Anna. "Where is yours?"
"Mine is over by the gate," Juan explains.

Use Pronouns

Write two sentences about a school project. Use a possessive pronoun in each one. Share your sentences with a partner.

Write as a Storyteller

Write a Story ✏️

Write a story about people who work together to make something happen. Add your story to a class magazine about cooperation.

Study a Model

Realistic fiction is a story that can happen in real life. Read Cal's story about what happens when friends cooperate.

Max's Bath

By Cal Jackson

Jaime's dog Max has been digging in the garden again. He is all muddy.

"I want you to give that dog a bath," says Jaime's mom. There is one problem. **Max weighs more than Jaime**!

Jaime calls some of his friends. He tells them all to wear swimsuits and meet in his **backyard**. He and Max are waiting.

Jaime picks up the soap and sponge. His friends aim the hose. Ten minutes later, everyone is wet and laughing. But Max the dog is clean!

The **beginning** tells who the **main character** is.

The reader learns about a **problem** that the characters need to solve.

The **middle** tells what happens next. It has more **details** about the characters and the **setting**.

The **end** tells how the problem is solved.

Prewrite

1. **Choose a Topic** What story will you tell? What happens when people cooperate? Talk with a partner to get ideas.

Language Frames	
Tell Your Ideas	**Respond to Ideas**
People cooperate so they can _____ .	I'm not sure how _____ shows cooperation. Tell me more.
I'd like to show how cooperation can _____ .	Maybe your characters could work together to _____ .

2. **Gather Information** Who will your characters be? What problem will they try to solve? What setting will you use? Write down your ideas.

3. **Get Organized** Use a story map to show your story ideas.

Story Map

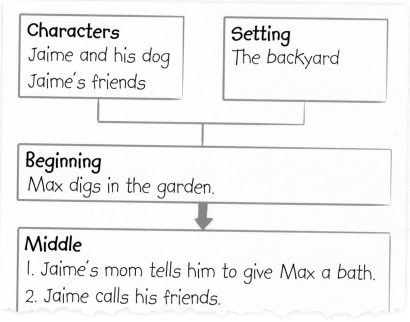

Characters
Jaime and his dog
Jaime's friends

Setting
The backyard

Beginning
Max digs in the garden.

Middle
1. Jaime's mom tells him to give Max a bath.
2. Jaime calls his friends.

Draft

Make sure your story has a beginning, middle, and end. Use details to tell more about your characters and setting.

Revise

1. **Read, Retell, Respond** Read your draft aloud to a partner. Your partner listens and then retells the story. Next, talk about ways to make your writing better.

Language Frames	
Retell	**Make Suggestions**
The story takes place in/at _____. The main characters are _____.	I can't really picture the setting. Could you add details about _____?
The characters in the story work together to _____.	I didn't understand why _____. Maybe you need to explain that more.
At the end, _____.	

2. **Make Changes** Think about your draft and your partner's ideas. Then use the Revising Marks on page 563 to mark your changes.

    *   Make sure your readers can picture your characters and setting.

        > Jaime's dog Max has been digging in the garden again. He is all muddy. ∧

    *   Do you tell every important event? Add any missing details.

        > Jaime tells them all to wear swimsuits and meet in his backyard. He and Max are waiting. ∧
        > Jaime picks up the soap and sponge.

400

Edit and Proofread

Work with a partner to edit and proofread your story. Be sure to use the correct form of pronouns. Use the marks on page 563 to show your changes.

Publish

On Your Own Make a final copy of your story. Read it aloud to your classmates. You can also retell it from memory.

Presentation Tips	
If you are the speaker...	**If you are the listener...**
Use your hands to help your listeners picture what's happening in the story.	Listen for details about character and setting. Try to picture them.
If you are retelling your story, make sure you tell events in order.	Is the speaker a good storyteller? See what you can learn as you watch and listen.

With a Group Publish your stories in a class magazine. Think of a good title. Make copies. Then share the magazine with your friends and family. Show them what cooperation is all about!

Talk Together

In this unit, you found lots of answers to the **Big Question**. Now use
your concept map to discuss the **Big Question** with the class.

Concept Map

They help
each other
succeed.

What happens
when people
work together?

Share Your Ideas

Choose one of these ways to share your ideas about the **Big Question**.

Write It!

Make a Booklet

With a partner, make a booklet about places or groups in your community that help people.

Talk About It!

Storytelling Performance

Work with a partner to tell your own version of "Stone Soup." Act out your version of the story for the class. Speak clearly and with expression. Move your hands and your body as you act out the story.

Do It!

Create a Mural

Work with a group to paint a mural on bulletin board paper. Show what is special about your community. Post the mural in the classroom for all to enjoy.

Write It!

Make a Poster

Pretend you need help from your community to clean the park. Make a poster to ask all your neighbors to help.

Best Buddies

BIG Question How do living things depend on each other?

Unit at a Glance
▶ **Language**: Express Likes and Dislikes, Retell a Story
▶ **Literacy**: Synthesize
▶ **Content**: Partnerships in Nature

Unit 7

Share What You Know

Do It!

❶ Choose your two favorite animals. Think about how the two animals could be friends. How could they help each other?

❷ Make a comic strip. Show your two animal friends helping each other.

❸ Share your comic strip with the class.

Build Background: Watch a video about animals working together.
🌐 NGReach.com

Express Likes and Dislikes

Listen and sing.

Spiders and Wolves

Song (((MP3)))

Do **you like** spiders?

Yes, I like helpful spiders.
I like to find their beautiful webs.
They can trap bugs in their sticky webs so
Spiders are members of the food chain.

Do you like gray wolves?

No, I don't like the gray wolves.
They are so strong and often they kill.

But wolves are cousins to
    your dog Juno.
They have to kill so they can
    survive.

Tune: "Morning Has Broken"

Key Words

Plants have important **roles** in nature. A **chain** can show how they **relate** to animals and each other.

Wildlife eat fruit from plants.

They drop the fruit's seeds.

The plants grow new fruit.

The seeds grow into new **vegetation**.

Talk Together

Look at the pictures. How do plants and animals work together in nature?

Characters' Motives

Characters do things in stories. You can figure out why they do these things. You can figure out their **motives**. Use a character map to show what a character does and why.

Character Map

Character	What the Character Does	Why the Character Does It
Sergio	feeds his dog	He loves his dog and wants to take good care of her.

Write the character's name here. **Write what the character does here.** **Write why the character acts this way here.**

Talk Together

Choose a picture card. Make up a story about the animal on your card. Work with your partner to fill in a character map. Show what the animal does and why.

More Key Words

accept
(ak-**sept**) *verb*

Her mother **accepts** the flowers and a hug. She loves getting both!

connect
(ku-**nekt**) *verb*

He **connects** the wires to make the computer work.

important
(im-**por**-tunt) *adjective*

Firefighters have an **important** job.

necessary
(**ne**-su-sair-ē) *adjective*

A seatbelt is **necessary** to stay safe in a car.

others
(**u**-thurz) *noun*

Casey stands away from the **others**.

Talk Together

Write a sentence for each **Key Word**. Take turns reading your sentences with a partner.

Parents have an <u>important</u> job.

It is <u>important</u> for neighbors to work together.

Add words to My Vocabulary Notebook.
NGReach.com

Learn to Synthesize

Look at the pictures. What do you see that you think is important? Think about how these pictures go with one another. Then **draw a conclusion**, or decide what you think the pictures are about.

Conclusion: Squirrels and trees are good for each other.

When you read, you **draw conclusions**, too.

How to Draw Conclusions

👁	**1.** Notice an important idea in the text.	*I read _____ .*
👁	**2.** Look for another idea that you think is important.	*I also read _____ .*
🧩	**3.** Put the ideas together. Draw a conclusion about the text.	*I conclude _____ .*

Talk Together

Read Sergio's and Joshua's description. Read the sample and draw your own conclusions. Then use **Language Frames** to tell a partner about them.

Description

The Oak Tree and the Squirrel

It is easy to **accept** the idea that trees are **important** to squirrels. Do you know that squirrels are also important to oak trees? You probably know that oak trees provide a place for squirrels to run, play, nest, and live. The trees also have acorns. Acorns are one of the foods that squirrels like best. In fact, acorns let squirrels help regrow oak trees.

Squirrels know that there may be no food once winter comes. So it's **necessary** to collect acorns and nuts during autumn. Then, the squirrels bury the food they find. During the winter, squirrels uncover and eat some of the acorns. **Others** are misplaced. They stay in the ground.

In the spring, shoots of a small oak tree may grow. Does a squirrel that **connects** with an acorn help to build a tree? Yes, and one day, squirrels may have a new place to build a nice, large nest.

Sample Conclusion

"I read that there may be no food when winter comes.

I also read that in autumn squirrels bury acorns they find.

I conclude that those acorns help squirrels survive the winter."

◄ = A good place to draw a conclusion

411

Read a Folk Tale

Genre

A **folk tale** is a story that has been told for many years. Many of the same folk tales are told around the world. This folk tale is told in Bali, India, and Congo.

Characters and Setting

The characters in this story are animals.

Elephant

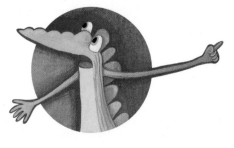

Gecko

This story happens at night in Bali. That's the setting.

ASIA

BALI

AUSTRALIA

Go to Sleep, Gecko!

Retold by **Margaret Read MacDonald**

illustrated by **Geraldo Valério**

Comprehension Coach

▶ **Set a Purpose**
Gecko cannot go to sleep!
Find out why.

One night, Elephant **was awakened by** a loud noise
right under his window.

"GECK-o! GECK-o! GECK-o!"

"Gecko, what are you doing here? It is the middle of
the night. Go home and go to bed."

In Other Words

was awakened by woke up
because he heard

414

"I can't sleep," said Gecko. "The fireflies are **flitting** all around my house. They're blinking their lights on and off . . . on and off . . . You've got to make them stop. You're the **village boss**. Do something about it."

"I'll talk to the fireflies in the morning," said Elephant. "Now go home and go to bed."

Gecko **dragged himself grumpily** home.

"Geck-o . . . geck-o . . . geck-o . . ."

In Other Words
flitting flying
village boss leader of our town
dragged himself grumpily walked slowly and unhappily

Next morning, Elephant called the fireflies.
"Is it true that you have been **flashing** your lights
on and off . . . on and off . . . all night long? Have you
been keeping Gecko awake?"

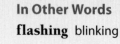

In Other Words
flashing blinking

"Oh, yes," said the fireflies. "We have to blink our lights on and off all night. Rain makes holes in the road. Without our lights, someone would step in a hole!"

"Why, that is very **thoughtful** of you," said Elephant. "Just keep on doing what you've been doing. You can go home now." So the fireflies went home.

In Other Words
thoughtful nice; kind

▶ **Before You Move On**

1. **Cause/Effect** Why can't Gecko go to sleep?
2. **Setting** Look at the pictures on pages 414–415. What can you tell about the setting of the story?

417

▶ **Predict**
Will Elephant find a way to
help Gecko go to sleep?

That night at midnight, Elephant was
awakened again.

"GECK-o! GECK-o! GECK-o!"

Elephant leaned out his window.

"Gecko, go home and go to bed."

In Other Words

That night at midnight
In the middle of the night

418

"But I can't sleep. The fireflies are still blinking their lights on and off . . . on and off . . . You said **you'd** make them stop."

"Gecko, the fireflies need to blink their lights. Rain makes holes in the road every afternoon. Without their lights, someone might step in a hole. You'll just have to **put up with** the fireflies."

"Then talk to Rain! You're the village boss. Do something about it!"

In Other Words
you'd you would
put up with accept

In the morning, Elephant called Rain.

"Is it true you wash holes in the road every afternoon?"

"Oh, yes. I rain hard every afternoon to make **puddles** for the mosquitoes. If the puddles **dried up**, the mosquitoes would die. If the mosquitoes died, there would be nothing for Gecko to eat. So I rain very hard every day."

"I see," said Elephant. "Rain, you may go home."

In Other Words

puddles water on the ground

dried up did not have water in them

420

▶ **Before You Move On**

1. **Confirm Prediction** Think about your prediction. Did it come true? Why or why not?

2. **Character's Motive** Why does Rain make puddles in the road every afternoon?

421

That night at midnight, Elephant was
awakened yet again.

"GECK-o! GECK-o! GECK-o!"

He leaned out his window. "Gecko, go home
and go to bed!"

"I still can't sleep. The fireflies are blinking their lights on and off . . . on and off . . . You said you'd do something about it!"

"Gecko, listen carefully. If Rain doesn't rain every afternoon, there will be no puddles. If there are no puddles, there will be no mosquitoes. If there are no mosquitoes, YOU, Gecko, will have nothing to eat. Now what do you think of that?"

Gecko thought.

If Elephant told Rain to stop raining, there would be no holes and puddles in the road. If there were no holes and puddles in the road, the fireflies would stop flashing their lights . . . but Gecko would have nothing to eat!

"Gecko," said Elephant. "This world is all **connected**. Some things you just have to put up with. Now go home and go to sleep."

So Gecko went home. Gecko
closed his eyes and went to sleep.
Outside the fireflies blinked on
and off . . . on and off . . .
Some things you just have
to put up with. ❖

▶ **Before You Move On**

1. **Confirm Prediction** Does Gecko **accept**
   the **role** of the fireflies? Explain.
2. **Draw Conclusions** Think about how
   Elephant treats Gecko. What does this show
   about Elephant's character?

Meet the Illustrator
Geraldo Valério

AWARD WINNER

Geraldo Valério loves art. When he was a boy growing up in Brazil, he liked to draw. At first he used colored pencils and pens. Then when he was ten years old, he began painting.

Now, it is Mr. Valério's job to illustrate children's books. He reads the stories and then paints pictures for them. "Most of all, I love playing with colors while painting the illustrations," he said.

Artist's Craft

Find places in the story where Mr. Valério's illustrations help you see and feel what the words say. Then make your own drawing. Try to show something that the author describes.

Talk About It

1. How do you know this selection is a **folk tale**?

   It is a folk tale because _____ .

2. At first, Gecko does not like the fireflies. Then he learns why fireflies are **necessary** . How do you feel about bugs? Explain.

   I like/don't like bugs because _____ .

3. What **lesson** does Gecko learn about the way things **connect** ?

   Gecko learns _____ .

Learn test-taking strategies.
⊘ **NGReach.com**

Write About It ✏

Work with a partner. Write a short letter to your favorite character from the folk tale. Tell him what you think about his actions in the story. Use **Key Words** in your letter.

May 12, 2010

Dear _____ ,

I like/don't like the way _____ . I agree/disagree that _____ .

Yours truly,

<your name>

Characters' Motives

What do the characters do in "Go to Sleep, Gecko!"? Why? Make a character map.

Character Map

Character	What the Character Does	Why the Character Does It
Gecko	He complains about the fireflies.	He can't sleep.

Now use your character map. Tell a partner about your favorite character in "Go to Sleep, Gecko!"

My favorite character is _____ . This character _____ because _____ .

Fluency  Comprehension Coach

Use the Comprehension Coach to practice reading with correct expression. Rate your reading.

Use a Dictionary

You can **use a dictionary** to find out what a word means. The words in the dictionary are in alphabetical order. Find the word **connect** in the dictionary.

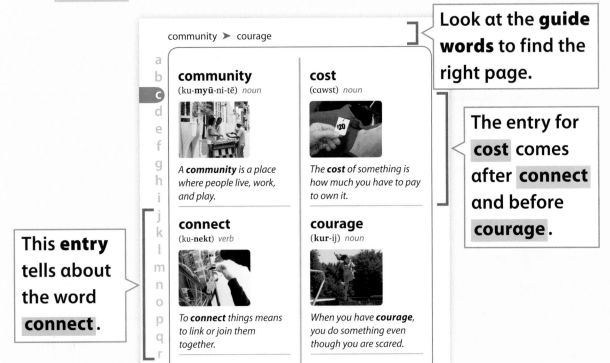

Look at the **guide words** to find the right page.

The entry for **cost** comes after **connect** and before **courage**.

This **entry** tells about the word **connect**.

community ➤ courage

a b **c** d e f g h i j k l m n o p q r

community
(ku-**myū**-ni-tē) *noun*

*A **community** is a place where people live, work, and play.*

connect
(ku-**nekt**) *verb*

*To **connect** things means to link or join them together.*

cost
(cawst) *noun*

*The **cost** of something is how much you have to pay to own it.*

courage
(**kur**-ij) *noun*

*When you have **courage**, you do something even though you are scared.*

Try It Together

Read the sentences. Then answer the questions.

Elephant explains to Gecko that the world is connected.
Animals help each other in different ways. Gecko **accepts** this and leaves Elephant to go back to his house.
"I can **relate** to that," he said. "I won't bother Elephant again!"

1. Look in a dictionary for the word **relate**. Write the definition of the word.

2. Write a sentence with the word **accept**. Use a dictionary if necessary.

Connect Across Texts Now read about other living things in nature and how they **connect** to one another.

Genre A **profile** tells about a person and what the person does.

Enric Sala
Marine Ecologist

by Kristin Cozort

Enric Sala has always wondered about things that live in the ocean. When he was young, he loved to swim. He liked to watch all kinds of animals and plants through his mask. He wanted to be an **underwater explorer**.

Today, Mr. Sala is a marine ecologist. He studies how underwater plants and animals **relate** to each other. He learns how they need each other to stay alive.

In Other Words
underwater explorer person who looks for new things in the ocean

▶ **Before You Move On**
1. **Draw Conclusions** What do you think Mr. Sala did to become a marine ecologist?
2. **Make Connections** Does Mr. Sala's job sound interesting to you? Why or why not?

Underwater Cities

Mr. Sala studies coral reefs in the Pacific Ocean. A coral reef is like an underwater city. Thousands of plants and animals live there. They **compete for** food and space. Coral reefs are beautiful. They are also easily harmed.

▲ **Many different kinds of plants and animals live in a coral reef.**

In Other Words
compete for try to be the first to find

Reefs and Humans

Mr. Sala also studies how people's actions can change coral reefs. Sometimes people **pollute the water or overfish**. That changes the way all the living things **connect** to one another.

Coral reefs can become **damaged**. Then, many animals must find new homes. Some animals just disappear. Mr. Sala wants to **prevent this**.

▼ **This reef is damaged. Many animals can't find food here.**

▶ **Before You Move On**

1. **Ask Questions** You ask yourself, "What is it that Mr. Sala wants to prevent?" What can you do to find the answer?

2. **Make Inferences** How does Mr. Sala feel about the coral reefs? How do you know?

433

All Parts Matter

Mr. Sala believes that all living things in a coral reef should be kept safe. "Underwater **ecosystems** are like airplanes," Mr. Sala says. "They need all of their parts to **function**. Who wants to travel on a plane knowing five or ten parts are missing?"

"To take better care of marine **habitats**, we first have to study them. It's the only way to understand **the full impact humans have on** these places," Mr. Sala says. ❖

In Other Words

ecosystems neighborhoods of plants and animals
function work correctly
habitats homes
the full impact humans have on all the ways people can change

Enric Sala swims with a green turtle. They are at Dirty Rock off Coco's Island in Costa Rica.

▶ **Before You Move On**

1. **Draw Conclusions** Does Mr. Sala spend a lot of time underwater? Why do you think so?

2. **Topic/Main Idea** What is the topic of this selection? What is the main idea?

Compare Genres

"Go to Sleep, Gecko!" is a folk tale and "Coral Reef Connections" is a profile. How are they the same? How are they different?

Folk Tale

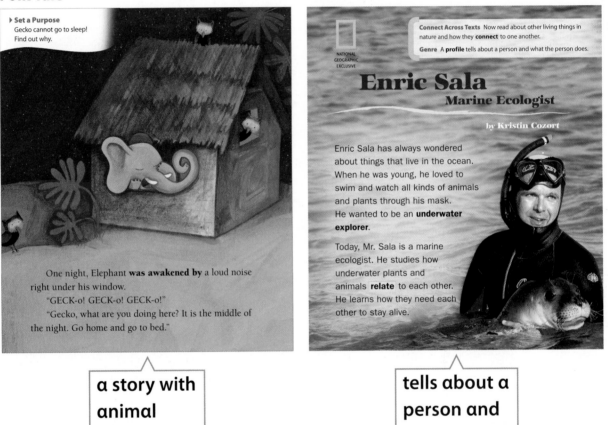

> ▶ **Set a Purpose**
> Gecko cannot go to sleep!
> Find out why.

One night, Elephant **was awakened by** a loud noise right under his window.
"GECK-o! GECK-o! GECK-o!"
"Gecko, what are you doing here? It is the middle of the night. Go home and go to bed."

a story with animal characters

Profile

Connect Across Texts Now read about other living things in nature and how they **connect** to one another.

Genre A **profile** tells about a person and what the person does.

NATIONAL GEOGRAPHIC EXCLUSIVE

Enric Sala
Marine Ecologist

by Kristin Cozort

Enric Sala has always wondered about things that live in the ocean. When he was young, he loved to swim and watch all kinds of animals and plants through his mask. He wanted to be an **underwater explorer**.

Today, Mr. Sala is a marine ecologist. He studies how underwater plants and animals **relate** to each other. He learns how they need each other to stay alive.

tells about a person and what the person does

Look at the pictures in the folk tale with your partner. Take turns telling how each group of characters in the story depends on the next group. Use **Key Words**.

Past-Tense Verbs

All action verbs show when the action happens. **Past-tense verbs** show that the action happened in the past.

Grammar Rules	Past Tense Verbs	
Regular Past Tense	Add **-ed** to the end of many verbs to show an action in the past.	**Examples:** walk + **-ed** = walk**ed** jump + **-ed** = jump**ed**
Irregular Past Tense	Some verbs have special forms to show past tense. You have to remember the forms.	**Example:** begin → began say → said

Read Past-Tense Verbs

Read these sentences from "Go to Sleep, Gecko!" Identify one irregular past-tense verb and one regular past-tense verb.

> Elephant leaned out his window. "Gecko, go to bed."
>
> "But I can't sleep. The fireflies are still blinking their lights on and off... on and off... You said you'd make them stop."

Use Past-Tense Verbs

Write two sentences about how animals help one another. Use at least one regular and one irregular past-tense verb. Share your sentences with a partner.

437

High Frequency Words
after
before
when
while

Retell a Story

Listen and read along.

Partners

Poem (((MP3)))

Before this small bird flies onto its back,
The rhino's too itchy to play.
After the bird eats the bugs on its hide,
The rhino is feeling okay.

When this little bird helps a rhino,
It eats many bugs off its back.
While the rhino enjoys a good cleaning
The little bird has a good snack.

Key Words

How do animals **respond** to other **species**?

Some animals are **partners**. They help each other.

Some animals are **enemies**. They **threaten** each other.

Why do you think some animals are **partners** and others are **enemies**?

Topic and Main Idea

The **topic** is what a selection is mostly about. The **main idea** is the most important idea about the topic. Look at these pictures.

Topic and Main Idea Chart

Topic	Main Idea
The oxpecker	The oxpecker gets its food by pecking the buffalo's body
The clownfish	The clownfish gets protection from the sea anemone.

Write the topic here.

Write the main idea here.

Talk Together

Read a nonfiction text with a partner. Work together to find the topic and main idea. Then write the information in a chart.

More Key Words

ability
(u-**bi**-lu-tē) *noun*

She has great **ability** in art. Her pictures show a lot of skill.

danger
(**dān**-jur) *noun*

If you walk too close to the edge, you are in **danger** of falling.

difficult
(**di**-fi-kult) *adjective*

It can be **difficult** to learn some new things.

unusual
(un-**yū**-zhu-wul) *adjective*

This tiny animal is very **unusual**. It has big eyes and long fingers.

useful
(**yūs**-ful) *adjective*

Tools are **useful** for fixing things.

Talk Together

Make a Word Map for each **Key Word**. Then compare your maps with a partner's.

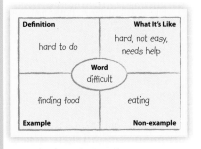

Definition	What It's Like
hard to do	hard, not easy, needs help
Word difficult	
finding food	eating
Example	Non-example

Add words to My Vocabulary Notebook.

⬤ NGReach.com

Learn to Synthesize

Look at the pictures. What kind of relationship do the ants and flower have? Can you think of other things that have this kind of relationship? If so, then you can form a **generalization**.

The ants keep other bugs away from the flower.

The flower makes food that the ants like.

A generalization is a statement that has to do with many situations. When you read, you **form generalizations**, too.

How to Form Generalizations

👁	**1.** Think about the important ideas in the text.	I read _____ .
💭	**2.** Think about how they go together. How are they like things you know from your own life?	I know _____ .
👄	**3.** Make a statement that seems true for both the text and what you know. Use words like *some*, *many*, *most*, or *all*.	Most of the time, it is true that _____ .

Talk Together

Read Graciela's and Emily's blog entry. Read the sample and form your own generalizations. Then use **Language Frames** to tell a partner about them.

Blog Entry

Read 'n Share Blog

Today's Posts | Calendar | Announcements | News | Search   REGISTER | SIGN IN

December 16, 2010

| This Week's Selection: | **Graciela & Emily: The Science Blog** |

December 16, 2010

Before today, we had never even heard of the trap-jaw ant or the costus flower. Both of these **unusual species** live in the rainforest. Do you want to know what makes them special? They are great **partners**.

While we were researching our science report, this is what we found out. When the trap-jaw ant visits a costus, it gets a good meal by sucking nectar from the flower. Yum.

But how is the ant **useful** to the flower? The trap-jaw ant has a special **ability**. Its bite is full of **danger**, since it has a very large jaw that it can open and shut very fast. That means it can injure other small creatures. If we got bit, we would feel a painful sting. Ouch!

If another insect wanders too close, the trap-jaw ant bites it. Then that insect will not do any damage to the flower. We could all use such a good partner!

Sample Generalization

"I read that the trap-jaw ant and costus flowers are great partners.

I know of other plants and animals that are partners, like trees and squirrels.

Most of the time, it is true that partners in nature help each other somehow."

◀ = A good place to form a generalization

443

Read a Science Article

Genre

A **science article** gives facts about a topic.

Text Features

Look for **headings**. They tell you what each section, or part, of the article is about.

Keeping Clean ⟨heading⟩

Some animals help others stay clean. Cleaner shrimps do that. They live in the sea at cleaning stations.

NATIONAL
GEOGRAPHIC

Odd Couples

by Amy Sarver

Comprehension Coach

▶ **Set a Purpose**
Find out about some **unusual**
ways that animals work together.

Pairing Up in the Wild

Animals in the wild have a **difficult** life.
They need to find food, stay healthy, and
hide from **danger**.

mongoose

▲ **A mongoose eats ticks
off a warthog.**

In Other Words
Pairing Up Becoming **Partners**

446

To make life easier, some animals pair up. The two kinds of animals may be very different. Yet these **odd couples** live together. This is called a symbiotic relationship. Each animal helps the other. Let's see how this works

Keeping Clean

Some animals help others stay clean. Cleaner shrimps do that. They live in the sea at **cleaning stations**.

To get clean, a dirty fish stops by. A shrimp climbs onto the fish. The shrimp has tiny **claws**. The claws pick dead skin and **pests** off the fish. The hungry shrimp eats what it picks. The fish gets cleaned.

A cleaner shrimp cleans a moray eel's mouth. ▶

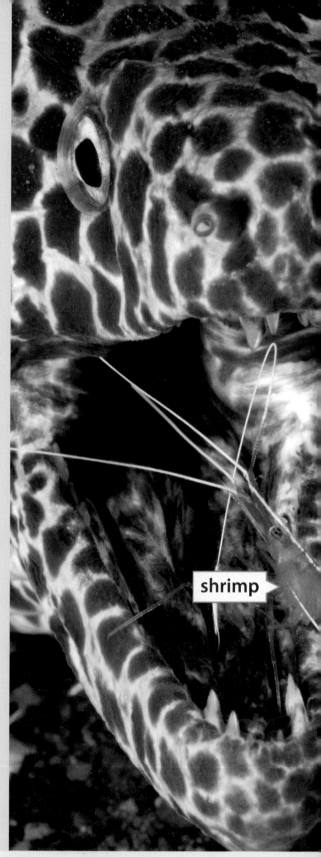

shrimp

In Other Words
cleaning stations places where many animals come to get clean
◀ **claws** sharp nails on its toes
pests harmful bugs

448

Shrimps are not the only cleaners. So are plovers. These brave birds clean crocodile teeth. **Crocs** cannot do that themselves.

Plovers eat tiny animals stuck to a croc's teeth. **It's a good trade.** Birds get food. Crocs get clean teeth.

plover

▶ **Before You Move On**

1. **Use Text Features** Is "Keeping Clean" a good heading for pages 448–449? Explain.

2. **Generalize** Think about animal **partners**. What does it mean to make a good trade?

Riding Along

Like plovers, oxpeckers are birds. They ride on giraffes, **rhinos**, and other big **buddies**.

The big animals don't mind. Why not? Well, the birds eat bugs. That's good for the big animals. **In return**, the birds get plenty of food. It's a perfect **pairing**!

oxpecker

▲ **One big buddy for an oxpecker bird is an antelope.**

In Other Words
rhinos rhinoceroses
buddies friends
In return As a trade
pairing way to be **partners**

remora

Some remora fish get a ride from a shark!

Sea animals also work together. Some fish ride on other sea animals. The remora is a fish that **attaches** itself to sharks. It sticks to the shark's body. The shark gives the fish a ride. In return, the fish eats **the shark's leftover food**.

In Other Words

attaches sticks

the shark's leftover food the food the shark has not eaten

▶ **Before You Move On**

1. **Problem/Solution** How do antelopes and sharks solve a problem for their animal buddies?

2. **Compare** How are the oxpecker and remora the same? How are they different?

Finding Food

Some animals like the same food. Both the honeyguide bird and the ratel love honey. So they **team up**.

The bird finds a **beehive**. Then the ratel uses sharp claws to tear it open. Both animals get **a sweet treat**.

▶ This honeyguide bird finds a beehive. ▶

▲ The ratel is also called a honey badger.

452

Coyotes and badgers also team up as hunting **partners**. Both like to catch small animals such as ground squirrels.

When the squirrel is above the ground, the coyote runs fast and catches it. Sometimes the squirrel **darts** into a hole. That's when the badger uses its long claws to dig under the ground and catch it.

◀ **A coyote usually hunts alone, unless a badger is around.**

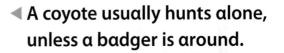

A badger's long claws help it dig. ▶

In Other Words
darts runs quickly

▶ **Before You Move On**

1. **Generalize** Ratels and honeyguide birds like the same food. How can having the same interests help make good partners? Give an example.

2. **Explain** How do coyotes and badgers work together to get food?

Keeping Safe

The sea anemone (u-**nem**-u-nē) and the clownfish make a great underwater team. Sea anemones have tentacles (**ten**-tu-kuls) that catch fish and sting them.

Most fish stay away from the tentacles, but the clownfish hides in them. The tentacles don't sting the clownfish. Its body has a thick **layer of mucus** that protects the clownfish from stings.

tentacles on a sea anemone

▲ **A clownfish hides from its enemies in a sea anemone.**

In Other Words
layer of mucus slippery covering
enemies fish that want to eat it

How does the clownfish help the anemone? It helps the anemone get food. The clownfish is colorful. Hungry fish can **spot it** easily.

Sometimes a hungry fish chases a clownfish into the anemone. Then the anemone stings the fish and eats it.

▼ **An anemone eats a shrimp.**

In Other Words

spot it see it

▶ **Before You Move On**

1. **Explain** How do the clownfish and the sea anemone make an **unusual** team?
2. **Generalize** The clownfish is a **useful partner** for the sea anemone. What does it mean to be a useful partner?

Helping Each Other Live

All animals try to survive. For some, that means living with or near other kinds of animals.

At first, these odd couples may seem strange, but look again.

These partners help one another find food, get clean, and stay safe. Each animal helps the other **get the most out of life**.

▲ **A shrimp helps this fish stay clean.**

Remoras get plenty of food from a shark.

An oxpecker helps keep pests off an impala.

In Other Words

get the most out of life live happily and safely

▶ **Before You Move On**

1. **Generalize** How does living together help animal **partners** get the most out of life?

2. **Main Idea** Tell a partner the most important things you learned about "Odd Couples." What is the main idea?

Talk About It

1. What facts did you learn from the **science article**? Read them aloud.

   I learned _____ .

2. What are the ways animal **partners** help each other? Make a **generalization**.

   Most animal partners help each other by _____ , _____ , and _____ .

3. Working together can make life easier for many animals. How can working together make life easier for people, too?

   Working together can _____ .

Learn test-taking strategies.
NGReach.com

Write About It

Write two questions about the animal pairs in the selection. Use at least one **Key Word**. Trade papers with a partner. Write answers to your partner's questions.

Question: *What does the _____ do? Why?*

Answer: *The _____ does _____ because _____ .*

Topic and Main Idea

Make a topic and main idea chart for "Odd Couples." Add details to the chart. Use them to figure out the topic of the selection.

Topic and Main Idea Chart

Topic:	Main Idea: Animal partnerships help both animals survive.
Details: Cleaner shrimp keep other fish clean	
Details:	

Now use your topic and main idea chart. Tell your partner about "Odd Couples."

> One detail is _____. Another detail is _____. The selection is mostly about _____.

Fluency  Comprehension Coach

Use the Comprehension Coach to practice reading with correct intonation. Rate your reading.

Use Context Clues

If you read a word that you do not know, look at all the words around it. These clues from the text, or **context clues**, can help you figure out the meaning of the word.

Cleaner shrimp have the **ability** to clean a dirty fish. They **can pick off tiny pieces of food** from the fish.

context clues

The words "can pick off tiny pieces of food" give clues about what **ability** means.

Try It Together

Read these sentences. Look for context clues to tell what the words **species** and **pattern** mean.

There are over 17,000 **species** of butterflies in the world. These groups of butterflies all have different **patterns** and designs on their wings.

Working Together

by Lori Wilkinson

There are many interesting **partnerships** in nature. One **unique pair** is the honeybee and the flower. Each does a job the other cannot do on its own. Honeybees and flowers need each other to **thrive**.

In Other Words
partnerships teams
unique pair special team
thrive live and grow

▶ **Before You Move On**

1. **Set Purpose** What do you already know about bees and flowers? Why will you read the article?

2. **Clarify** Find words that tell what a partnership is. Then say it in your own words.

Honeybees Need Flowers

Honeybees get their food from flowers. Flowers make a sweet juice called nectar. Bees drink the nectar. They fly to their hives. There they turn the nectar into honey for their babies to eat.

Flowers also make pollen. Pollen helps new flowers grow. But for a honeybee, pollen is good food. It has all the **vitamins, minerals, and protein** a bee needs.

pollen

▲ **A honeybee collects nectar and pollen from a flower.**

In Other Words
vitamins, minerals, and protein
healthy things

▲ A bee takes pollen from one flower to another.

Flowers Need Honeybees

Plants need honeybees to help them make more plants. When a bee sits on a flower, some pollen sticks to it. When the bee flies to other flowers, it spreads the pollen around. Without the honeybee, **fewer** new flowers would grow!

In Other Words
fewer not many

▶ **Before You Move On**

1. **Topic/Main Idea** What is the topic of this article? What is the main idea?

2. **Generalize** Think about what you know and what you read about insects and plants. Do all insects and plants help each other?

463

Compare Topics and Main Ideas

"Odd Couples" and "Working Together" both have **topics** and **main ideas**. How are these ideas the same? How are they different? Work with a partner to complete the chart.

Comparison Chart

Title	Topic	Main Idea
"Odd Couples"		
"Working Together"		

The topic is what the selection is mostly about. Write the topic here.

The main idea is the most important message. Write the main idea here.

Talk Together

Talk with a partner. Name some pairs of animals. Use **Key Words** to tell how the pairs of animals help each other.

Grammar

Skills Trace: ▶ Future Tense with *will*
　　　　　　　 ▶ Future Tense with *going to*
　　　　　　　 ▶ **Future Tense**

Future Tense

Future-tense verbs tell what will happen in the future. There are two ways to make a verb tell about the future.

Grammar Rules Future Tense

Future Tense with *will*	Examples:
will sing	The badger **will hunt** later.
will sleep	The ratel **will eat** honey.
Future Tense with *going to*:	**Examples:**
am going to	I **am going to** visit the aquarium.
is going to	It **is going to** be fun.
are going to	We **are going to** see clownfish.

Read Future Tense Verbs

Read these sentences with a partner. Find three verbs that show what will happen in the future.

Sea animals will help each other. Some fish are going to ride on other sea animals. The remora is one fish that will attach itself to a shark

Use Future Tense Verbs

Look at the photograph of the giraffe. Write two sentences telling what you think the giraffe is about to do. Use future tense verbs.

465

Write as a Researcher

Write a Science Report ✏️

Write a report about a partnership in nature. You will publish your report in a classroom science magazine.

Study a Model

When you write a report, you gather information from different places. You organize the information and share it with others.

Open House

By Amy Lin

Hermit crabs and sea anemones sometimes work as partners. They make a very strange pair.

A **hermit crab** has a **soft body**. It needs protection. So it **lives in shells** it picks up from the ocean floor.

A **sea anemone** is an animal that looks like a plant. It **sticks on rocks or coral**. When it's hungry, it has to wait for smaller animals to float by. Then it **stings them** with its poison tentacles and eats them.

Sometimes, a **crab and an anemone team up**. A **crab will pick up an anemone** and put it on its shell. The **anemone gets to eat** the crab's leftover food. The **crab is protected** by the anemone's tentacles. Both win!

The first paragraph presents the **topic** of the report.

The report is well organized. Each paragraph has a different **main idea**.

Facts and **details** support the main idea in each paragraph.

Prewrite

1. **Choose a Topic** What will your report be about? Get ideas from books and websites. Talk about those ideas with a partner.

Language Frames	
Tell Your Ideas	**Respond to Ideas**
I know about _____ and _____ . I once saw a show about _____ . I could write about that. I'd like to learn more about _____ .	_____ sounds interesting. I'd like to read about that! What do _____ and _____ do? Tell me more about _____ .

2. **Gather Information** What do you want to find out? Write questions. Find the answers in books or on the Internet. Talk to someone who knows about the topic.

3. **Get Organized** Use a main idea and details chart to help you organize your information.

Topic, Main Idea, and Details Chart

Topic: Hermit crabs and sea anemones work as partners.

Main Idea 1: Hermit crab needs protection	Details: Soft body Lives in shells to protect itself
Main Idea 2:	Details:

Draft

Use your chart and notes to write your draft. Begin by telling about the topic. Write about each main idea in a new paragraph. Add facts and details. Include a picture if you can.

Revise

1. **Read, Retell, Respond** Read your draft aloud to a partner. Your partner listens and then retells the main points. Next, talk about ways to make your writing better.

Language Frames	
Retell	**Make Suggestions**
Your report is about _____ .	I didn't understand _____ .
The main ideas I heard are _____ .	Can you say it in a different way?
Some interesting facts and details are _____ .	Can you add more details about _____ ?

2. **Make Changes** Think about your draft and your partner's ideas. Then use the Revising Marks on page 563 to mark your changes.

   - Did you explain each idea clearly? Add details if you need to.

     It needs protection. So
     A hermit crab has a soft body. It lives in shells it picks up from the ocean floor.

   - Put your details in an order that makes sense.

     them
     When it's hungry, it stings smaller animals with its poison tentacles and eats them. It has to wait for smaller animals to float by. Then

Edit and Proofread

Work with a partner to edit and proofread your report. Pay special attention to verb tense. Use the marks on page 563 to show your changes.

Spelling Tip

✔ Remember that some verbs, like *dig*, have irregular past tense forms. Spell them correctly.

Publish

On Your Own Make a final copy of your report. Present it out loud to your class. Invite your listeners to ask questions.

Presentation Tips	
If you are the speaker…	**If you are the listener…**
Speak clearly. Pronounce all words correctly.	Think about what you should be learning from the report.
If your listeners have questions, answer them with more details from your notes.	Listen for the main ideas and the details that support them.

With a Group Collect all of the reports. Publish them in a magazine called "Nature's Partners." Make copies of the magazine and share them with another class.

Nature's Partners

BIG Question

How do living things depend on each other?

Talk Together

In this unit, you found lots of answers to the **Big Question**. Now, use your concept map to discuss the **Big Question** with the class.

Concept Map

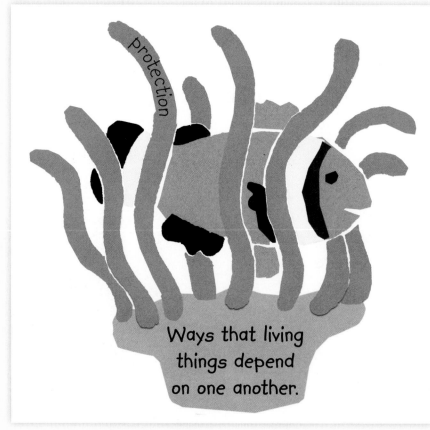

protection

Ways that living things depend on one another.

Share Your Ideas

Choose one of these ways to share your ideas about
the **Big Question**.

Write It!

Write a Song

Work with a partner to write
a song about how living
things depend on each other.
Prepare to sing the song for
your class. Teach the song to
your classmates so they can
sing along.

Talk About It!

Give a Radio Report

Work with a partner to write
a report about a partnership
in nature. Record your report.
Remember to keep your voice
natural and speak slowly and
clearly. Then play the report
for the class.

Do It!

Perform a Puppet Show

Create paper bag puppets
of different animals that
help each other. Then write
dialogue for a skit about the
animals.

Write It!

Make a Booklet

Make a booklet that asks
people to protect coral reefs
and the animals
that live there.

Our United States

BIG Question

What does America mean to you?

Unit at a Glance
- ▸ **Language**: Make a Request, Express Intentions
- ▸ **Literacy**: Reading Strategy Review
- ▸ **Content**: Patriotism

Unit
8

Share What You Know

Do It!

> My square tells about my family.

① **Make** a quilt square that tells about you, your family, or your culture.

② **Put** all the squares together to make a class quilt.

③ **Tell** the class about your square. What does the quilt say about the United States?

Build Background: Watch a video about America's national identity and symbols.
 NGReach.com

High Frequency
Words

may

please

we

will

Make a Request

Listen and sing.

Independence Days

Song ((MP3))

 A Mexican tradition is Independence Day.
It's on September 16. That's when **we** celebrate.
There's dancing and there's music, and good
food to eat.

 May I help you make some?

 Yes, thank you. That's sweet.

 The U.S. also has an Independence Day.
July Fourth is a time for picnics and parades.

 Please tell me what **will** happen
on July the Fourth.

 We'll go to see some fireworks,
And we'll play some sports.

Tune: "Corre, Nino"

474

Key Words

What do the pictures tell you about **American** **culture**?

belief in freedom

history

holidays

American
Culture

people

language

traditions

Talk **Together**

What other things are part of American culture? Which parts
are most important to you?

Character's Feelings

A character is a person in a story. A **character has feelings**. Use a character map to name the feelings. Then tell why the character has those feelings.

Character Map

Character	How the Character Feels	Why the Character Feels This Way
Anita I wonder.	Anita is curious.	Anita wants to find out more about the Liberty Bell and why it has a crack in it.
Patrick I feel good.	Patrick is happy.	Patrick likes marching in a parade and holding a flag.

Write the name of the character here.	Describe how the character feels here.	Explain why the character feels that way here.

Talk **Together**

Tell your partner about a story that you like. Talk about the main character's feelings. Then, fill in a character map.

More Key Words

alike
(u-lĭk) *adjective*

These dogs look **alike**.

celebrate
(**se**-lu-brāt) *verb*

Many people **celebrate** the Fourth of July by watching fireworks.

difference
(**di**-fur-uns) *noun*

One apple is red. That is the **difference**.

expect
(ik-**spekt**) *verb*

I **expect** the clouds will turn into rain today.

variety
(vu-**rī**-u-tē) *noun*

I have a **variety** of crayons. They are many colors.

Talk Together

Make a study card using each **Key Word**. Write the word on the front. Write the meaning and a sentence on the back. Use the cards to quiz your partner.

difference | how things are not alike

We learn about the difference between eagles and hawks.

Add words to My Vocabulary Notebook.
◉ NGReach.com

Strategic Reading

Choose Reading Strategies

Good readers use reading strategies. You can use more than one strategy. It is important to know what strategies to use and when to use them. As you read:

- Think about the strategies. Each one is a different tool. It can help you understand what you read.

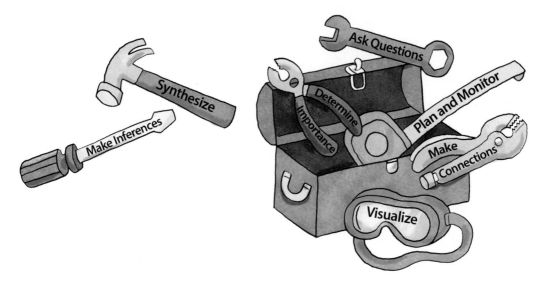

When you read, choose a reading strategy to help you understand.

How to Choose a Reading Strategy

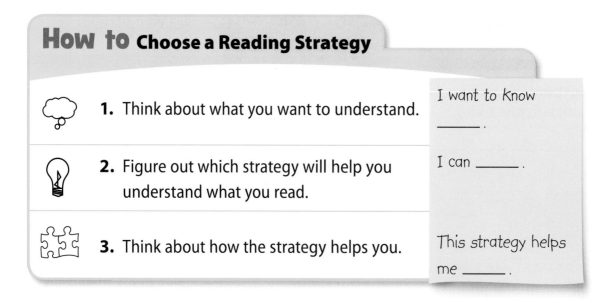

1. Think about what you want to understand.

2. Figure out which strategy will help you understand what you read.

3. Think about how the strategy helps you.

I want to know _____ .

I can _____ .

This strategy helps me _____ .

Reading Strategies

- Plan and Monitor
- Make Inferences
- Ask Questions
- Make Connections
- Visualize
- Determine Importance
- Synthesize

Talk Together

Practice using at least two reading strategies.

Description

An American Holiday

My favorite **holiday** is Thanksgiving. We **celebrate** the Pilgrims who settled Plymouth Colony in 1620. We celebrate the Wampanoag who helped the Pilgrims survive in the New Land. And we celebrate all the good things we have today.

Today, the best part of the holiday is having a big family dinner. We eat a **variety** of food, such as turkey, stuffing, yams, and green beans. Then we have yummy desserts. No two pies are ever **alike**! Slowly, the food disappears from our plates. After dinner, the children get impatient to go and play. The grown-ups stay inside and watch football.

Even when we don't know what to **expect** next, it's good to give thanks for what we have. I wonder if the Pilgrims would ever have predicted that people would remember them with a feast nearly 400 years after they came to America.

Read a Story

Genre

This story is **realistic fiction**. It tells about things that could really happen.

Features of Fiction

A fiction story has characters, a setting, and a plot.

The plot tells what happens.

So, I **straighten** the milk and the videos and **sample** a few new candy bars

until five o'clock,

when two hungry customers walk inside for some Chinese food **to go**.

This setting is in a store on July 4.

The girl is a character in the story.

Apple Pie 4th of July

by **Janet S. Wong**

illustrated by **Margaret Chodos-Irvine**

▶ **Set a Purpose**
A family's store is almost always open. Will it stay open on **the Fourth of July**?

Seven days a week, fifty-two weeks, three hundred sixty-four days a year (and three hundred sixty-five in **a leap year**), our store is open.

Christmas is the only day we close.

Even on Thanksgiving we open the store. Even on New Year's Day. Even today, the Fourth of July.

In Other Words

the Fourth of July the United States of America's birthday

a leap year the year when February has an extra day

482

I hear the **parade**
coming this way—
boom, boom, boom.

I smell apple pie in Laura's
oven upstairs and—
chow mein in our kitchen.
Chow mein!
Chinese food on the Fourth of July?

In Other Words
parade people walking and playing music
◀ **chow mein** thin noodles

484

No one wants Chinese food
on the Fourth of July, I say.

Fireworks are Chinese, Father says,
and **hands** me a pan full of **sweet-and-sour pork**.

▶ **Before You Move On**

1. **Clarify** How can you tell this story is fiction? Name two things.
2. **Visualize** What do you see, hear, and smell in your mind when you read about the family's store?

485

▶ **Predict**
Do you think anyone will want
Chinese food on the Fourth of July?

I hear the parade—
BOOM, BOOM, BOOM.

I hear the parade passing by.

486

Noon, and **customers** come
for soda and potato chips.

One o'clock,
and they buy ice cream.

Two o'clock.
The **egg rolls** are getting hard.

Three o'clock.
Ice and matches.

Four o'clock,
and the noodles feel like shoelaces.

No one wants Chinese food on the
Fourth of July, I say.

In Other Words
customers shoppers
egg rolls small Chinese meals

487

Mother **piles** noodles on my plate.
My parents do not understand all **American** things.
They were not born here.

Even though my father has lived here
since he was twelve,
even though my mother loves apple pie,
I cannot **expect** them to know
Americans
do not eat Chinese food
on the Fourth of July.

So, I **straighten** the milk and the videos
and **sample** a few new candy bars

until five o'clock,

when two hungry customers
walk inside
for some Chinese food **to go**.

▶ **Before You Move On**

1. **Confirm Prediction** Was your prediction correct? Did anyone want Chinese food? Explain.

2. **Clarify** What does the girl want her parents to understand?

▶ **Predict**
Will the girl's feelings change?

I tell them no one—no one—came,
so we ate it up ourselves

but the customers smell food in the
kitchen now—
and Mother walks through the
swinging door
holding a tray of chicken chow mein,

and Father follows her
step for step
with a **brand-new** pan of
sweet-and-sour pork—

In Other Words
step for step close behind
brand-new hot and fresh

490

and three more people **get in line**,
eleven more at six o'clock,
nine at seven,
twelve by eight,
more and more and more and more

In Other Words
get in line wait to buy food

until it's time to close the store—

time to climb to our **rooftop chairs**,
way up high, **beyond the crowd**,

where we sit and watch the fireworks show—

and eat our apple pie. ❖

In Other Words
rooftop chairs chairs on the roof
beyond the crowd above all the people

▶**Before You Move On**

1. **Confirm Prediction** Why did the girl's feelings change? Was your prediction correct?

2. **Make Connections** Describe how you **celebrate** a favorite **holiday**. How is it like a holiday in this story?

Meet the Author
Janet S. Wong

Janet Wong knows that the word "American" can mean many things. Although she was born in California, her father is Chinese and her mother is Korean.

As a college student, Ms. Wong started a special art program for children who were new to the United States. Later, she became a popular children's book writer. Ms. Wong was even invited to the White House to read a part of *Apple Pie 4th of July*.

▲ Janet S. Wong

Writer's Craft ✏️

Janet Wong uses some long sentences and some short ones to make her writing interesting. Try writing a description of your favorite holiday. Mix up the length of your sentences to make it really interesting to read!

Talk About It

1. What parts of this **realistic fiction** story could really happen?

   The parts that could really happen are _____ .

2. Describe what the girl in the story wants her parents to do. How is it different from what they usually do?

   The girl wants her parents to _____ instead of _____ .

3. How could the girl **ask for** what she wants? What could she say to her parents?

   The girl could say, "_____ ."

Learn test-taking strategies.
NGReach.com

Write About It

Do you think everyone should **celebrate** the 4th of July in the same way? Why or why not? Write a sentence. Try to convince the girl in the story to agree with your way of thinking. Use **Key Words**.

I think _____ because _____ .
You should/shouldn't _____ because _____ .

494

Character's Feelings

Think about how the characters feel and why. Then fill in a character map for "Apple Pie 4th of July."

Character Map

Character	How the Character Feels	Why the Character Feels This Way
The girl telling the story.	Unhappy	She thinks no one will want Chinese food on the 4th of July.

Now use your character map. Tell your partner about the other characters in "Apple Pie 4th of July."

> The main character is _____.
> She feels _____ because _____.

Fluency  Comprehension Coach

Use the Comprehension Coach to practice reading with the correct intonation. Rate your reading.

Use a Dictionary

You can **use a dictionary** to find out how to spell and say words. You can also learn what words mean. Use alphabetical order to find the word **celebrate** in the dictionary.

Look at the guide words to find the right page.

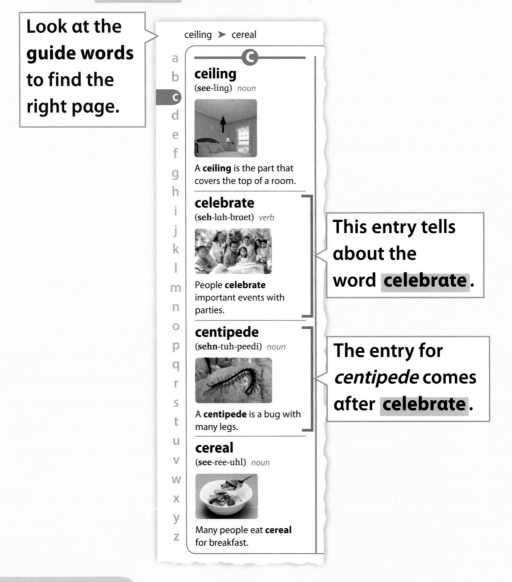

ceiling ➤ cereal

ceiling
(**see**-ling) *noun*

A **ceiling** is the part that covers the top of a room.

celebrate
(**seh**-lah-braet) *verb*

People **celebrate** important events with parties.

centipede
(**sehn**-tuh-peedi) *noun*

A **centipede** is a bug with many legs.

cereal
(**see**-ree-uhl) *noun*

Many people eat **cereal** for breakfast.

This entry tells about the word celebrate.

The entry for *centipede* comes after celebrate.

Try It Together

1. What word comes before **celebrate** on this dictionary page?

2. Where would you find the words **before** and **belong**? Between the guide words **beet** ➤ **begin** or **bell** ➤ **below**?

Connect Across Texts Find out what America means to some other children.

Genre A **poem** tells about feelings and ideas in a special way. Sometimes, the words don't mean exactly what they say.

AMERICA
a weaving
by Bobbi Katz

Have you ever seen a weaving

With colors woven through it?

Different colors all together

Making beauty as they do it.

In Other Words

weaving a cloth made by passing different threads over and under each other

▶ **Before You Move On**

1. **Plan and Monitor** What do you think this poem is going to be about?
2. **Visualize** What do you picture in your mind when you read the title?

497

Could a country be a weaving—

Different tongues, different faces,

People coming, always coming

From so many different places?

People bringing, always bringing

Special foods and special things:

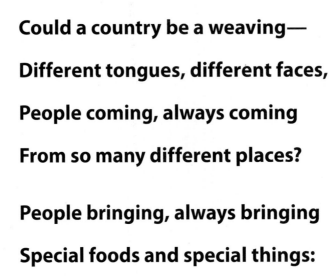

In Other Words
tongues languages
embraces welcomes; includes

Sushi, chili, spring rolls, curry

Enchiladas, lamb kebabs!

Different dances, different rhythms

Different songs that they are singing!

America, America: a never-ending

weaving!

A never-ending blending that

embraces all who come.

▶ **Before You Move On**

1. **Confirm Prediction** In what way is America a weaving? What are its threads?
2. **Clarify** The poet lists many kinds of foods. What country does each one come from?

We all contribute to this country

Built by those who came before.

We're connected to that weaving

Bit by bit, then more and more!

We buy blue jeans! We make pizza!

We eat hot dogs on soft buns.

We speak the English language.

And we speak our native tongues.

In Other Words
contribute give our best
We're connected to We become part of

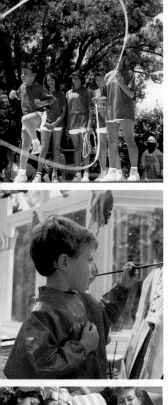

Watch us play baseball,

See us jumping Double Dutch.

We work, we play, we study,

Learning, learning oh, so much!

We become part of the weaving

Bit by bit, then more and more.

We are blending with the blending

Made by those who came before.

America, America: a never-ending weaving

A never-ending blending that embraces everyone.

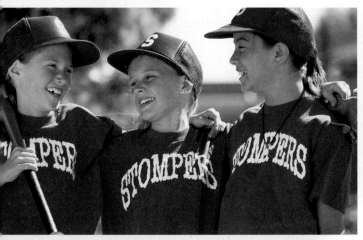

In Other Words
Double Dutch a jump rope game

▶ **Before You Move On**

1. **Explain** Who is the "We" in this poem? How can you tell?

2. **Visualize** What do you picture when you think of the words "We are blending with the blending made by those who came before"?

501

Compare Language

Sometimes words mean exactly what they say. Sometimes they mean something else. Read the sentences from "Apple Pie 4th of July" and "America: A Weaving." Does each sentence mean exactly what it says? If not, tell what the sentence really means.

Comparison Chart

These words mean just what they say.

"Apple Pie 4th of July"	"America: A Weaving"
I hear the parade passing by. This means exactly what it says.	America, America, a never-ending weaving. Meaning: Many cultures and traditions make America.
My parents do not understand all American things.	

These words do not mean exactly what they say.

Talk Together

Draw a picture that shows exactly what these words say:

"A never-ending blending that embraces everyone."

Then write a caption that tells what the words really mean. Try to use **Key Words**.

Prepositions

A **preposition** links a noun or pronoun to the other words in the sentence.

Grammar Rules Prepositions	
• A preposition often tells where.	The fireworks burst **over** the buildings.
• Prepositions that are used often: *over, under, beside, between, in, out, on, off, up, down, through, across, around,* and *into*.	Then the lights shine **in** the sky.

Read Prepositions

Read these sentences from "Apple Pie 4th of July" with a partner. Find three prepositions. Explain or show what they mean.

I smell apple pie in Laura's oven and chow mein in our kitchen.
Chow mein!
Chinese food on the Fourth of July?

Write Prepositions 🖉

Write two sentences about going to a fireworks show. Use prepositions to tell about a place or direction. Share your sentences with a partner.

503

High Frequency Words

going

there

these

Express Intentions

Listen and read along.

Poem (((**MP3**)))

 ## Trips We'll Take

This summer, I plan to see Utah.
I am **going** to Bryce Canyon **there**.
I hear they have landforms called hoodoos.
I'll be sure to take photos to share.

I will visit the state of Nevada
Where the sky is so blue and so clear.
We will stay near a body of water.
Lake Tahoe is super, I hear.

 Both states have **these** beautiful landforms.
There are hoodoos and mesas and more.
We are lucky to live in a country
With such wonderful parks to explore!

hoodoos

504

Key Words

Look at the map. What things can you see in America?

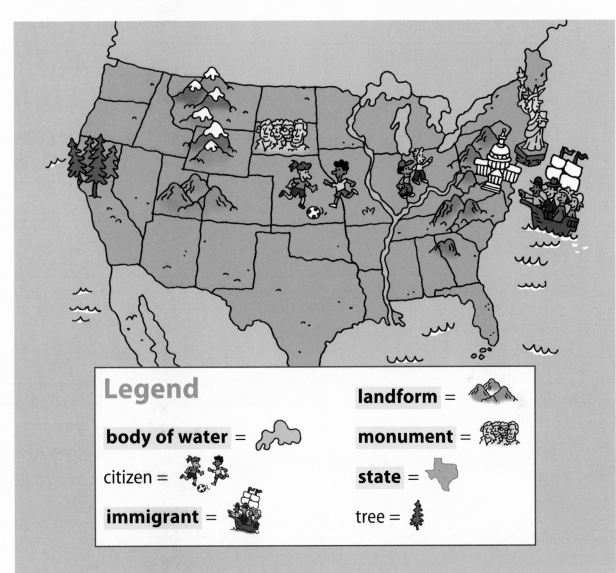

Legend

body of water =

citizen =

immigrant =

landform =

monument =

state =

tree =

Talk Together

What would you like to visit in the United States? Explain your answer to a partner.

Author's Purpose

The **author's purpose** tells why the author wrote the text.

Author's Purpose Chart

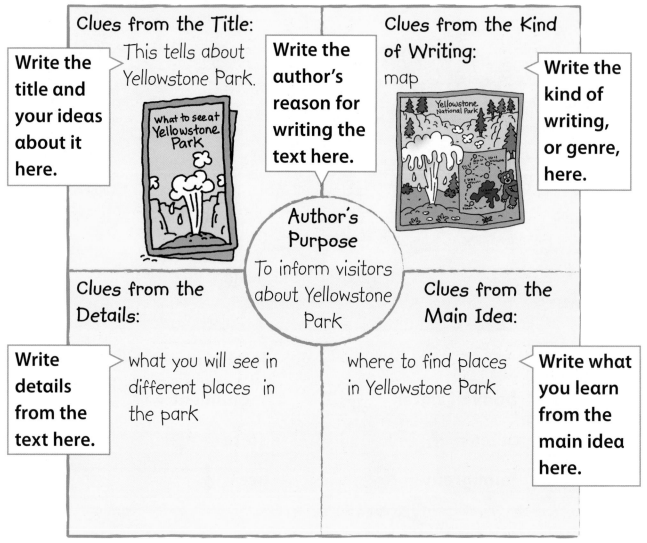

Clues from the Title:
This tells about Yellowstone Park.

what to see at Yellowstone Park

Write the title and your ideas about it here.

Write the author's reason for writing the text here.

Clues from the Kind of Writing:
map

Yellowstone National Park

Write the kind of writing, or genre, here.

Author's Purpose
To inform visitors about Yellowstone Park

Clues from the Details:

what you will see in different places in the park

Write details from the text here.

Clues from the Main Idea:

where to find places in Yellowstone Park

Write what you learn from the main idea here.

Read a magazine article or other nonfiction text with a partner. Then, use an author's purpose chart to figure out why the author wrote the text.

More Key Words

freedom
(**frē**-dum) *noun*

We have the **freedom** to say what we want.

remember
(ri-**mem**-bur) *verb*

Remember to call and say, "Happy birthday!"

seek
(**sēk**) *verb*

The girl **seeks** the piñata with a stick. She finds it.

symbol
(**sim**-bul) *noun*

Each candle on a birthday cake is a **symbol** for one year of your life.

united
(yū-**nī**-tud) *adjective*

When we play soccer, we are **united** as a team.

Talk Together

Tell a partner what a **Key Word** means. Then your partner uses the word in a sentence.

> A **symbol** is something that stands for something else.

> The Statue of Liberty is a **symbol** of the United States.

Add words to My Vocabulary Notebook.
NGReach.com

507

Use Reading Strategies

Use reading strategies before, during, and after you read.

- Before: look through the text quickly. What is the text mostly about? Decide on your purpose, or reason, for reading.

- During: as you read, stop now and then. Ask yourself: *Does this make sense?* Use a reading strategy to help you understand better.

- After: when you finish reading, stop and think. Decide what you learned from reading the text. Share your ideas with others.

How to Use a Reading Strategy

?	**1.** Before you start to read, stop and ask: *What strategies will help me get ready to read?*	Before I read I will _____ .
☁	**2.** During reading, think about what strategies will help you understand.	As I read, I can _____ .
⧇	**3.** After reading, ask yourself: *What strategies can I use? How will they help me think about what I read?*	Now that I'm done, I think _____ .

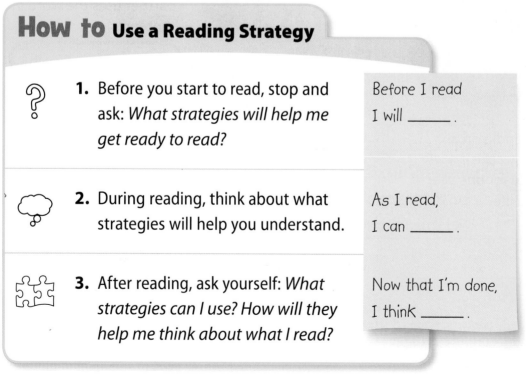

Reading Strategies

- Plan and Monitor
- Make Inferences
- Ask Questions
- Make Connections
- Visualize
- Determine Importance
- Synthesize

Talk Together

Practice using at least two reading strategies.

Description

National Parks and Monuments

Did you know that the **United** States was the first country to use land for national parks? It's true. Yellowstone was the first national park. It was created in 1872. Since then, 57 more parks have been named. There are also 334 monuments. Some are historic structures. Others are battlefields where we **remember** soldiers who died in war. Still others are beautiful seashores. One of the monuments is the Statue of Liberty. It's a **symbol** of hope and **freedom** everywhere.

The national park system helps protect places like Great Smoky Mountains and the Grand Canyon. These parks and monuments are national treasures. Millions of people are going to take their vacations at one of these places. Why don't you?

Read Literary Nonfiction

Genre

Literary nonfiction gives facts about a topic in a way that sounds a lot like a story or a poem.

Features of Nonfiction

All nonfiction tells about real people, places, and events. It uses facts to explain or describe a topic.

Literary Nonfiction

America is fifty states. It reaches from the Atlantic coast to the Pacific Ocean and beyond.

Textbook Nonfiction

America is a country made up of fifty states. Most of its land is between the Atlantic and the Pacific Oceans.

America Is...

written by **Louise Borden**
illustrated by **Stacey Schuett**

America is our country. It is the place we call home. We are a nation whose name means **freedom** to people all over the world.

◀ **Statue of Liberty**

America is fifty **states**. **It reaches** from the Atlantic coast to the Pacific Ocean and **beyond**. America is the **United States** of America. Some states are big, and some states are small. Thirteen of the states are very old. The rest came later, one by one.

These are the fifty states that make up the United States of America.

In Other Words

It reaches The land in America goes

beyond even farther

America is a flag of stars and stripes. Fifty stars **are for** the fifty **states** . Thirteen stripes are for the thirteen states that began our nation.

In Other Words

are for are **symbols** that stand for

America is the **pledge** we say at school. It is the song we sing, hands over our hearts.

In Other Words
pledge promise

▶ **Before You Move On**

1. **Use Text Features** Find and name three facts about America from the text.
2. **Details** Many **symbols** stand for America. What details on pages 512–515 support this main idea?

▶ **Predict**
Who are the workers that make
America special?

America is old barns and country roads. It is fields of corn and wheat. It is the farmers who work **sunup to sundown**.

America is teachers and their students in schools in every **state** . It is **miners and factory workers**. It is **artists and musicians**. It is bakers and bankers. It is millions of people who work many different jobs every day.

In Other Words

sunup to sundown all day

miners and factory workers people
  who work with their hands

artists and musicians people who
  make art and music

America is tall **skyscrapers** with many windows that go up, up, up. It is the people in cities who **rush** to and from work in cars, buses, and taxicabs, and on **subways** and fast trains. From New York City to Los Angeles, this is America.

In Other Words

skyscrapers buildings
rush hurry
subways underground trains in the city

▶ **Before You Move On**

1. **Main Idea** The topic of this section is America's workers. What is the main idea?

2. **Make Connections** Name other workers you have seen or read about. How do they make America special?

America is the **swamps and bayous** of the Deep South. It is the ponds that **glimmer** from east to west. It is lakes so huge and deep, they look like they are as big as an ocean. It is **rushing streams**, **creeks**, **and brooks**. It is rivers that bring our **states** together as one **vast** land.

In Other Words
swamps and bayous wet land
glimmer shine in the sunlight
rushing streams, creeks, and brooks bodies of water
vast very large

America is the **prairie** and tall grass, and wind, and stars. Listen. This is America. America is the stone walls of New England and the forests of the Northwest. The West and its ranches are a part of this nation, too. This is America.

In Other Words
prairie flat, grassy land

America is **rugged** mountains with **caps of snow** and deserts that are hot and dry. It is Niagara Falls, the Grand Canyon, and sandy beaches. There is so much to see in every **state** .

In Other Words
rugged rough-looking
caps of snow tops that are covered with snow

America is roads that take us east, west, north, and south. It is old towns with old names and new towns, too. They tell **our history** then and now. It is a nation where states meet. It is a place where we are all one.

In Other Words
our history about what happened

▶ **Before You Move On**

1. **Confirm Prediction** Was your prediction correct? Why or why not?
2. **Author's Purpose** Reread pages 518–521. What does the author want you to know? Find the text that supports your answer.

▶ **Predict**

Look at the pictures on the next four pages. What is important to people in America?

America is the land where we are free
to live, to **speak out**, to **worship**, to work,
to play, to **follow our dreams**. America is
holidays we **call our own**. It is Thanksgiving
in November to **honor** the Pilgrims and the
Native Americans. It is Fourth of July,
when fireworks light up our sky.
"Happy birthday, America!"

In Other Words

speak out say what we want
worship believe
follow our dreams do what
  we want

call our own have and
  celebrate as Americans
honor remember

America is letters, phone calls, e-mails, and faxes from family and friends across the fifty **states,** both near and far. It is **vacations and reunions**. We **connect** across the rivers and mountains and reach out across the miles.

America is home to its very first people. And America is those of us who came later. It is many kinds of people from many countries of the world. We are one family and one team. We are Americans.

America is the stories of all of us, told together. **From continent to continent** across the world, we are a nation whose name means **freedom**. America is our country. It is the place we call home.

▶ **Before You Move On**

1. **Summarize** Think about this selection. Explain what makes America special.
2. **Generalize** Have you ever been a part of a team? Tell a partner what it means to be a part of something like America.

Talk About It

1. How do you know this selection is **nonfiction**?

   It is nonfiction because _____ .

2. Think of a **monument** that you want to visit. **Give a reason why** you want to visit this place.

   I want to visit _____ because _____ .

3. Why do you think it is important to learn more about the **symbols** of the **United** States? Explain your answer.

   I think it is important to learn more about United States symbols because _____ .

Learn test-taking strategies.
⊘ NGReach.com

Write About It

Write a brief poem that tells what America means to you. Tell how America looks, sounds, feels, smells, and tastes. Use **Key Words** in your poem.

America looks _____ .

It feels _____ .

It sounds _____ .

It smells _____ .

Author's Purpose

Think about the author's reasons for writing "America Is . . ."

Author's Purpose Chart

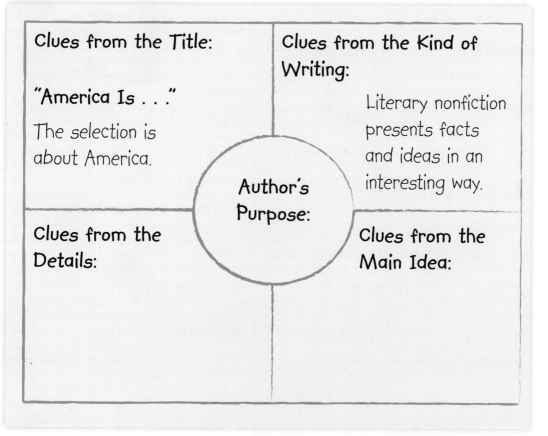

Clues from the Title:

"America Is . . ."
The selection is about America.

Clues from the Kind of Writing:

Literary nonfiction presents facts and ideas in an interesting way.

Author's Purpose:

Clues from the Details:

Clues from the Main Idea:

Now work with a partner and use your author's purpose chart to figure out the author's reason for writing "America Is. . . ."

The author tells me _____ .
The author wrote this selection to _____ .
The author's purpose is _____ .

Fluency   Comprehension Coach

Use the Comprehension Coach to practice reading with correct phrasing. Rate your reading.

Prefixes

A **prefix** is a word part that is added to the beginning of a word. A prefix can change the meaning of the word.

My grandparents were **immigrants** from Korea.

Prefix: **im**-	Word: **migrant**	**im** + migrant = **immigrant**
Meaning: into	Meaning: a person who moves around	Meaning: a person who has moved from one place to live in another place

She inputs numbers into the computer.

Prefix: **in**-	Word: **put**	**in** + put = **input**
Meaning: into	Meaning: place	Meaning: place into

Try It Together

Read the sentences. Then answer the questions.

> America is vacations and <u>reunions</u>. We connect across the rivers and mountains and reach out across the miles.

1. The prefix <u>**re**</u>- means again. What does the word <u>**reunion**</u> mean?

2. Write a sentence with a word that begins with a prefix.

Connect Across Texts Find out what the people of the **United States** share.

Genre **Song lyrics** are the words of a song. They often use rhyme, rhythm, and repetition like poems do.

THIS LAND IS YOUR LAND

words and music by **Woody Guthrie**
photos by **Sam Abell**

This land is your land. This land is my land.

From California to the New York Island.

From the Redwood Forest to the Gulf Stream waters

This land was made for you and me.

In Other Words
the Redwood Forest a big park in California full of redwood trees
Gulf Stream waters warm Atlantic Ocean waters

▶ **Before You Move On**
1. **Analyze Genre** Read the song lyrics aloud. How are they like a poem?
2. **Main Idea** What is the most important idea of this verse? Tell it in your own words.

As I was walking that ribbon of highway,

I saw above me that endless skyway.

I saw below me that golden valley.

This land was made for you and me.

▶ Before You Move On

1. **Ask Questions** What question do you have about this verse of the song? Look for an answer in the text or photos.

2. **Figurative Language** Reread the first line on page 530. Was the speaker really walking on a ribbon? Explain.

531

I've roamed and rambled and I followed my footsteps

To the sparkling sands of her diamond deserts;

And all around me a voice was sounding:

This land was made for you and me.

▶ **Before You Move On**

1. **Make Inferences** What can you tell about the speaker from the song lyrics? How does he feel about the **United States**?

2. **Visualize** Which words help you see, feel, and hear the places the song describes?

533

When the sun came shining, and I was strolling,

And the wheat fields waving and the dust
   clouds rolling,

As the fog was lifting a voice was chanting:

This land was made for you and me.

In Other Words
strolling walking
was lifting leaving
chanting singing

MORE ABOUT SAM ABELL

Sam Abell travels across the **United States** and around the world, taking photos of many places and people. He has provided photos for National Geographic Society for almost 40 years.

Mr. Abell learned **photography** from his father when he was very young.

"For me, photography means, **'Andiamo!'**" he said. "It's what gets me out the door."

In Other Words
photography how to take photos
Andiamo! Let's go! (in Italian)

▶ **Before You Move On**
1. **Make Inferences** The song tells about a singing voice. What do you think the speaker means?
2. **Draw Conclusions** How are the speaker and Sam Abell alike?

Respond and Extend

Compare Author's Purpose

Authors have a purpose, or reason, for writing texts. What do you think the authors of "America Is. . ." and "This Land is Your Land" are trying to do?

Comparison Chart

	"America Is. . ." by Louise Borden	"This Land Is Your Land" by Woody Guthrie
persuade readers		✔
inform readers	✔	
entertain readers		
share experiences		
express feelings		
express creativity		

Authors can have more than one purpose.

Put a check if the statement is true for the selection.

Talk Together

With your partner, take turns choosing picture cards. Use the cards and **Key Words** to tell about America.

Prepositional Phrases

A **prepositional phrase** starts with a preposition and ends with a noun or pronoun. Prepositional phrases add details to a sentence.

Grammar Rules Prepositional Phrases

Use prepositional phrases • to show where something is *above, below, between, in, out*	**in** Yosemite National Park **below** the waterfall
• to show direction ➝ *up, down, through, around, into*	**through** the woods **around** the big boulder
• to show time 🕐 *before, during, after, until*	**until** our next visit **during** summer vacation
• to add details *at, for, of, to, about, with, without*	**about** the park **without** our backpack

Read Prepositional Phrases

Read these sentences from "This Land is Your Land" with a partner. Identify two prepositional phrases.

I saw above me
that endless skyway.
I saw below me that
golden valley.
This land was made for you and me.

Use Prepositional Phrases ✎

Write two sentences using the two prepositional phrases you found in the song above.

Write About Yourself

Write a Personal Narrative 🖊

Tell what America means to you or someone you know. Put your story into a class scrapbook.

Study a Model

A personal narrative tells about a real event that means a lot to you. Read about Vijay's first 4th of July.

Everyone's Flag

by Vijay Kumar

My family moved to the United States three years ago. On **our first 4th of July**, we went to a parade. **My mom started crying**.

My mom said when she was growing up in India, people couldn't put up their own flags. Only the government could do that.

Here, everyone had a flag! There were flags on houses and flags on floats. People wore flag pins and flag shirts. **Even little babies waved flags**!

That's when I learned that **America belongs to everyone**. I'm glad that this country is my home.

The **beginning** tells what **event** Vijay is writing about.

The middle tells more about what happened. Vijay uses **words that sound like him**. He writes using his own voice.

The end tells why the event was **important**.

Prewrite

1. **Choose a Topic** What will you write about? Talk with a partner. Choose an event from your life that is important to you.

2. **Gather Information** Think about the event. What happened? Who was there? What did you see, hear, and feel?

3. **Get Organized** Use a Feelings Chart to help you organize details.

Feelings Chart

Character	How the Character Feels	Why the Character Feels This Way
My mom.	She cries when she sees the flag.	

Draft

Use your details and chart to write your draft. Remember to tell why the event is important. Use words and sentences that sound like you.

Revise

1. **Read, Retell, Respond** Read your draft aloud to a partner. Your partner listens and then retells the story. Next, talk about ways to make your writing better.

Language Frames

Retell	Make Suggestions
You tell about _____ . I think this story is important to you because _____ .	I'm not sure why _____ is special. Can you explain that more? The writing doesn't sound like you. Maybe you could change _____ .

---

2. **Make Changes** Think about your draft and your partner's ideas. Then use the Revising Marks on page 563 to mark your changes.

   - Do your words and sentences sound like you? If not, change some.

   - Do you tell why the event is important? Add details that will help your reader understand.

Edit and Proofread

Work with a partner to edit and proofread your personal narrative. Look for prepositional phrases. If one starts a sentence, you may need to add a comma after it. Use the marks on page 563 to show your changes.

Spelling Tip

✔ Watch out for words that sound alike: *through* is a preposition, but *threw* is a verb.

Publish

On Your Own Make a final copy of your personal narrative. Read it aloud to your classmates. You could also send it in an e-mail to a friend or family member.

Presentation Tips	
If you are the speaker…	**If you are the listener…**
Listen to how you're telling the story. You should sound like you're talking to a friend.	As you listen, think of something similar that happened to you.
Change your voice when events are funny or sad or serious.	Think about why the event is important to the reader.

With a Group Collect all of the personal narratives. Put them in a scrapbook. Add photographs, drawings, and decorations. Take turns bringing the book home to share with your families.

541

?
BIG
Question

What does America mean to you?

Talk Together

In this unit, you found lots of answers to the **Big Question**. Now, use your concept map to discuss the **Big Question** with the class.

Concept Map

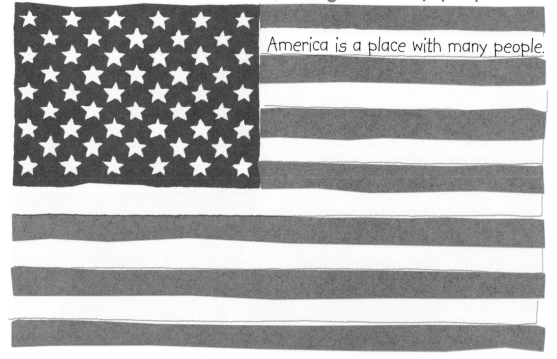

America means many things to many people.

America is a place with many people.

542

Share Your Ideas

Choose one of these ways to share your ideas about the **Big Question**.

Write It!

Write a Song

Work with a partner to write your own song about America. Perform your song for the class. Tell what America means to you.

Talk About It!

Give a News Report

Pretend that you and your partner are reporters on the local news. Give a news report about a famous American landmark close to where you live. Share your report with the class.

Do It!

Perform a Skit

Make up a skit about another holiday. Use the characters from "Apple Pie 4th of July." Assign roles and think of lines for each character to say. Make props to use in the skit. Then perform the skit for your class.

Write It!

Write a Recipe

Write the recipe for a favorite meal that you enjoy at home.

543

Strategies for Learning Language

These strategies can help you learn to use and understand the English language.

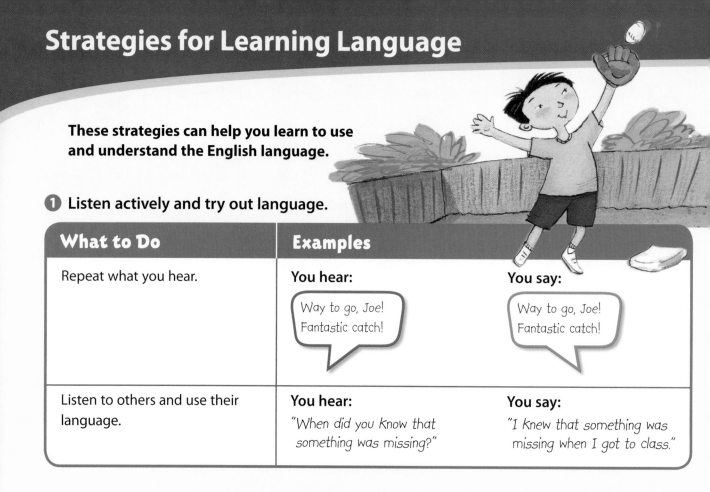

① **Listen actively and try out language.**

What to Do	Examples	
Repeat what you hear.	**You hear:** Way to go, Joe! Fantastic catch!	**You say:** Way to go, Joe! Fantastic catch!
Listen to others and use their language.	**You hear:** "When did you know that something was missing?"	**You say:** "I knew that something was missing when I got to class."

② **Ask for help.**

What to Do	Examples	
Ask questions about how to use language.	Did I say that right? Did I use that word in the right way? Which is correct, "bringed" or "brought"?	
Use your native language or English to make sure that you understand.	**You say:** "Wait! Could you say that again more slowly, please?"	**Other options:** "Does 'fluffy' mean 'soft'?" "Is 'giant' another way to say 'big'?"

3 **Use gestures and body language, and watch for them.**

What to Do	Examples
Use gestures and movements. That will help others understand your ideas.	I will hold up five fingers to show that I need five more minutes.
Look at people as they speak. Watch how they move. That can help you understand what their words mean.	Let's give him a hand. / Everyone is clapping. "Give him a hand" must mean to clap for him.

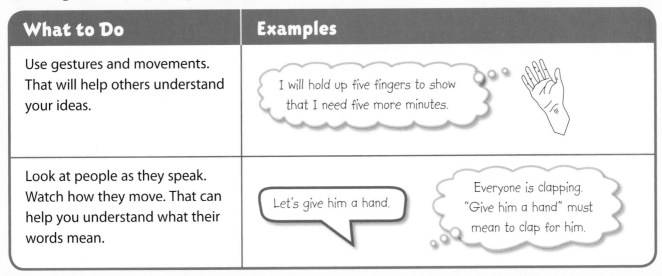

4 **Think about what you are learning.**

What to Do	Examples
Ask yourself: Are my language skills getting better? How can I improve?	Was it correct to use "they" when I talked about my parents? / Did I add **s** to show more than one?
Take notes. Use your notes to practice using English.	How to Ask Questions • I can start a question with "is," "can," or "do": Do you have my math *book*? • I can start a question with "who," "what," "where," "when," "how," or "why" to get more information: Where did you put my math *book*?

Vocabulary Strategies

When you read, you may find a word you don't know. But, don't worry! There are many things you can do to figure out the meaning of an unfamiliar word.

Use What You Know

Look at the word. Does it look like a word you know?

- Some words are in the same word family. So the new word might have a similar meaning. The words *build*, *builder*, and *rebuild* are in the same word family.

- Some words look the same in English and another language. If you know the word in your native language, you'll know the English word, too. The English word *problem* and the Spanish word *problema* look alike. They mean the same thing, too!

On the Top of the World

Mount Everest is the highest mountain in the world. It is 29,028 feet (8,848 meters) high. This **magnificent** mountain is covered in permanently frozen snow and ice. But this doesn't stop **adventurous** climbers from trying to reach its peak.

> This English word looks like **magnifico**. That means "beautiful" in Spanish. I think that meaning makes sense here, too.

> I know that **adventure** means "an exciting event" and that an **adventurer** is "someone who takes risks." So, **adventurous** probably means "willing to be a part of risky activities."

Use Context Clues

Sometimes you can figure out a word's meaning by looking at other words and phrases near the word. Those words and phrases are called **context clues.**

There are different kinds of context clues. Look for signal words such as *means, like, but,* or *unlike* to help you find the clues.

Extremely cold temperatures are hazardous to mountain climbers.

Kind of Clue	Signal Words	Example
Definition Gives the word's meaning.	*is, are, was, refers to, means*	Hazardous ***refers to*** something that causes harm or injury .
Restatement Gives the word's meaning in a different way, usually after a comma.	*or*	Mountain climbing can be hazardous**,** *or* result in injuries to climbers .
Synonym Gives a word or phrase that means almost the same thing.	*like, also*	Sudden drops in temperature can be hazardous. ***Also*** dangerous are very high altitudes that make it hard to breathe.
Antonym Gives a word or phrase that means the opposite.	*but, unlike*	The subzero temperatures can be hazardous, ***but*** special gear keeps the climbers safe .
Examples Gives examples of what the word means.	*such as, for example, including*	Climbers prepare for hazardous situations. ***For example***, they carry extra food, equipment for heavy snowfall, and first-aid kits .

Vocabulary Strategies, *continued*

Use Word Parts

Many English words are made up of parts. You can use these parts as clues to a word's meaning.

When you don't know a word, look to see if you know any of its parts. Put the meaning of the word parts together to figure out the meaning of the whole word.

laptop

keyboard

Compound Words

A compound word is made up of two or more smaller words. To figure out the meaning of the whole word:

1. Break the long word into parts.

keyboard = key + board

2. Put the meanings of the smaller words together to predict the meaning of the whole word.

key = button
+
board = flat surface

keyboard = flat part of computer with buttons

3. If you can't predict the meaning from the parts, use what you know and the meaning of the other words to figure it out.

lap + top = laptop

laptop means "small portable computer," not "the top of your lap"

Prefixes

A prefix comes at the beginning of a word. It changes the word's meaning. To figure out the meaning of an unfamiliar word, look to see if it has a prefix.

1. Break the word into parts. Think about the meaning of each part.

I need to **rearrange** the files on my computer.

re- + arrange

The prefix *re-* means "again." The word *arrange* means "to put in order."

2. Put the meanings of the word parts together.

The word *rearrange* means "to put in order again."

Some Prefixes and Their Meanings

Prefix	Meaning
co-	together
in-	not, into
im-	not
re-	again, back
un-	not

Suffixes

A suffix comes at the end of a word. It changes the word's meaning and part of speech. To figure out the meaning of new word, look to see if it has a suffix.

Some Suffixes and Their Meanings

Suffix	Meaning
-able	can be done
-ation	act, process
-er, -or	one who
-ful	full of
-less	without
-ship	state or quality of

1. Break the word into parts. Think about the meaning of each part.

My **teacher** helps me find online articles.

teach + -er

verb

The word *teach* means "to give lessons."
The suffix -*er* means "one who."

2. Put the meanings of the word parts together.

A *teacher* is "a person who gives lessons."

noun

Vocabulary Strategies, *continued*

Look Beyond the Literal Meaning

Writers use colorful language to keep their readers interested. They use words and phrases that mean something different from their usual definitions. Figurative language and idioms are kinds of colorful language.

Figurative Language: Similes

A simile compares two things that are alike in some way. It uses the words *like* or *as* to make the comparison.

Simile	Things Compared	How They're Alike
Cory hiked across the desert **as sluggishly as a snail**.	Cory and a snail	They both move very slowly.
His skin was **like sheets of sandpaper.**	skin and sandpaper	They are both rough and very dry.

Figurative Language: Metaphors

A metaphor compares two things without using the words *like* or *as*.

Metaphor	Things Compared	Meaning
The **sun's rays were a thousand bee stings** on his face.	sun's rays and bee stings	The sun's rays blistered his face.
His only **companion was thirst.**	friend and thirst	His thirst was always there with him.

Figurative Language: Personification

When writers use personification they give human qualities to nonhuman things.

Personification	Object	Human Quality
The **angry sun** kept punishing him.	sun	has feelings
A **cactus reached out to** him.	cactus	is able to be friendly

Idioms

An idiom is a special kind of phrase that means something different from what the words mean by themselves.

What you say:

If the topic is Mars, **I'm all ears.**

Break a leg!

Rachel had **to eat her words.**

Give me a break!

Hang on.

I'm **in a jam.**

The joke was so funny, Lisa **laughed her head off.**

Juan was **steamed** when I lost his video game.

Let's **surf the Net** for ideas for report ideas.

I'm so tired, I just want to **veg out.**

Rob and Zak are together **24-seven**.

You can say that again.

Zip your lips!

What you mean:

If the topic is Mars, **I'll listen very carefully**.

Good luck!

Rachel had **to say she was wrong.**

That's ridiculous!

Wait.

I'm **in trouble.**

The joke was so funny, Lisa **laughed very hard.**

Juan was **very angry** when I lost his video game.

Let's **look around the contents of the Internet** for report ideas.

I'm so tired, I just want to **relax and not think about anything.**

Rob and Zak are together **all the time.**

I totally agree with you.

Be quiet!

Reading Strategies

Good readers use a set of strategies before, during, and after reading. Knowing which strategy to use and when will help you understand and enjoy all kinds of text.

Plan and Monitor

Good readers have clear plans for reading. Remember to:

- **Set a purpose** for reading. Ask yourself: Why am I reading this? What do I want to find out?

- **Preview** the text. Read the title. Look at the pictures.

- **Make predictions**, or guess, what comes next. Check your predictions as you read. Change them as you learn new information.

Monitor, or keep track of, your reading. Remember to:

- **Clarify ideas and vocabulary** to make sure you understand what everything means. Stop and ask yourself: Does that make sense?

- **Reread, read on,** or **change your reading speed** if you are confused.

Determine Importance

To help you remember all the facts and details as you read:

- Look for the most important details. Put them together to figure out the **main idea**.

- **Summarize**, or tell the most important ideas in your own words.

Ask Questions

Ask yourself questions as you read.

- Look in the text for the answers. Some answers might **right there** in the text. For other answers, you may have to **think and search**.

- Sometimes you won't find the answers in the book. Then you'll need to **use what you know** and **what the author tells you** to figure out the answers.

Visualize

Think about the writer's words. What do you see, hear, feel, taste, or smell? Use all your senses to **visualize**, or picture in your mind, what the writer describes.

Make Connections

When you read, you make connections to things you already know. You use all these things to help you understand what the writer says:

- **your own ideas and experiences**
- what you learn about the **world** from TV, songs, and school
- **other texts** you've read.

Make Inferences

Sometimes a writer doesn't tell a reader everything. To figure out what a writer means:

- Look for details in the text.
- Think about what you already know.
- Put the details and your ideas together to figure out what the author means.

Synthesize

As you read, think about what the text tells you and what you know. Then you can **synthesize**, or put together, all the ideas. You can

- decide what to think about a topic, or **draw a conclusion**.
- make a statement that seems true for a lot of situations, or **form a generalization**.

Writing and Research

Writing is a good way to express yourself. Follow these steps to help you say want you want clearly, correctly, and in your own special way.

Prewrite

When you prewrite, you choose a topic. Then you collect all the details and information you need for writing.

1 **Choose a Topic and Make a Plan** Think about what you will write.

- Make a list. Then choose the best idea to use for your topic.

- Think about your writing role, audience, and form. Add those to a RAFT chart.

- Jot down any research questions, too. Those will help you look for the information you need.

RAFT Chart

Role: scientist

Audience: my teacher and classmates

Form: report

Topic: honeybees

2 **Gather Information** List details you know about your topic. Or, use resources like those on pages 557–560 to find information that answers your questions. Take notes.

Use Information Resources

Books

Book Cover

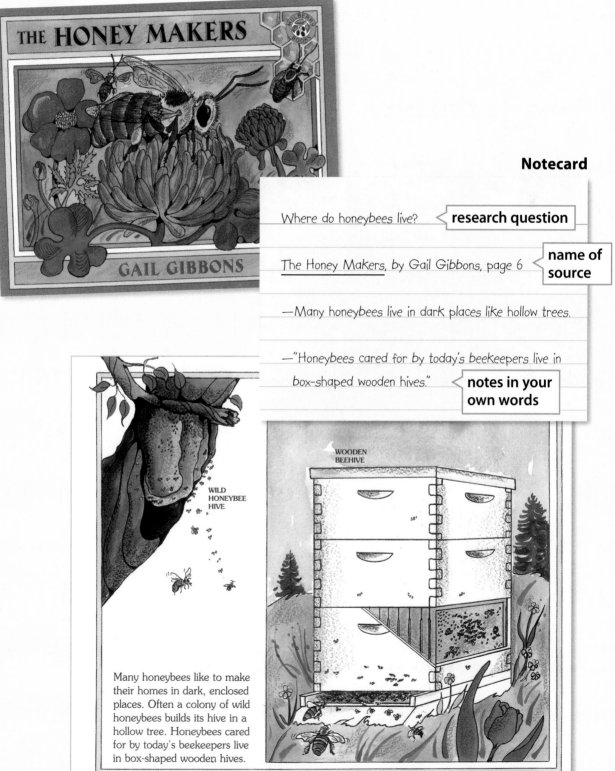

THE HONEY MAKERS

GAIL GIBBONS

Notecard

Where do honeybees live? [research question]

The Honey Makers, by Gail Gibbons, page 6 [name of source]

—Many honeybees live in dark places like hollow trees.

—"Honeybees cared for by today's beekeepers live in box-shaped wooden hives." [notes in your own words]

WILD HONEYBEE HIVE

WOODEN BEEHIVE

Many honeybees like to make their homes in dark, enclosed places. Often a colony of wild honeybees builds its hive in a hollow tree. Honeybees cared for by today's beekeepers live in box-shaped wooden hives.

Writing and Research, *continued*

Encyclopedias

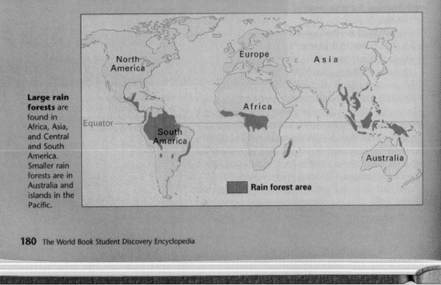

● Rain forest

Rain forest

Rain forests are thick forests of tall trees. They are found where the weather is warm the year around, and there is plenty of rain. Most rain forests grow near the equator, a make-believe line around Earth's middle. Africa, Asia, and Central and South America have large rain forests. Smaller rain forests are found in Australia and islands in the Pacific.

Tropical rain forests have more kinds of trees than anywhere else in the world. More than half of all the kinds of plants and animals on Earth live in tropical rain forests.

The tallest rain forest trees are as tall as 165 feet (50 meters). The treetops form a leafy covering called the canopy

Tropical rain forests have more kinds of trees than anywhere else in the world.

Large rain forests are found in Africa, Asia, and Central and South America. Smaller rain forests are in Australia and islands in the Pacific.

North America
Europe
Asia
Equator
South America
Africa
Australia

◼ Rain forest area

180 The World Book Student Discovery Encyclopedia

1. What is the first letter of your topic? Find the volume for that letter. Or, find the correct section on the **CD-ROM**.

2. Read the **guide words**. Use alphabetical order to look up your topic.

3. Read the **article** and take notes.

Magazines

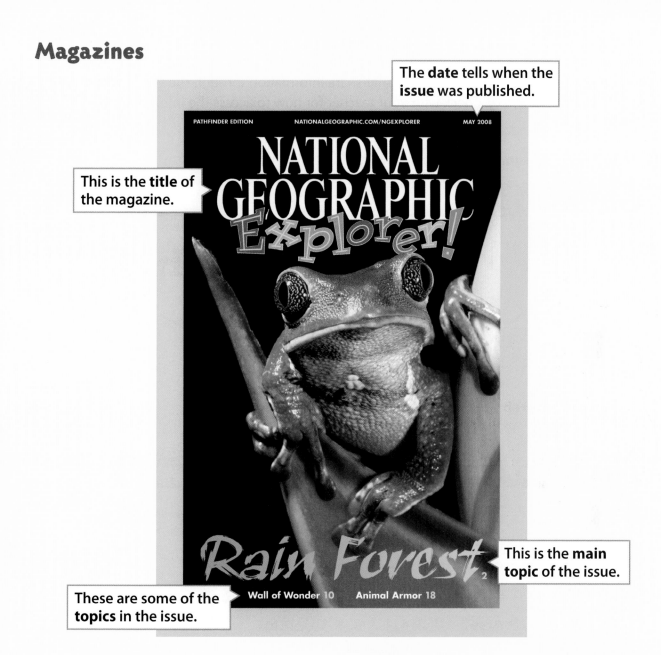

The **date** tells when the **issue** was published.

This is the **title** of the magazine.

This is the **main topic** of the issue.

These are some of the **topics** in the issue.

... and Experts

Talk to an **expert,** or someone who knows a lot about your topic. Find out when you can meet.

- Prepare questions you want to ask.
- Ask your questions.
- Write down the person's answers.
- Say thank you.
- Choose the notes you'll use for your writing

Writing and Research, *continued*

Internet

The Internet is a connection of computers that share information through the World Wide Web. It is like a giant library. Check with your teacher for how to access the Internet from your school.

1. **Go to a search page.** Type in your key words. Click search.

2. **Read the list of Web sites, or pages, that have your key words.** The underlined words are links to the Web sites.

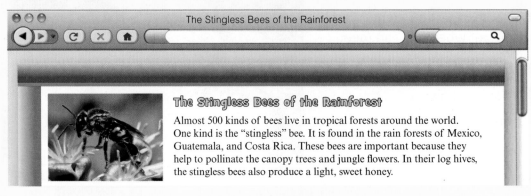

3. **Click on a link to go directly to the site, or Web page.** Read the article online or print it if it is helpful for your research. Later on, you can use the article to take notes.

560

4. Get Organized Think about all the details you've gathered about your topic. Use a list, a chart, or other graphic organizer to show what you'll include in your writing. Use the organizer to show the order of your ideas, too.

Cluster

compound eyes

3 pairs of legs

antennae

1

2

head

honeybee parts

thorax

slender, hairy tongue

3

abdomen with stinger for females

2 sets of wings

Outline

The Helpful, Sweet Honeybee

I. Important insects

  A. help pollinate plants

    1. flowers and trees

    2. fruits

  B. turn nectar into honey

II. Honeybee homes

  A. around the world

  B. hives

Draft

When you write your first draft, you turn all your ideas into sentences. You write quickly just to get all your ideas down. You can correct mistakes later.

Cluster

Turn your main idea into a topic sentence. Then add the details.

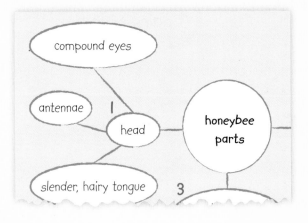

Outline

Turn the main idea after each Roman numeral into a topic sentence. Then turn the words next to the letters and numbers into detail sentences that tell more about the main idea.

> The Helpful, Sweet Honeybee
>
> I. Important insects
>   A. help pollinate plants
>   1. flowers and trees
>   2. fruits

Beginning of Description

> One main part of a honeybee is the head. The bee's head seems to be mostly eyes! They are called compound eyes and have a lot of tiny lenses in them.

Beginning of Report

> **The Helpful, Sweet Honeybee**
>
> You may think that all the honeybee does is make honey. But, believe it or not, this insect is always busy with another important job.
>
> A honeybee helps keep plants growing. It helps to spread the pollen flowers and trees need to start new plants.

Revise

When you revise, you make changes to your writing to make it better and clearer.

1 **Read, Retell, Respond** Read your draft aloud to a partner. Your partner listens and then retells your main points.

You are describing a honeybee's hive. Isn't a bee's nest the same as a hive?

Yes, it is. I don't need the word "nest," so I'll take it out.

Your partner can help you discover what is unclear or what you need to add. Use your partner's suggestions to decide what you can to do to make your writing better.

2 **Make Changes** Think about your draft and what you and your partner discussed. What changes will you make? Use Revising Marks to mark your changes.

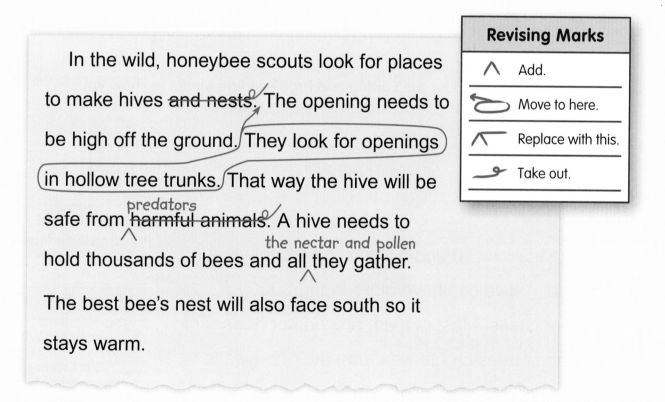

Revising Marks	
∧	Add.
↶	Move to here.
⋀	Replace with this.
⟋	Take out.

In the wild, honeybee scouts look for places to make hives ~~and nests.~~ The opening needs to be high off the ground. They look for openings in hollow tree trunks. That way the hive will be safe from ~~harmful animals.~~ predators A hive needs to hold thousands of bees and all the nectar and pollen they gather.

The best bee's nest will also face south so it stays warm.

563

Edit and Proofread

When you edit and proofread, you look for mistakes in capitalization, grammar, and punctuation.

❶ Check Your Sentences Check that your sentences are clear, complete, and correct. Add any missing subjects or predicates

❷ Check Your Spelling Look for any misspelled words. Check their spelling in a dictionary or a glossary.

❸ Check for Capital Letters, Punctuation, and Grammar Look especially for correct use of

- capital letters in proper nouns
- apostrophes and quotation marks
- subject-verb agreement
- pronouns
- verb tenses

❹ Mark Your Changes Use the Editing and Proofreading Marks to show your changes.

❺ Make a Final Copy Make all the corrections you've marked to make a final, clean copy of your writing. If you are using a computer, print out your corrected version.

It is crowded and busy inside a honeybee hive. A hive can have more than 50,000 honeybees. Most of them are worker bees. The worker bees create wax from their bodies to build combs. The combs are layers of cells, or holes. The cells hold nectar, pollen, or larvae.

Editing and Proofreading Marks

∧	Add.
୶	Take out.
⋏	Replace with this.
◯	Check spelling.
≡	Capitalize.
/	Make lowercase.
¶	Make new paragraph.

Publish

When you publish your writing, you share it with others.

1 **Add Visuals** Visuals can make your writing more interesting and easier to understand. Maybe you will

- import photographs or illustrations
- insert computer clip art
- add graphs, charts, or diagrams

2 **Present Your Writing** There are a lot of ways to share your finished work. Here are just a few ideas.

- E-mail it to a friend or family member.
- Send it to your favorite magazine or publication.
- Turn it into a chapter for a group book about the topic.
- Make a video clip of you reading it to add to a group presentation.

A Home for the Honeybee

In the wild, honeybee scouts look for places to make hives. They look for openings in hollow tree trunks. The opening needs to be high off the ground. That way the hive will be safe from predators. A hive also needs to big enough for thousands of bees and all the nectar and pollen they gather. The best hive will also face south so it stays warm.

Writing Traits

Good writing is clear, interesting, and easy to follow. To make your writing as good as it can be, check your writing to be sure it has the characteristics, or traits, of good writing.

Focus and Coherence

Writing is focused when the main idea is clear. It is coherent when all the ideas work together to tell about the same idea. What score can you give your or your partner's writing for focus and coherence? How can you make it better?

	Are the ideas related?	Is the writing complete?
4	❏ All of the ideas are about the same topic.	❏ There is a beginning and an end. ❏ All of the details in the middle are important.
3	❏ Most of the ideas are about the same topic.	❏ There is a beginning and an end. ❏ Most of the details in the middle are important.
2	❏ There are many ideas that don't go together. It is hard to tell what the writing is all about.	❏ The writing has a beginning or an end, but it doesn't have both. ❏ Some of the details in the middle don't belong there.
1	❏ The ideas don't go together. I can't tell what the writing is really about.	❏ The writing does not have a beginning. ❏ The writing does not have an end.

Development of Ideas

Writing is well-developed when the ideas are interesting and supported by plenty of details. What score can you give your or your partner's writing for development of ideas? What can you add to develop the ideas better?

	Is the writing interesting?	How well do you understand the ideas?
4	❏ The writer has thought about the topic carefully. ❏ The ideas are presented in a very interesting way.	❏ The writing answered all of my questions. There were enough details to help me understand.
3	❏ The writer has thought about the topic. ❏ The ideas are presented in an interesting way.	❏ The writing answered most of my questions. There were enough details to help me understand.
2	❏ The writer doesn't seem to have thought about the topic very much. ❏ The writing is OK, but not interesting.	❏ I have some questions that were not answered.
1	❏ The writer doesn't seem to have thought about the topic at all. ❏ The ideas are presented in a boring way.	❏ I have a lot of questions. The writing didn't tell me enough.

Organization

Writing is organized when it is easy to follow. All the ideas make sense together and flow from one idea to the next in an order that fits the writer's purpose.

	Is the whole thing organized?	Does the writing flow?
4	☐ The writing is very well-organized. It fits the writer's purpose.	☐ The writing is very smooth. Each idea flows into the next one.
3	☐ The writing is organized. It fits the writer's purpose.	☐ Most of the writing is smooth. There are only a few places where it jumps around.
2	☐ The writing is organized, but doesn't fit the writer's purpose.	☐ The writing jumps from one idea to another idea, but I can follow it a little.
1	☐ The writing is not organized. Maybe the writer forgot to use a chart to plan.	☐ I can't follow the ideas at all. I can't tell what the writer wants to say.

Organized

Not organized

Voice

Every writer has a special way of saying things, or voice. Readers can always tell who the writer is by the words the writer uses and how the sentences are put together.

	Does the writing sound real?	Do the words fit the purpose and audience?
4	❑ The writing shows who the writer is. ❑ The writer is talking right to me.	❑ The writer uses words that really fit the purpose and audience.
3	❑ The writing shows who the writer is. ❑ The writer sounds real.	❑ The writer uses good words for the purpose and audience.
2	❑ It's hard to tell who the writer is. ❑ The writer isn't talking to me.	❑ The writer uses some words that fit the purpose and audience.
1	❑ I can't tell who the writer is. The writer doesn't seem to care.	❑ The words don't fit the purpose and audience.

Hello. This is Sonja.

Yes. I know it's you, Sonja. I can tell from your voice!

Written Conventions

Good writers always follow the rules of grammar, punctuation, and spelling.

	Are the sentences complete?	Is the writing correct?
4	❑ Every sentence has a subject and a predicate.	❑ All the punctuation, capitalization, and spelling is correct.
3	❑ Most of the sentences have a subject and a predicate.	❑ Most of the punctuation, spelling, and capitalization is correct.
2	❑ Some of the sentences are missing subjects or predicates.	❑ The writing has several errors. I can't tell what some of the sentences mean.
1	❑ Several sentences are missing subjects or predicates.	❑ There are many errors. The writing is very confusing.

Grammar, Usage, Mechanics, and Spelling

Sentences

A sentence expresses a complete thought.

Kinds of Sentences

There are four kinds of sentences.

A **statement** tells something. It ends with a **period**.	Ned is at the mall now**.** He needs a new shirt**.**
A **question** asks for information. It ends with a **question mark**.	Where can I find the shirts**?**

Kinds of Questions

Some questions ask for "Yes" or "No" answers. They start with words such as **Is**, **Do**, **Can**, **Are**, and **Will**.	**Do** you have a size 10**?** **Answer:** Yes **Are** these shirts on sale**?** **Answer:** No
Other questions ask for more information. They start with words such as **Who**, **What**, **Where**, **When**, and **Why**.	**What** colors do you have**?** **Answer:** We have red and blue. **Where** can I try this on**?** **Answer:** You can use this room.

An **exclamation** shows strong feeling. It ends with an **exclamation mark**.	This is such a cool shirt**!** I love it**!**
A **command** tells you what to do or what not to do. It usually begins with a **verb** and ends with a **period**. If a command shows strong emotion, it ends with an exclamation mark.	**Please** bring me a size 10**.** **Don't open** the door yet**.** Wait until I come out**!**

Negative Sentences

A negative sentence means "no."

| A **negative sentence** uses a **negative word** to say "no." | That is **not** a good color for me. |
| | I **can't** find the right size. |

Complete Sentences

A complete sentence has two parts.

The **subject** tells whom or what the sentence is about.	<u>My friends</u> buy clothes here.
	<u>The other store</u> has nicer shirts.
The **predicate** tells what the subject is, has, or does.	My friends <u>buy clothes here.</u>
	The other store <u>has nicer shirts.</u>

Sentences *(continued)*

Compound Sentences

When you join two sentences together, you can make a compound sentence.

Use a **comma** and the word **and**, **but**, or **or** to join the sentences.	Tina went to the pool. Then she went shopping. Tina went to the pool**, and** then she went shopping.
Use **and** to put together two ideas that are alike.	My friends walk to the mall. I go with them. My friends walk to the mall**, and** I go with them.
Use **but** to put together two ideas that show a difference.	My friends walk to the mall. I ride my bike. My friends walk to the mall**, but** I ride my bike.
Use **or** to show a choice between two ideas.	You can walk to the mall with me. You can ride with Dad. You can walk to the mall with me**, or** you can ride with Dad.

Nouns

Nouns name people, animals, places, or things.

Common Nouns and Proper Nouns

There are two kinds of nouns.

A **common noun** names any person, animal, place, or thing of a certain type.	I know that **girl**. She rides a **horse**. I also see her at the **gym**. She plays for the **team**.
A **proper noun** names a particular person, animal, place, or thing. • Start all the important words in a proper noun with a capital letter. • Use capital letters for city and state names. Also use them when you abbreviate state names.	I know **Marissa**. Her horse is **Brownie**. I also see her at the **Sports Center**. She plays for the **Sting Rays**. Her family is from **Dallas, Texas**. They live on **Crockett Lane**.

Abbreviations for State Names in Mailing Addresses

Alabama	AL	Hawaii	HI	Massachusetts	MA	New Mexico	NM	South Dakota	SD
Alaska	AK	Idaho	ID	Michigan	MI	New York	NY	Tennessee	TN
Arizona	AZ	Illinois	IL	Minnesota	MN	North Carolina	NC	Texas	TX
Arkansas	AR	Indiana	IN	Mississippi	MS	North Dakota	ND	Utah	UT
California	CA	Iowa	IA	Missouri	MO	Ohio	OH	Vermont	VT
Colorado	CO	Kansas	KS	Montana	MT	Oklahoma	OK	Virginia	VA
Connecticut	CT	Kentucky	KY	Nebraska	NE	Oregon	OR	Washington	WA
Delaware	DE	Louisiana	LA	Nevada	NV	Pennsylvania	PA	West Virginia	WV
Florida	FL	Maine	ME	New Hampshire	NH	Rhode Island	RI	Wisconsin	WI
Georgea	GA	Maryland	MD	New Jersey	NJ	South Carolina	SC	Wyoming	WY

Nouns *(continued)*

Nouns that Name More than One

Count nouns name things that you can count. A singular count noun shows "one." A plural count noun shows "more than one."

Add **-s** to most nouns to show more than one.	bicycle ➞ bicycle**s** club ➞ club**s**	
Add **-es** to nouns that end in **x**, **ch**, **sh**, **ss**, **z**, and sometimes **o**.	box ➞ box**es** bench ➞ bench**es** wish ➞ wish**es** loss ➞ loss**es** potato ➞ potato**es**	
For nouns that end in **y**, change the **y** to **i** and then add **-es**. For nouns that end in a vowel plus **y**, just add **-s**.	berry**i** ➞ berr**ies** family**i** ➞ famil**ies** boy ➞ boy**s** day ➞ day**s**	
A few nouns change in special ways to show more than one.	man ➞ men woman ➞ women foot ➞ feet tooth ➞ teeth child ➞ children	

Noncount Nouns

Noncount nouns name things that you cannot count.
Noncount nouns have one form for "one" and "more than one."

Weather Words	heat lightning thunder rain **YES:** **Thunder** and **lightning** scare my dog. **NO:** Thunders and lightnings scare my dog.
Food Words Use a measurement word such as **cup, slice, glass**, or **head** and the word **of** to make a food word name more than one.	bread milk rice soup **YES:** I'm thirsty for **milk**. I want **two glasses of milk.** **NO:** I'm thirsty for milks. I want milks.
Ideas and Feelings.	fun help luck work **YES:** I need **help** with my homework. **NO:** I need helps with my homework.
Category Nouns	clothing mail money time **YES:** Did you get **mail** today? **NO:** Did you get mails today?
Materials	air gold paper water wood **YES:** Is the **water** in this river clean? **NO:** Is the waters in this river clean?
Activities or Sports	baseball dancing golf singing soccer **YES:** I played **soccer** three times this week. **NO:** I played soccers three times this week.

575

Nouns *(continued)*

Words that Signal Nouns

The articles *a*, *an*, *some*, and *the* help identify a noun. They often appear before count nouns.

Use **a, an,** or **some** before a noun to talk about something in general. Use **an** instead of **a** before a word that begins with a vowel or silent **h**. Do <u>not</u> use **a** or **an** before a noncount noun.	**Some jokes** are funny. Do you have **a favorite joke**? I have **an uncle** who knows a lot of jokes. It is **an event** when my uncle comes to visit. He lives about **an hour** away from us. He drives in ~~a~~ snow, ~~a~~ fog, or ~~an~~ ice to get here.
Use **the** to talk about something specific.	Uncle Bill takes me to **the** park. We feed **the** ducks there.

The words *this*, *that*, *these*, and *those* point out nouns. Like other adjectives, they answer the question "Which one?"

Use **this** or **these** to talk about things that are near you. Use **that** or **those** to talk about things that are far from you.	We sit on **this** bench. **That** duck must be hungry.

	Near	Far
One thing	this	that
More than one thing	these	those

Possessive Nouns

A possessive noun is the name of an owner. An apostrophe (') is used to show ownership.

For one owner, add **'s** to the **singular noun**.	This is Raul**'s'** cap. The cap**'s** color is a bright red.
For more than one owner, add just the apostrophe (') to the **plural noun**.	The boys**'** T-shirts are the same. The players**'** equipment is ready.
For some plural nouns that have special forms, add **'s** to the **plural noun**.	Do you like the **children's** uniforms? The **men's** scores are the highest.

Pronouns

A pronoun takes the place of a noun or refers to a noun.

Pronoun Agreement

When you use a pronoun, be sure you are talking about the right person.

Use a capital **I** to talk about yourself.

Use **you** to speak to another person.

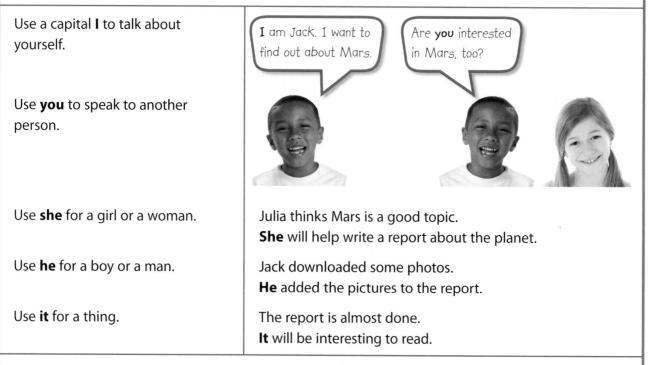

I am Jack. I want to find out about Mars.

Are you interested in Mars, too?

Use **she** for a girl or a woman.

Julia thinks Mars is a good topic.
She will help write a report about the planet.

Use **he** for a boy or a man.

Jack downloaded some photos.
He added the pictures to the report.

Use **it** for a thing.

The report is almost done.
It will be interesting to read.

Be sure you are talking about the right number of people or things.

Use **you** to talk about two or more people.

Use **we** for yourself and another person.

Are you prepared for tomorrow?

Yes. Sam and I are ready. We give a report tomorrow.

Use **they** for other people or things.

Scott and Tyrone set up the video camera.
They will record each presentation.

Subject Pronouns

Subject pronouns take the place of the subject in the sentence.

Subject pronouns tell who or what does the action.	Julia is a good speaker. **She** tells the class about Mars. The photo shows the planet Mars. **It** is an image from NASA.

Object Pronouns

Object pronouns replace a noun that comes after a verb or a preposition.

An **object pronoun** answers the question "What" or "Whom." Object pronouns come after a verb or a preposition such as **to**, **for**, **at**, **of**, or **with**.	The class asked Jack and Julia about Mars. The class asked **them** about Mars. Jack put the report online. Jack put **it** online. Did you look for the report? Did you look for **it**?

Possessive Pronouns

A possessive pronoun tells who or what owns something.

To show that you own something, use **mine.**	**I** wrote a report about the sun. The report about the sun is **mine.**
Use **ours** to show that you and one or more people own something.	**Meg, Bob, and I** drew diagrams. The diagrams are **ours.**
Use **yours** to show that something belongs to one or more people.	Have you seen my report, **Matt**? Yes, that report is **yours.**
Use **his** for one boy or man. Use **hers** for one girl or woman.	Here is **Carole's** desk. The desk is **hers.**
For two or more people, places, or things, use **theirs.**	**Ross and Clare** made posters. The posters are **theirs.**

Adjectives

An adjective describes, or tells about, a noun.

How Adjectives Work

Usually, an **adjective** comes before the noun it tells about.	You can buy **delicious** fruits at the market.
But, an **adjective** can also appear after verbs such as *is, are, look, feel, smell,* and *taste*.	All the fruit looks **fresh**. The shoppers are **happy**.
Adjectives describe • what something is like • the size, color, and shape of something • what something looks, feels, sounds, or smells like	The market is a **busy** place. size Look at all the **big** baskets. color Did you see the **green** peppers? shape I see the **round** apples. The **shiny** peppers are in one basket. Another basket has **crunchy** cucumbers. The pineapples are **sweet** and **juicy**.
Some **adjectives** tell "how many" or "in what order."	The sellers have **two** baskets of green beans. The **first** basket is near the limes. The **second** basket is by the cucumbers.
When you don't know the exact number of things, use the adjectives in the chart.	The women have **a few** onions to sell. When there's **a lot of** sun, the sellers sit in the shade.

If you can count what you see, use:		If you can't count what you see, use:	
many	several	much	not much
a lot of	only a few	a lot of	only a little
few	not any	a little	not any
some	no	some	no

Adjectives That Compare

Adjectives can help you make a comparison, or show how things are alike or different.

To compare two things, add **-er** to the adjective. You will often use the word **than** in your sentence, too.	This is a **small** pineapple. The guava is **smaller than** the pineapple.
To compare three or more things, add **-est** to the adjective. Always use **the** before the adjective.	The lime is **the smallest** fruit of them all.
For some adjectives change the spelling before you add **-er** or **-est**. • If the adjective ends in silent **e**, drop the final **e** and add **-er** or **-est**.	large larger largest nice nicer nicest
• If the adjective ends in **y**, change the **y** to **i** and add **-er** or **-est**.	pretty i crazy i prettier crazier prettiest craziest
• If the adjective ends in one vowel plus one consonant, double the final consonant and add **-er** or **-est**.	big g sad d bigger sadder biggest saddest
A few adjectives have special forms for comparing things.	good bad little better worse less best worst least
For long adjectives, do not use **-er** or **-est** to compare. Use **more**, **most**, **less**, or **least**.	**YES:** Of all the fruit, the guavas are the **most colorful**. **NO:** Of all the fruit, the guavas are the colorfulest. **YES:** The oranges are **more delicious** than the pears. **NO:** The oranges are deliciouser than the pears.
When you make a comparison, use either **-er** or **more**; or **-est** or **most**. Do not use both.	The oranges are the ~~most~~ juiciest of all the fruits.

Verbs

Verbs tell what the subject of a sentence is, has, or does. They show if something happened in the past, is happening now, or will happen in the future.

Action Verbs

An **action verb** tells what someone or something does.	The children **ride** bikes. They **wear** helmets for safety. They **pedal** as fast as they can.	

The Verbs *Have* and *Be*

The verb **to have** tells what the subject of a sentence has.	I **have** a bicycle. It **has** twelve gears. My friend Pedro **has** a bicycle, too. Sometimes we **have** races.	**Forms of the Verb *have*** have has had
The verb **to be** does not show action. It tells what the subject of a sentence is (a noun) or what it is like (an adjective).	I **am** a fan of bicycle races. Pedro **is** excited about our next race.	**Forms of the Verb *be*** am was are were is

Helping Verbs

A **helping verb** works together with an action verb. A **helping** verb comes before a **main verb**. Some helping verbs have special meanings.

- Use **can** to tell that someone is able to do something.
- Use **could**, **may,** or **might** to tell that something is possible.
- Use **must** or **should** to tell that somebody has to do something.

We **can work** as a team.

We **may reach** the finish line first.

We **must pedal** hard to win!

Contractions with Verbs

You can put a subject and verb together to make a **contraction**. In a contraction, an apostrophe (') shows where one or more letters have been left out.

They are riding a
They are
They're riding fast.

You can make a contraction with the verbs **am**, **are**, and **is**.

Contractions with *Be*			
I + am =	**I'm**	she + is =	**she's**
you + are =	**you're**	where + is =	**where's**
we + are =	**we're**	what + is =	**what's**

You can make a contraction with the helping verbs **have**, **has**, and **will**.

Contractions with *Have*			
I + have =	**I've**	he + has =	**he's**
you + have =	**you've**	I + will =	**I'll**
they + have =	**they've**	it + will =	**it'll**

In contractions with a verb and **not**, the word **not** is shortened to **n't**.

Contractions with *Not*			
do + not =	**don't**	have + not =	**haven't**
did + not =	**didn't**	has + not =	**hasn't**
are + not =	**aren't**	could + not =	**couldn't**
was + not =	**wasn't**	should + not =	**shouldn't**

The contraction of the verb **can** plus **not** has a special spelling.

can + not = **can't**

Verbs, *(continued)*

Actions in the Present

All action verbs show when the action happens. Verbs in the **present tense** show • that the action is happening now. • that the action happens all the time.	Pedro **eats** his breakfast. Then he **takes** his bike out of the garage. Pedro and I **love** to ride our bikes on weekends.
To show the present tense for the subjects **he, she,** or **it**, add -**s** to the end of most action verbs. • For verbs that end in **x, ch, sh, ss,** or **z**, add -**es.** • For most verbs that end in **y**, change the **y** to **i** and then add -**es**. For verbs that end in a vowel plus **y**, just add -**s**. • For the subjects **I, you, we,** or **they**, do <u>not</u> add -**s** or -**es**.	**Pedro checks** the tires on his bike. **He finds** a flat tire! Pedro **fixes** the tire. A pump **pushes** air into it. "That should do it," he **says** to himself. He **carries** the pump back into the garage. I **arrive** at Pedro's house. We **coast** down the driveway on our bikes.

Actions in the Past

Verbs in the **past tense** show that the action happened in the past.	Yesterday, I looked for sports on TV.
The past tense form of a **regular verb** ends with -**ed**. • For most verbs, just add -**ed**. • For verbs that end in silent **e**, drop the final **e** before you add -**ed**. • For verbs that end in one vowel plus one consonant, double the final consonant before you add -**ed**. • For verbs that end in **y**, change the **y** to **i** before you add -**ed**. For verbs that end in a vowel plus **y**, just add -**ed**.	I watch**ed** the race on TV. The bikers **arrived** from all different countries. They **raced** for several hours. People **grabbed** their cameras. They **snapped** pictures of their favorite racer. I **studied** the racer from Italy. I **stayed** close to the TV.
Irregular verbs do not add -**ed** to show the past tense. They have special forms.	The Italian racer **was** fast. He **broke** the speed record!

Some Irregular Verbs

Present Tense	Past Tense
begin	began
do	did
have	had
make	made
take	took
ride	rode
win	won

Verbs, *(continued)*

Actions in the Future

Verbs in the **future tense** tell what will happen later, or in the future.	Tomorrow, Shelley **will clean** her bike.
To show the future tense, you can • add the helping verb **will** before the **main verb**. • use **am going to**, **are going to**, or **is going to** before the **main verb**.	She **will remove** all the dirt. She **is going to remove** all the dirt. I **am going to help** her.
If the **main verb** is a form of the verb **to be**, use **be** to form the future tense.	The bike **will be** spotless. Shelley **is going to be** pleased!
To make negative sentences in the future tense, put the word **not** just after **will**, **am**, **is**, or **are**.	We are **not** going to stop until the bike shines. Pedro is **not** going to believe it. Her bike will **not** be a mess any longer.

Adverbs

An adverb tells more about a verb.

How Adverbs Work	
Many **adverbs** tell **how** something happens. These adverbs often with **-ly.**	Josh **eats fast**. Josh **walks quickly** to the train.
Some **adverbs** tell **where** something happens.	He **will travel downtown** on the train.
Some **adverbs** tell **when** or **how often** something happens.	He **will arrive** at school **soon**. (when) Josh **never misses** a day of school. (how often)

Prepositions

A preposition links a noun or pronoun to other words in a sentence. A preposition is the first word in a prepositional phrase.

Prepositions

Some prepositions tell **where** something is.	above / over under / below / beneath beside / next to / by / near in front of in back of / behind between in out inside outside on off
Some prepositions show **direction**.	up down through across around into
Some prepositions tell **when** something happens.	**before** lunch **in** 2003 **on** September 16 **during** lunch **in** September **at** four o'clock **after** lunch **in** the afternoon **from** noon to 3:30
Other prepositions have many uses.	**about** **among** **for** **to** **against** **at** **from** **with** **along** **except** **of** **without**

Prepositional Phrases

A **prepositional phrase** starts with a **preposition** and ends with a **noun** or a **pronoun**. Use prepositional phrases to add information or details to your writing.	**At our school**, we did many activities **for Earth Day**. We picked up the trash **along the fence**. Then we planted some flowers **next to it**.

Capital Letters

A word that begins with a capital letter is special in some way.

How to Use Capital Letters

A word that begins with a capital letter is special in some way.

Use a **capital letter** at the beginning of a sentence.	**O**ur class wants to go to the airplane museum. **W**e will go there next week.
Always use a capital letter for the pronoun **I**.	My friends and **I** can't wait!
Use a capital letter for a person's • first and last name • initials • title	Class Trip List Students Parents **B**illy **R**oss **M**rs. Lane Luisa Díaz Ms. Kelly **J**. **J**. Kelly Dr. Díaz

Use a capital letter for the names of • the days of the week • the twelve months of the year and their abbreviations	We're going the first **S**aturday in **J**anuary.

Days of the Week

		Months of the Year	
Sunday	**S**un.	**J**anuary	**J**an.
Monday	**M**on.	**F**ebruary	**F**eb.
Tuesday	**T**ue.	**M**arch	**M**ar.
Wednesday	**W**ed.	**A**pril	**A**pr.
Thursday	**T**hurs.	**M**ay	
Friday	**F**ri.	**J**une	These months are not abbreviated.
Saturday	**S**at.	**J**uly	
		August	**A**ug.
		September	**S**ep.
		October	**O**ct.
		November	**N**ov.
		December	**D**ec.

Use a capital letter for each important word in the names of special days and holidays.	That will be after **C**hristmas, **K**wanzaa, and **N**ew **Y**ear's **D**ay. **E**arth **D**ay **F**ourth of **J**uly **H**anukkah **T**hanksgiving

Capital Letters, (continued)

More Ways to Use Capital Letters

Use a capital letter for each important word in the names of	
• public places, buildings, and organizations	The **W**ilson **A**irplane **M**useum is in the **V**eterans **M**emorial **H**all. It's in the middle of **V**eterans **P**ark.
• streets, cities, and states	The museum is on **F**light **A**venue. It is the biggest airplane museum in **F**lorida. It's the biggest in the whole **U**nited **S**tates!
• landforms and bodies of water, continents, and planets and stars	**Landforms and Bodies of Water**: **R**ocky **M**ountains, **S**ahara **D**esert, **G**rand **C**anyon, **P**acific **O**cean, **C**olorado **R**iver, **L**ake **E**rie **Continents**: **A**frica, **A**ntarctica, **A**sia, **E**urope, **S**outh **A**merica **Planets and Stars**: **E**arth, **M**ars, the **B**ig **D**ipper, the **M**ilky **W**ay
Use a capital letter for the names of countries and adjectives formed from the names of countries.	My friend Magdalena is **C**hilean. She says they don't have a museum like that in **C**hile.
Use a capital letter for each important word in the title of a book, a story, a poem, or a movie.	We are reading *First Flight* about the Wright brothers. Magdalena wrote a poem about Amelia Earhart. She called it "**V**anished from the **S**ky." What a great title!

Punctuation Marks

Punctuation marks make words and sentences easier to understand.

period

question mark

exclamation point

comma

quotation marks

apostrophe

Period .

Use a **period** at the end of a statement or a command.	I don't know if I should get a dog or a cat. Please help me decide. I saw a cute little dog last week.
Also use a **period** when you write numbers.	It only weighed 1.3 pounds. But it costs $349.99!
Use a **period** after an initial in somebody's name, and after most abbreviations. But, don't use a period after state abbreviations.	The salesperson gave me this business card: 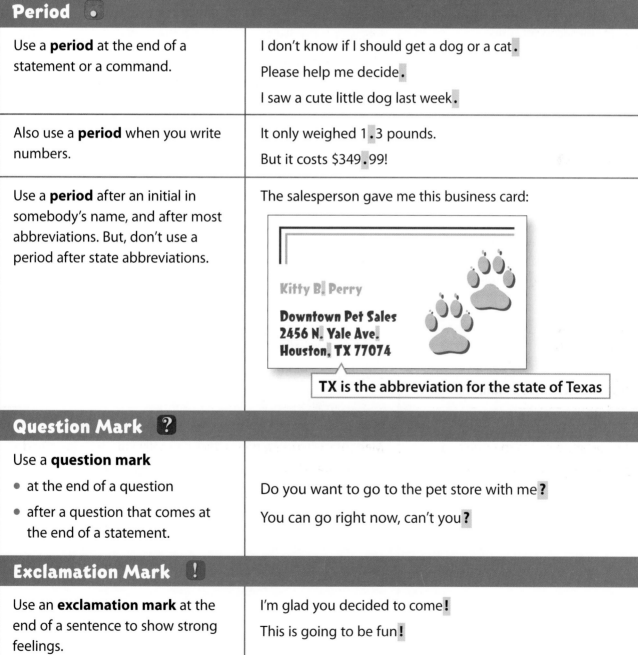 Kitty B. Perry **Downtown Pet Sales** **2456 N. Yale Ave.** **Houston, TX 77074** **TX is the abbreviation for the state of Texas**

Question Mark ?

Use a **question mark** • at the end of a question • after a question that comes at the end of a statement.	Do you want to go to the pet store with me? You can go right now, can't you?

Exclamation Mark !

Use an **exclamation mark** at the end of a sentence to show strong feelings.	I'm glad you decided to come! This is going to be fun!

591

Punctuation *(continued)*

Commas ,

Use a **comma**	
• when you write large numbers	There are more than 1,300 pets at this store.
• to separate three or more things in the same sentence	Should I get a dog, a cat, or a parrot?
• before the words **and**, **but**, or **or** in a compound sentence.	I came to the store last week, and the salesperson showed me some dogs. She was very helpful, but I couldn't make a decision.
Use a **comma** to set off	
• short words like **Oh**, **Yes**, and **Well** that begin a sentence	Oh, what a hard decision! Well, I better choose something.
• someone's exact words	The salesperson said, "This little dog wants to go with you." I said, "I like it, but I like those cats, too!"
Use a **comma** between two or more adjectives that tell about the same noun.	Do I get a big, furry puppy? Or, do I get a cute, tiny kitten?
Use a **comma** in letters • between the city and state • between the date and the year • after the greeting in a friendly letter • after the closing	177 North Avenue New York, NY 10033 October 3, 2010 Dear Aunt Mia, Can you help me? I want a pet, but don't know which is easier to care for, a cat or a dog? I need your advice. Your niece, Becca

Quotation Marks

Use quotation marks	
• to show a speaker's exact words	"Ms. Perry, this is the dog for me!" Becca said.
• to show the exact words from a book or other printed material	The ad said "friendly puppies" for sale.
• the title of a magazine or newspaper article	I saw the idea in the article "Keeping Your Pet Happy."
• the title of a chapter from a book	Now I'm on the chapter "Working Dogs" in my book.
Use periods and commas inside quotation marks.	"Many dogs are good with people," Ms. Perry said. "You just have to decide if you want to big dog or a little one."

> Ms. Perry, this is the dog for me!

Apostrophes

Use an **apostrophe** when you write a **possessive noun**.	My **neighbor's** dog is huge. The **Smith s'** yard is just big enough for him.
Use an **apostrophe** to replace the letter left out in a **contraction.**	**Let's** go back to the pet store. **I'll** look some more for the best pet for me.

Picture Dictionary

The definitions are for the words as they are introduced in the selections of this book.

Pronunciation Key

Say the sample word out loud to hear how to say, or pronounce, the symbol.

Symbols for Consonant Sounds

b	box		p	pan
ch	chick		r	ring
d	dog		s	bus
f	fish		sh	fish
g	girl		t	hat
h	hat		th	Earth
j	jar		th	father
k	cake		v	vase
ks	box		w	window
kw	queen		wh	whale
l	bell		y	yarn
m	mouse		z	zipper
n	pan		zh	treasure
ng	ring			

Symbols for Short Vowel Sounds

a	hat
e	bell
i	chick
o	box
u	bus

Symbols for Long Vowel Sounds

ā	cake
ē	key
ī	bike
ō	goat
yū	mule

Symbols for R-controlled Sounds

ar	barn
air	chair
ear	ear
īr	fire
or	corn
ur	girl

Symbols for Variant Vowel Sounds

ah	father
aw	ball
oi	boy
oo	book
ü	fruit

Miscellaneous Symbols

shun	fraction	$\frac{1}{2}$
chun	question	?
zhun	division	$2\overline{)100}^{50}$

Parts of an Entry

The **entry** shows how the word is spelled.

The **pronunciation** shows you how to say the word and how to break it into syllables.

The **picture** helps you understand more about the meaning of the word.

variety

(vu-**rī**-u-tē) *noun*

A mix of the same kind of thing is called a **variety**.

*I have a **variety** of crayons. They are many colors.*

part of speech

The **definition** gives the meaning of the word.

The **sample sentence** uses the word in a way that shows its meaning.

ability
(u-**bi**-lu-tē) *noun*
When you are able to do something, you have an **ability**.

*She has great **ability** in art.*

absorb
(ub-**zorb**) *verb*
To **absorb** is to take in or soak up.

*The mop **absorbs** the water.*

accept
(ik-**sept**) *verb*
When you **accept** something, you take a thing that is offered to you.

*Her mother **accepts** the flowers and a hug.*

adaptation
(a-dap-**tā**-shun) *noun*
An **adaptation** is a feature of an animal that helps it live.

*A turtle's hard shell is an **adaptation** that keeps it safe.*

add
(ad) *verb*
To **add** means to put things together.

*When you **add** things to a group, you make the group bigger.*

affect
(u-**fekt**) *verb*
When you **affect** something, you change it.

*The hot sun **affects** the ice cream. It makes the ice cream melt.*

aid
(ād) *verb*
To **aid** is to help someone.

*The police officer **aids** the girl. She helps the girl find her way home.*

alike
(u-**līk**) *adjective*
Things that are **alike** look the same.

*These dogs look **alike**.*

alone
(u-**lōn**) *adverb*
Alone means to be without anyone else.

*She likes to be **alone**.*

American

(u-**mer**-u-cun) *adjective*

American means having to do with the United States.

*This is the **American** flag.*

animal

(a-**nu**-mul) *noun*

An **animal** is any living creature that can breathe and move around.

*A horse is an **animal** you can ride.*

appear

(u-**pēr**) *verb*

When something **appears**, it comes into sight.

*The whale **appears** above the water.*

area

(**air**-ē-u) *noun*

An **area** is a part of a place.

*Water covers a large **area** of Earth.*

attack

(u-**tak**) *verb*

When animals **attack** something, it means they try to hurt it.

*Some animals **attack** other animals to say, "Go away!"*

attract

(u-**trakt**) *verb*

To **attract** something means to get it to come close.

*The light from a bulb will **attract** a moth to it.*

autumn

(**ah**-tum) *noun*

Autumn is the season between summer and winter. It is also called fall.

__Autumn__ is when the leaves on trees turn color and fall to the ground.

become

(bē-**kum**) *verb*

To **become** means to turn into or grow to be something.

*A caterpillar **becomes** a butterfly.*

begin
(bi-**gin**) *verb*
To **begin** means to start.

When the sun rises, the day ***begins***.

belief
(bu-**lēf**) *noun*
A **belief** is a strong feeling that something is true.

*Her **belief** that people should share helped her to give half of her lunch to her friend.*

belong
(bē-**long**) *verb*
To **belong** is to be part of a group.

*These girls **belong** to a softball team.*

body of water
(**bah**-dē uv **wah**-tur) *noun*
A **body of water** is a large amount of water, such as an ocean, lake, or river.

ocean

lake

river

*The Pacific Ocean is the largest **body of water** on Earth.*

build
(**bild**) *verb*
When you **build** something, you make or create it.

*He uses wood and tools to **build** a birdhouse.*

building
(**bil**-dēng) *noun*
A **building** is a house, or a school, or anything that has a roof and walls.

*This tall **building** is called a skyscaper.*

C

care
(**kair**) *verb*
To **care** is to feel love for a person or thing.

*People in families **care** for each other.*

a
b
c
d
e
f
g
h
i
j
k
l
m
n
o
p
q
r
s
t
u
v
w
x
y
z

carry
(**kair**-ē) *verb*
To **carry** something is to hold onto it and take it somewhere.

*The friends **carry** their boat to the water.*

celebrate
(se-lu-**brāt**) *verb*
We **celebrate** events like birthdays and holidays to show how special they are to us.

*Many people **celebrate** the Fourth of July by watching fireworks.*

chain
(chān) *noun*
A **chain** is a series of things that are connected.

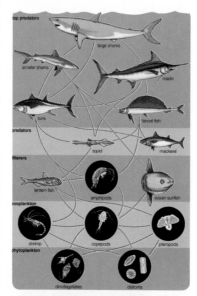

*Food **chains** show how animals and plants are connected.*

chance
(chans) *noun*
When something has a **chance**, it is possible.

*She takes care of the plant so it has a **chance** to grow.*

change
(chānj) *verb*
When you **change** something, you make it different.

*He **changes** the color of the wall from white to red.*

character
(**kair**-ik-tur) *noun*
Character is the special way someone feels, thinks, and acts.

*She helps her brother. This shows good **character**.*

choice
(chois) *noun*
When you have a **choice**, it means you have to pick between two or more things.

*He will make a **choice** between the apple and the hotdog.*

citizenship
(**si**-tu-zen-ship) *noun*
Citizenship is belonging to a country. Citizenship also gives you the rights and duties of that country.

*Her **citizenship** makes her proud and happy.*

clean
(**klēn**) *adjective*
If something is **clean**, it is not dirty.

*The dog is **clean** after her bath.*

cloud
(**klowd**) *noun*
A **cloud** is a mass of tiny drops of water floating in the air.

*The **clouds** look light and fluffy.*

color
(**ku**-lur) *noun*
Color is the way things look due to the way light reflects off them.

*You can make the **color** green. Mix together yellow and blue.*

community
(ku-**myū**-nu-tē) *noun*
A **community** is a place where people live, work, and play.

*These people live in a small **community**.*

connect
(ku-**nekt**) *verb*
To **connect** things means to link or join them together.

*He **connects** the wires to make the computer work.*

cook
(**kook**) *noun*
A **cook** is someone who prepares food for people to eat.

*The **cook** chops the peppers.*

a b c d e f g h i j k l m n o p q r s t u v w x y z

a
b
c
d
e
f
g
h
i
j
k
l
m
n
o
p
q
r
s
t
u
v
w
x
y
z

cooperate

(kō-**ah**-pu-rāt) *verb*

When you **cooperate**, it means you work with or help others.

*Two girls **cooperate** with each other to plant trees.*

cost

(**cawst**) *noun*

The **cost** of something is how much you have to pay to own it.

*The **cost** of the shirt is twenty dollars.*

courage

(**kur**-ij) *noun*

When you have **courage**, you do something even though you are scared.

*She jumps into the pool. She has **courage**!*

culture

(**kul**-chur) *noun*

Culture is the way of life, art, ideas, and customs of a group of people.

*He likes traveling and meeting people from different **cultures**.*

D

danger

(**dān**-jur) *noun*

Something is a **danger** when it can hurt you.

*If you walk too close to the edge, you are in **danger** of falling.*

day

(**dā**) *noun*

The time between sunrise and sunset is **day**.

*The sun can be seen in the sky during the **day**.*

decide

(di-**sīd**) *verb*

When you **decide**, you make a choice about something.

*She and her mom **decide** what to get at the store.*

defend

(di-**fend**) *verb*

To **defend** something means to keep it from being hurt.

*The mother **defends** her baby so that it stays safe.*

difference
(**di**-fur-uns) *noun*
The **difference** is the way that one thing is not the same as the other thing.

*One apple is red. That is the **difference**.*

difficult
(**di**-fi-kult) *adjective*
When something is **difficult**, it is hard to do.

*It can be **difficult** to learn some new things.*

doctor
(**doc**-tur) *noun*
A **doctor** is someone who treats people who are sick or injured.

*The **doctor** will check the boy's heart.*

draw
(**drah**) *verb*
To **draw** means to pull up or pull out.

*The girls **draw** up juice through their straws.*

dream
(**drēm**) *noun*
A **dream** is something you hope to do or succeed at in the future.

*His **dream** is to win a medal at the track meet.*

E

Earth
(**urth**) *noun*
Earth is the planet we live on.

*What does **Earth** look like from space?*

education
(e-ju-**kā**-shun) *noun*
To get an **education** means to learn things you didn't know before.

*You go to school to get an **education**.*

end
(**end**) *verb*
The **end** is the last part of something.

*We turned off the TV at the **end** of the program.*

enemy
(e-ne-**mē**) *noun*
An **enemy** is someone who hates you and wants to harm you.

*The opposite of an **enemy** is a friend.*

a b c **d e** f g h i j k l m n o p q r s t u v w x y z

601

enough

(ē-**nuf**) *adjective*

To say you have **enough** means you have all that you need.

*There is just **enough** milk to fill the glass.*

example

(ig-**zam**-pul) *noun*

To set an **example** is to do something good that other people might do too.

*They set an **example** by cleaning up the park.*

expect

(ik-**spekt**) *verb*

When you **expect** something, you think it is likely to happen.

*I **expect** it will rain today.*

explain

(ik-**splān**) *verb*

To **explain** is to talk about an idea so that someone else can understand it.

*She **explains** the math problem to her student.*

F

fall

(**fawl**) *noun*

Fall is another word for autumn. It is the season between summer and winter.

*In the **fall** children like to play in piles of leaves.*

features

(**fē**-churs) *noun*

Features are the important or interesting parts of something.

*The giraffe's long neck is a **feature** that helps it eat leaves on trees.*

food

(**füd**) *noun*

Food is something that people, animals and plants eat to stay alive and grow.

*Fruit and vegetables are healthy **foods** to eat.*

freedom
(**frē**-dum) *noun*
Freedom means you can do the things you want to do.

*We have the **freedom** to say what we want.*

G

generous
(**je**-nu-rus) *adjective*
Someone who is **generous** is willing to share what they have.

*She is **generous** and shares with her friends.*

grateful
(**grāt**-ful) *adjective*
When you are **grateful,** you are thankful.

*She is **grateful** for the gift.*

H

habitat
(**ha**-bu-tat) *noun*
A **habitat** is a place where an animal or plant can live and do well.

*The **desert** is a very dry habitat.*

happen
(**ha**-pun) *verb*
*When something **happens,** it takes place.*

*They watch what **happens** in the game.*

healthy
(**hel**-thē) *adjective*
Someone who is **healthy** is not sick.

*Eating fruit helps you stay **healthy**.*

hero
(**hear**-ō) *noun*
A **hero** is a brave person who many other people admire.

*The firefighter who saved the child is a **hero**.*

a b c d e f g h i j k l m n o p q r s t u v w x y z

a
b
c
d
e
f
g
h
i
j
k
l
m
n
o
p
q
r
s
t
u
v
w
x
y
z

hide
(**hīd**) *verb*
To **hide** is to put something where no one will find it.

*She **hides** the gift so her dad cannot see it.*

history
(**his**-tu-rē) *noun*
History is the study of people and events from the past.

*George Washington was the first president in U.S. **history**.*

holiday
(**hah**-lu-dā) *noun*
A **holiday** is a special day when many people do not work.

*In America, the Fourth of July is a **holiday**.*

home
(**hōm**) *noun*
Your **home** is the place you live.

house

houseboat

Homes can come in different shapes and sizes. Your home might be a house, or an apartment, or even a houseboat on the water!

hospital
(hos-**pi**-tul) *noun*
A **hospital** is a building in which doctors and nurses help people who are sick or injured.

*This is the **hospital's** emergency entrance.*

idea
(ī-**dē**-u) *noun*
An **idea** is something you think, believe, or imagine.

*She had good **idea** for reaching the book.*

identify
(ī-**den**-ti-fī) *verb*
To **identify** something is to recognize what or who it is.

*Mom helps Ana **identify** places on a map.*

immigrant
(**im**-u-grunt) *noun*
An **immigrant** is someone who comes to a foreign country to live.

*These **immigrants** came to the United States in the early 1900s.*

important
(im-**por**-tunt) *adjective*
If something is **important**, you care about it a lot.

*Firefighters have an **important** job.*

insect
(**in**-sekt) *noun*
An **insect** is a small creature with six legs and three main sections of its body.

bee

beetle

butterfly

grasshopper

praying mantis

*Some **insects** also have wings.*

invention
(in-**ven**-shun) *noun*
An **invention** is something new or a new way of doing something.

*The cell phone is a new **invention**.*

J

job
(job) *noun*
A **job** is the work someone does to earn money.

*His **job** is to walk the dog.*

join
(join) *verb*
To **join** means to become a member of a group.

*He was happy to **join** a Little League team.*

L

lake
(lāk) *noun*
A **lake** is a large body of water with land all around it.

*We fish for trout in the **lake**.*

a
b
c
d
e
f
g
h
i
j
k
l
m
n
o
p
q
r
s
t
u
v
w
x
y
z

landform
(**land**-form) *noun*
A **landform** is the way that the surface of the land is shaped.

*This **landform** is called a valley.*

language
(**lāng**-gwij) *noun*
A **language** is a system of words and grammar used by people to talk and write to each other.

*These people are using sign **language**.*

leader
(**lē**-dur) *noun*
Being a **leader** means that you lead or guide others.

*The President of the United States is the **leader** of the country.*

library
(**lī**-brair-ē) *noun*
A **library** is a room or a building that has books, DVDs, magazines, and newspapers to read or to borrow.

*People check out books at the **library**.*

*People also use the computers at the **library** to get information.*

locate
(**lō**-kāt) *verb*
When you **locate** something, you find it.

*The girl **locates** the books she is looking for.*

machine
(mu-**shēn**) *noun*
A **machine** is something with moving parts that usually uses power to do a job.

*A bicycle is a kind of **machine**.*

*My bicycle is a **machine** I can ride!*

mean
(**mēn**) *adjective*
A **mean** person is not kind or nice.

*It is **mean** to leave someone out.*

measure

(**me**-zhur) *verb*

To **measure** is to figure out the size or amount of something.

*He **measures** the doorway to see how big it is.*

message

(**me**-sij) *noun*

A **message** is information you give by speaking or writing.

*You can send a **message** for a friend to read.*

monument

(**mon**-yū-munt) *noun*

A **monument** is something that is built so that people remember something important.

*This is a **monument** to war heroes.*

moon

(**mūn**) *noun*

A **moon** is a natural satellite that travels around, or orbits, a planet.

*You can see our **moon** from Earth.*

motion

(**mō**-shun) *noun*

If something is in **motion**, it is moving.

*The man is in **motion**.*

necessary

(**ne**-su-sair-ē) *adjective*

When something is **necessary**, it is absolutely needed.

*A seatbelt is **necessary** to stay safe in a car.*

neighbor

(**nā**-bur) *noun*

A **neighbor** is someone who lives near you.

*Say "hello" to a **neighbor** who lives next door.*

night

(**nīt**) *noun*

Night is the time between sunset and sunrise.

*It is dark outside at **night**.*

nurse

(**nurs**) *noun*

A **nurse** is someone whose job is to take care of people who are sick or injured.

*The **nurse** takes the girl's temperature.*

a b c d e f g h i j k l **m** **n** o p q r s t u v w x y z

observe

(ub-**zurv**) *verb*

When you **observe** something, you watch it.

*She **observes** the insect.*

ocean

(**ō**-shun) *noun*

The **ocean** is the salt water that covers most of Earth's surface.

*There are big waves in the **ocean** today.*

*Earth's **ocean**s can be seen from outer space.*

opportunity

(ah-pur-**tü**-ni-tē) *noun*

An **opportunity** is a chance to do something.

*She has an **opportunity** to kick the ball.*

organize

(**or**-gu-nīz) *verb*

To **organize** means to put things neatly in order.

*She **organized** the robots on her shelf.*

others

(**u**-thurz) *noun*

Others are people apart from you.

*Casey stands away from the **others**.*

park

(**park**) *noun*

A **park** is a place with grass and trees, where people go to walk, bike, and play.

*We take a long walk in the **park** every weekend.*

*Picnics in the **park** are nice when the weather is sunny.*

partner

(**part**-nur) *noun*

A **partner** is someone you do something with, such as dancing.

*These people were famous dance **partners** in the movies.*

a b c d e f g h i j k l m n o p q r s t u v w x y z

pattern
(**pa**-turn) *noun*
When things are done in a **pattern**, they are done again and again in the same order or way.

*Orange, grey, and blue tiles make a **pattern** on this floor.*

pipe
(**pīp**) *noun*
Pipes are tubes used for carrying water or gas.

Pipes carry water to the crops.

place
(**plās**) *noun*
A **place** is a space where something is.

This cabin is in a quiet place by a lake.

plan
(**plan**) *noun*
A **plan** is a set of organized ideas that help you reach a goal.

> Plan to Cleam My Room
> 1. Make bed.
> 2. Fold clothes.
> 3. Put away clothes.
> 4. Clean desk..

This is a plan to clean my room.

population
(pah-pyu-**lā**-shun) *noun*
The **population** of a place is the number of people who live there.

Crowded cities have a very large population of people.

possible
(**pah**-su-bul) *adjective*
If something is **possible**, it means it could happen.

*Airplanes make it **possible** for people to fly.*

predator
(**pre**-du-tur) *noun*
A **predator** is an animal that hunts other animals for food.

Lions, sharks, and eagles are predators.

prey
(**prā**) *noun*
An animal is **prey** if another animal hunts it for food.

hunter

prey

*The cat hunts the mouse, its **prey**.*

a b c d e f g h i j k l m n o **p** q r s t u v w x y z

a b c d e f g h i j k l m n o **p** **q** **r** s t u v w x y z

project

(prah-jekt) *noun*

A **project** is work that you plan carefully.

*His school science **project** took a long time to finish.*

provide

(pru-vīd) *verb*

To **provide** means to give what is needed.

*A water fountain **provides** water to drink.*

pump

(**pump**) *noun*

A **pump** is a machine that makes liquids or gases go into or out of something.

*The **pump** moves water from the well.*

Ⓡ

rain

(rān) *noun*

Rain is drops of water that fall from clouds in the sky.

*The umbrella protects her from the **rain**.*

reason

(rē-zun) *noun*

A **reason** is why something is a certain way.

*Hard work and practice are the **reasons** she is a good dancer.*

recognize

(**re**-kig-nīz) *verb*

To **recognize** means to know who someone is or what something is.

*It's easy to **recognize** people that you know.*

---

relate

(rē-lāt) *verb*

When things **relate** to each other, there is a connection between them.

*All the questions **relate** to what our teacher said in class.*

remember

(ri-**mem**-bur) *verb*

To **remember** something means to think of it again or have a memory of it.

***Remember** to call and say, "Happy birthday!"*

repeat

(ri-**pēt**) *verb*

To **repeat** means to do or say the same thing again.

*She has to **repeat** what she said because her friend did not hear her.*

require

(ri-**kwīr**) *verb*

To **require** something means to need it.

*This ride **requires** two people.*

respect

(ri-**spekt**) *noun*

When you show **respect**, you are polite. You treat others the way you want to be treated.

*There are many different ways to show **respect**.*

respond

(ri-**spond**) *verb*

To **respond** is to answer someone by speaking or writing.

*He **responds** to the letter from his friend.*

responsible

(ri-**spon**-su-bul) *adjective*

A **responsible** person makes good decisions and can be trusted to do the right thing.

*These **responsible** children helped their mother without being asked.*

result

(rē-**zult**) *noun*

The **result** is what happens after a series of actions.

*If you trip and drop a cup, the **result** is broken pieces.*

right

(**rīt**) *adjective*

When you do good deeds, you do the **right** thing.

*It is not wrong to help others. It is **right**.*

rise

(**rīz**) *verb*

To **rise** means to go up.

*The buildings **rise** high up into the sky.*

a
b
c
d
e
f
g
h
i
j
k
l
m
n
o
p
q
r
s
t
u
v
w
x
y
z

role

(rōl) *noun*

Something's **role** is its job or its purpose.

*The guide dog's **role** is to help lead the blind man.*

safe

(sāf) *adjective*

When you are **safe**, you will not be hurt.

*He wears a helmet to keep his head **safe** in case he falls.*

save

(sāv) *verb*

When you **save** something, you keep it from being hurt or broken.

*He **saves** the boy from falling.*

S

school

(skool) *noun*

School is the place people go to learn.

*We learn to read and write in **school**.*

season

(sē-zun) *noun*

A **season** is one of the four parts of the year. The seasons are spring, summer, autumn or fall, and winter.

spring

summer

fall

winter

*Which one is your favorite **season**?*

seek

(sēk) *verb*

When you **seek** something, you are trying to find it.

*The girl **seeks** the piñata with a stick.*

seem
(sēm) *verb*
To **seem** means to look or act like.

*The game **seems** hard, but it is really easy to play.*

serve
(surv) *verb*
When you **serve** others, you help them.

*They **serve** their neighborhood. They plant a community garden.*

shadow
(shɑ-dō) *noun*
A **shadow** is a dark area that is made when something blocks the light.

*You can see the **shadow** of the palm tree on the wall.*

shape
(shāp) *noun*
A **shape** is the outline or form of something.

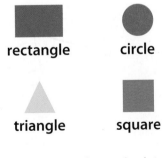

rectangle   circle

triangle   square

*The **shape** of our clock is a circle.*

share
(shair) *verb*
When you **share** you give someone part of something you have.

*The boy and girl **share** the ice cream.*

shelter
(shel-tur) *noun*
A **shelter** is a covered place where you are safe from the weather.

*A tent provides **shelter** in case it rains.*

size
(sīz) *noun*
Size is a measurement of how big or small something is.

*The popcorn comes in these two **sizes**.*

a
b
c
d
e
f
g
h
i
j
k
l
m
n
o
p
q
r
s
t
u
v
w
x
y
z

a b c d e f g h i j k l m n o p q r **s** t u v w x y z

skill
(skǐl) *noun*
A **skill** is the ability to something well.

*Rock climbing takes a lot of **skill**.*

sky
(skī) *noun*
The **sky** is the space above Earth. It's where you find the sun, clouds, and stars.

*The **sky** looks cloudy but bright.*

society
(su-sī-u-tē) *noun*
A **society** is a group of people who live in the same area or country. It can also be a group of people with the same interests and hobbies.

*In our **society** we salute the U.S. flag.*

*This chess **society** meets on Wednesdays.*

source
(sors) *noun*
A **source** is where something comes from.

*The sun is a **source** of heat and light.*

species
(spē-shēz) *noun*
A **species** is a group of animals or plants that have similar characteristics.

lion

house cat

cougar

*There are many different **species** of cats.*

spring
(sprēng) *noun*
Spring is one of the four seasons of the year. It comes between winter and summer.

blossoms

***Spring** is a time of regrowth.*

stars

(stɑrz) *noun*

Stars are very large balls of gas. From Earth, **stars** look like points of light in the night sky.

*The **stars** shine brightly at night.*

state

(stāt) *noun*

A **state** is a part of the United States of America. There are 50 states in all.

*Oregon is a **state** in the western part of the United States.*

success

(suk-**ses**) *noun*

Success is when you set out to do something and you get it done.

*They win the game. It is a big **success**!*

summer

(**su**-mur) *noun*

Summer is one of the four seasons of the year.

***Summer** comes after spring and before autumn.*

support

(su-**port**) *verb*

To **support** means to help.

*Friends **support** each other by listening.*

survive

(sur-**vīv**) *verb*

To **survive** means to live.

*Penguins **survive** cold weather by standing together to stay warm.*

symbol

(**sim**-bul) *noun*

A **symbol** is something that represents something else.

*Each birthday candle is a **symbol** for one year of your life.*

T

teacher

(**tē**-chur) *noun*

A **teacher** is someone whose job is to show others how to do something.

*My **teacher** writes math problems on the board.*

team member

(**tēm**-**mem**-bur) *noun*

Team members are the people who work together to get something done.

*These **team members** work together to win the game.*

a b c d e f g h i j k l m n o p q r **s t** u v w x y z

a b c d e f g h i j k l m n o p q r s **t u v** w x y z

teamwork
(**tēm**-wurk) *noun*
When people work well together, they are using **teamwork.**

*It takes **teamwork** to build a house.*

thoughtful
(**thawt**-ful) *adjective*
Someone who is **thoughtful**, thinks about others.

*He wrote a **thoughtful** note to his grandfather.*

threaten
(**thre**-tun) *verb*
If something or someone **threatens** you, it means you are afraid or in danger.

*The angry dog **threatens** by barking.*

together
(tu-**ge**-thur) *adverb*
People are **together** when they are with one another.

*This family likes to spend time **together**.*

tradition
(tre-**di**-shun) *noun*
A **tradition** is a custom or belief that is shared by a group of people.

*Dancing is part of their **tradition**.*

U

united
(yū-**nī**-tud) *adjective*
When a group is **united**, the people agree and work together.

*When we play soccer, we are **united** as a team.*

unusual
(un-**yū**-zhū-wul) *adjective*
Something **unusual** is odd or uncommon.

*This tiny animal is very **unusual**.*

useful
(**yūs**-ful) *adjective*
When something is **useful**, it helps you.

*Tools are **useful** for fixing broken things.*

V

variety
(vu-**rī**-u-tē) *noun*
A mix of the same kind of thing is called a **variety**.

*I have a **variety** of crayons. They are many colors.*

vegetation

(ve-ju-**tā**-shun) *noun*

Vegetation is all the plants of an area.

Can you name the different kinds of vegetation?

Ⓦ

water

(**wah**-tur) *noun*

Water is the clear liquid that falls from the sky as rain.

All living things need water to survive.

weather

(**we**-<u>th</u>ur) *noun*

Weather is the current condition of the air. Weather is how cold or hot it is or if it is raining, snowing, or sunny.

snow

The weather is cold today.

well

(**wel**) *noun*

A **well** is a deep hole in the ground from which you get water or oil.

How many gallons of oil did this well produce?

wildlife

(**wīld**-līf) *noun*

Animals that live in their natural environment are **wildlife**.

deer in forest

zebra in grasslands

Different wildlife live in different parts of the world.

winter

(**win**-tur) *noun*

Winter is one of the four seasons of the year. Winter comes after autumn and before the spring.

There are many fun things we can do in winter.

a
b
c
d
e
f
g
h
i
j
k
l
m
n
o
p
q
r
s
t
u
v
w
x
y
z

Index

W

Writing

answers **158**, **258**, **458**, **494**

paragraphs 60–63, 128–131, 133, 194–197, 199, 326–329, 398–401, 466–469, 471, 538–541, 543

questions **158**, **258**, **325**, **458**

sentences

complete **31**, **52**, **99**, **120**, **126**, **158**, **165**, **186**, **193**, **229**, **257**, **288**, **297**, **356**, **367**, **388**, **397**, **437**, **465**, **494**, **503**, **537**

simple **59**

Writing forms

article **128**

blog entry **443**

booklet 403, 471

caption 59, 90, 502

cartoon 331

chant 263

comic strip 405

commercial 65

comparison **326**

description 52

e-mail 541

essay **171**

explanation 222

fable 222

folk tale **194**

guide book 3

human-interest feature 248, 388

interview 65, 199, **258**

journal **9**, **73**, **207**

letter 199, **248**, **428**

list 24

map 65

nature log 331

newsletter 261

opinion essay **235**

oral report **105**

personal narrative **538**

photo-essay 52, **60**

play 366

poetry **318**, **526**

poster 403

proverb 263

realistic fiction 24, 90, 288, **398**, 494

recipe 543

report **466**, **471**, 543

riddle 133

science article 120, 458

scientific log 133

skit **471**, 543

song 65, 263, 471, 543

story **271**, **398**

study card 35

traditional tale 158

TV show 133

see also Researching

Writing process

drafting 61, 129, 195, 259, 327, 399, 467, 539, 562

editing 63, 131, 197, 261, 329, 401, 469, 541

capitalization 564

grammar 564

punctuation 564

revising 62, 130, 196, 260, 328, 400, 468, 540, 563

prewrite

planning 61, 129, 195, 259, 327, 399, 467, 539, 556

organizing 61, 129, 195, 259, 327, 399, 467, 539, 561

publishing 63, 131, 197, 261, 329, 401, 469, 541

add visuals 565

present writing 565

Writing traits

coherence 566

development of ideas 568

focus 566

organization 567

voice 569

written conventions 569

Acknowledgments, continued

Text Credits

Unit One

Children's Book Press: Excerpt from *Quinto's Neighborhood* by Ina Cumpiano, illustrated by Jose Ramirez. Text copyright © 2005 Children's Book Press. Illustrations © 2009 by Jose Ramirez. Reprinted by permission of the publisher, Children's Book Press, San Francisco, Calif., www.childrensbookpress.org.

Charlesbridge Publishing, Inc.: Adaptation of *Be My Neighbor* by Maya Ajmera and John D. Ivanko. Copyright © 2004 by Maya Ajmera and John D. Ivanko. Used with permission of Charlesbridge Publishing, Inc. All rights reserved.

Unit Two

Star Bright Books, Inc.: Excerpt from *Twilight Hunt* by Narelle Oliver. Copyright © 2002 by Narelle Oliver. Reprinted by permission of the publisher, Star Bright Books, Inc.

Weekly Reader: Adaptation of "Hide and Seek: animals and their habitats" from *Weekly Reader*, April 11, 2005. Copyright © 2005 by Weekly Reader. Special permission granted by Weekly Reader. All rights reserved.

Houghton Mifflin Harcourt: "The Firefly," from *Beast Feast* by Douglas Florian. Copyright © 1994 by Douglas Florian. Reprinted by permission of Houghton Mifflin Harcourt Publishing Company.

All rights reserved.

"The Diamond Rattlesnake," from *Lizards, Frogs, and Polliwogs: Poems and Paintings* by Douglas Florian. Copyright © 2001 by Douglas Florian. Reprinted by permission of Houghton Mifflin Harcourt Publishing Company. All rights reserved.

"The Io Moth," from *Insectlopedia* by Douglas Florian. Copyright © 1998 by Douglas Florian. Reprinted by permission of Houghton Mifflin Harcourt Publishing Company. All rights reserved.

Unit Four

Cable News Network: Excerpt from "Disabled Iraqi children get wheelchairs, big smiles" by Carol Jordan and Arwa Damon from CNN.com, February 13, 2008. Copyright © 2008 by Cable News Network, Inc. Reprinted courtesy of CNN.

Unit Five

HarperCollins Publishers: Excerpt from *When the Wind Stops* by Charlotte Zolotow, illustrated by Stefano Vitale. Text copyright © 1962, 1995 by Charlotte Zolotow, illustrations © by Stefano Vitale. Reprinted by permission of HarperCollins Publishers.

Penguin Group (USA) Inc.: Excerpt from *What Makes the Seasons?* by Megan Montague Cash. Copyright © 2003 by Megan Montague Cash. Reprinted by permission of Penguin Group (USA) Inc.

Unit Six

John Forster and Tom Chapin: Excerpt from the lyrics of "Stone Soup" by John Forster and Tom Chapin. Copyright © 1990 by Limousine Music Company and The Last Music Co. (ASCAP). Reprinted by permission of the authors.

Scholastic Library Publishing and George Ancona: Excerpt from *Mi barrio=My neighborhood* by George Ancona. Text and photographs copyright © 2004 by George Ancona. Reprinted by permission of Children's Press, an imprint of Scholastic Library Publishing and George Ancona. All rights reserved.

Unit Seven

Marian Reiner: Excerpt from *Go to Sleep, Gecko* by Margaret Read MacDonald, illustrated by Geraldo Valério. Text copyright © 2006 by Margaret Read MacDonald. Illustrations © 2006 by Geraldo Valério. Published by August House Publishers Inc. Used by permission of Marian Reiner.

Unit Eight

Houghton Mifflin Harcourt: *Apple Pie 4th of July* by Janet S. Wong, pictures by Margaret Chodos-Irvine. Copyright © 2002 by Janet S. Wong. Illustrations © 2002 by Margaret Chodos-Irvine. Reprinted by permission of Houghton Mifflin Harcourt Publishing Company. All rights reserved.

Simon and Schuster, Inc.: Excerpt from *America Is . . .* by Louise Borden, illustrated by Stacey Schuett. Copyright © 2002 by Louise Borden. Illustrations © 2002 by Stacey Schuett. Reprinted by permission of Simon and Schuster, Inc.

TRO: Excerpt from the lyrics of "This Land is Your Land" words and music by Woody Guthrie. Copyright © 1956 (renewed), 1958 (renewed), 1970 (renewed), 1972 (renewed), Ludlow Music, Inc. International copyright secured. Made in U.S.A. Used by permission of TRO. All rights reserved including public performance for profit.

▢ **NATIONAL GEOGRAPHIC SCHOOL PUBLISHING**

National Geographic School Publishing gratefully acknowledges the contributions of the following National Geographic Explorers to our program and to our planet:

Annie Griffiths Belt, National Geographic Contributing Photographer
Dennis Desjardin, National Geographic Writer
Jon Waterman, National Geographic Grantee
William Allard, National Geographic Contributing Photographer
Tyrone Hayes, 2004 National Geographic Emerging Explorer
Losang Rabgey, 2006 National Geographic Emerging Explorer
Enric Sala, National Geographic Fellow
Sam Abell, National Geographic Contributing Photographer

Photographic Credits

–iv (tl) Hans Lippert/Photolibrary. v (tc) David B. Fleetham/Visuals Unlimited. vi (tc) Bill Hatcher/National Geographic Image Collection. vii (tc) Photo courtesy CARE. viii (tc) Merijn van der Vliet/iStockphoto. ix (tc) Tsering Rabgey/Machik. x (tl) Jeff Hunter/Getty Images. xi (tl) Studio 1One/Shutterstock. xiii (tr) Tashi Rabgey/Machik. 2-3 Image Source/Getty Images. 5 (bl) bonnie jacobs/iStockphoto. (br) Catherine Yeulet/iStockphoto. (tl) Sean Locke/iStockphoto. (tr) Richard Nowitz/National Geographic Image Collection. 7 (bl) Jupiterimages/Getty Images. (br) John Lund/Drew Kelly/Sam Diephuis/Blend Images/Getty Images. (tc) Ariel Skelley/Blend Images/Getty Images. (tl) Brand X Pictures/Jupiterimages/Getty Images. (tr) Monkey Business Images/Shutterstock. 12 Andre Bonn/Shutterstock. 13 Ingram Publishing/Superstock. 23 Children's Book Press. 26 (r) Diane Diederich/iStockphoto. (tr) Stockbyte/Getty Images. 27 (bg) Annie Griffiths Belt. (inset) Linda Marakov/National Geographic Image Collection. 28-29 (bg) Annie Griffiths Belt/National Geographic Image Collection. 29 (br) Annie Griffiths Belt/National Geographic Image Collection. (cr, t) Annie Griffiths Belt. 30 (b, bg) Annie Griffiths Belt/National Geographic Image Collection. (c, t) Annie Griffiths Belt. 34 (bl) David Young-Wolff/PhotoEdit. (br) Tony Freeman/PhotoEdit. (tl) ARCO/Geduldig/age fotostock. (tr) Rudi Von Briel/PhotoEdit. 35 (bl) Pete Ryan/National Geographic Image Collection. (bl) Michael Shake/Shutterstock. (tc) Somos/Veer/Getty Images. (tl) Photos.com/Jupiterimages. (tr) Kenneth C. Zirkel/iStockphoto. 38 Gavin Hellier/Robert Harding World Imagery/Corbis. 38-39 (bg) Jamie Marcial/SuperStock. 40 imagebroker/Alamy Images. 41 (b) TravelStockCollection - Homer Sykes/Alamy Images. (t) Gavin Hellier/Robert Harding World Imagery/Corbis. 42 (b) Gary Cook/Alamy Images. (t) Hans Lippert/Photolibrary. 43 George Simhoni/Masterfile. 44 (b) Jeff Greenberg/Photolibrary. (t) George Hammerstein/Corbis. 45 (b) Hugh Sitton/Corbis. (t) Angelo Cavalli/SuperStock. 46 Chad Ehlers/Alamy Images. 47 (b) PhotoDisc/Getty Images. (t) Patrick Frilet/Hemis/Corbis. 48 (b) Wild Bill Melton/Corbis. (bg) Tim Pannell/Corbis. (inset) Liba Taylor/Corbis. 49 Stephane De Sakutin/AFP/Getty Images. 50 (b) Tony Arruza/Corbis. (t) Bob Krist/Corbis. 51 (b) Jean du Boisberranger/Getty Images. (t) James P. Blair/National Geographic Image Collection. 52 Chad Ehlers/Alamy Images. 54 (bl) Kenneth C. Zirkel/iStockphoto. (br) PhotoDisc/Getty Images. (cl) Somos/Veer/Getty Images. (cr) Pete Ryan/National Geographic Image Collection. (tl) Photos.com/Jupiterimages. (tr) Michael Shake/Shutterstock. 55 Ules Barnwell/iStockphoto. 56 (b) Image Source/Getty Images. (t) Masterfile. 57 Karen Givens/Shutterstock. 58 Jamie Marcial/SuperStock. 60 (bl) Katherine Moffitt/iStockphoto. (br) Marzanna Syncerz/iStockphoto. (t) Corbis. 64 Image Source/Getty Images. 65 Paul Burns/Fancy/Corbis. 66-67 Michael and Patricia Fogden/Minden Pictures/National Geographic Image Collection. 67 (b) Andre Bonn/Shutterstock. (t) Creatas/Jupiterimages. 69 (bl, tr) Creatas/Jupiterimages. (br) pixelman/Shutterstock. (cl) DigitalStock/Corbis. (cr, tl) Digital Vision/Getty Images. 71 (bl) Jupiterimages. (br) David Tipling/Getty Images. (tc) DigitalStock/Corbis. (tl) Hernan H. Hernandez/iStockphoto. (tr) Anthony Harris/Shutterstock. 76 Joe McDonald/Corbis. 77 Jim des Rivières. 79 Don Farrall/Getty Images. 81 Don Farrall/Getty Images. 83 David N. Davis/Photo Researchers, Inc. 84 Darlyne A. Murawski/National Geographic Image Collection. 85 Cyril Laubscher/Getty Images. 89 Narelle Oliver. 92 (b) Shutterschock/Shutterstock. (cb) Moira Lovell/Alamy Images. (t) Comstock Images/Jupiterimages. 93 AFP/Getty Images. 94 (bl) PhotoDisc/Getty Images. (r) Creatas/Jupiterimages. (tl) Jim Zuckerman/Corbis. 95 (b) It Stock Free/Polka Dot Images/age fotostock. (t) Kenzo Ohya/Dex Image/Photolibrary. 96 (b, t) Reinhard Dirscherl/Peter Arnold, Inc. 97 (b) Pete Oxford/Minden Pictures/National Geographic Image Collection. (t) Michael and Patricia Fogden/Minden Pictures/National Geographic Image Collection. 98 (b) It Stock Free/Polka Dot Images/age fotostock. (t) Kenzo Ohya/Dex Image/Photolibrary. 101 (b) Art Wolfe/Getty Images. (bl) AlaskaStock. (br) Anup Shah/Photodisc/Alamy Images. (t) DigitalStock/Corbis. (tl) Digital Vision/Getty Images. (tr) Gavriel Jecan/Getty Images. 102 (br) Flip Nicklin/Minden Pictures/National Geographic Image Collection. (cl) Ewan Chesser/Shutterstock. (cr) Corel. (tl) Mark Conlin/VWPics/Photoshot. (tr) Rena Schild/Shutterstock. 103 (bl) Eyecandy Images/Photolibrary. (br) Daniel Pangbourne/Digital Vision/Getty Images. (tc) PIER/Getty Images. (tl) Digital Vision/Getty Images. (tr) Jack Hollingsworth/Photodisc/Getty Images. 104 (l) Jeff Hunter/Getty Images. (r) Visuals Unlimited/Corbis. 106-107 Gregory G. Dimijian/Photo Researchers, Inc. 108 (bg) Thomas Marent/Minden Pictures. (inset) Ian Shive/Aurora/Getty Images. 109 (b) Masana Izawa/Minden Pictures. (t) Dr. Dennis Desjardin. 110 (l) Cassius V. Stevani/Dr. Dennis Desjardin. (r) Dr. Dennis Desjardin. 111 (bg) Jurgen Freund/Nature Picture Library. 112 (b) Steve Percival/Photo Researchers, Inc. (t) David Muench/Corbis. 113 (b) Brian Brake/Photo

626

International Images Limited/Alamy Images. 529 Sam Abell/National Geographic Image Collection. 530 Sam Abell/National Geographic Image Collection. 531 Sam Abell/National Geographic Image Collection. 532 Sam Abell/National Geographic Image Collection. 533 Sam Abell/National Geographic Image Collection. 534 Sam Abell/National Geographic Image Collection. 535 (bg, inset) Sam Abell/National Geographic Image Collection. 537 Sam Abell/National Geographic Image Collection. 538 PhotoDisc/Getty Images. 541 PhotoDisc/Getty Images. 542 Ariel Skelley/Getty Images. 548 Warren Morgan/Corbis. 549 Jupiterimages/Comstock Images/Getty Images. 550 Yuri Arcurs/Shutterstock. 556 Andersen Ross/Blend Images/Getty Images. 557 Copyright 1997 by Gail Gibbons. Used by permission of Harper Collins Publisher. 558 World Book Encyclopedia © 2010. 559 (b) David Young-Wolff/PhotoEdit. (t inset) Pete Oxford Photography. (t) National Geographic Explorer cover May 2008. 560 Anthony Bannister/Gallo Images/Getty Images. 561 Andrew Tichovolsky/Shutterstock. 565 (b) Pete Oxford/Minden Pictures/National Geographic Image Collection. (t) Andrew Tichovolsky/Shutterstock. 566 Semisatch/Shutterstock. 568 (l, r) icyimage/Shutterstock. 569 (l) Monkey Business Images/Shutterstock. (r) Russell Glenister/image100/Corbis. 570 (b) Graça Victoria/Shutterstock. (t) Stuart Miles/Shutterstock. 571 jocicalek/Shutterstock. 574 (b) LianeM/Shutterstock. (cb) Comstock/Jupiterimages. (cc, cl, cr) FoodCollection/StockFood America. (tcl, tcr, tl, tr) Stockbyte/Getty Images. 577 Image Source/Photolibrary. 578 (b) Comstock Images/Getty Images. (tc, tl) Jani Bryson/iStockphoto. (tr) Nathan Blaney/Photodisc/Getty Images. 579 Digital Vision/Getty Images. 580 PCL/Alamy Images. 581 (tc) Goodshoot/Jupiterimages. (tcr) Stockbyte/Getty Images. (tr) Medioimages/Photodisc/Getty Images. 582 Myrleen Pearson/Alamy Images. 584 David Young-Wolff/PhotoEdit. 585 Simone van den Berg/Shutterstock. 586 Dave King/Dorling Kindersley/Getty Images. 588 Jim West/Alamy Images. 593 Judy Kennamer/iStockphoto. 594 PhotoDisc/Getty Images. 595 (bc) Moira Lovell/Alamy Images. (bl) Comstock Images/Jupiterimages. (br) Gelpi/Shutterstock. (cc) PhotoDisc/Getty Images. (cl) Alexey Stiop/iStockphoto. (cr) Shutterschock/Shutterstock. (tc) Hernan H. Hernandez/iStockphoto. (tl) Jacek Chabraszewski/Shutterstock. (tr) Michael Newman/PhotoEdit. 596 (bc) PIER/Getty Images. (bl) Tory Kallman/National Geographic Image Collection. (br) Ralph A. Clevenger/Corbis. (cc) Digital Vision/Getty Images. (cl) Justyna Furmanczyk/Shutterstock. (tc) Photos.com/Jupiterimages. (tl) Big Cheese Photo LLC/Alamy Images. (tr) BrandX/Jupiterimages. 597 (bc) Ariel Skelley/Blend Images/Getty Images. (bl) Brand X Pictures/Jupiterimages/Getty Images. (br) Monkey Business Images/Shutterstock. (ccb) Janne Hämäläinen/Shutterstock. (cct) 2009fotofriends/Shutterstock. (cl) Jupiterimages/Getty Images. (tc) Image Farm Inc./Alamy Images. (tl) Yellowj/Shutterstock. (tr) Laurie Noble/Digital Vision/Getty Images. 598 (bc) George Doyle/Stockbyte/Getty Images. (bl) Photodisc/Getty Images. (br) Juanmonino/iStockphoto. (cc) Gary Meszaros/Photo Researchers, Inc. (cr) Judy Barranco/iStockphoto. (tc) Encyclopaedia Britannica/Universal Images Group Limited/Alamy Images. (tr) Emanuele Ferrari/iStockphoto. 599 (bc) Jupiterimages/Getty Images. (bl) Michael Pettigrew/Shutterstock. (br) visi.stock/Shutterstock. (cc) Stephen Oliver/Dorling Kindersley/Getty Images. (tc) John Eastcott and Yva Momatiuk/National Geographic Image Collection. (tl) Dave & Les Jacobs/Blend Images/Getty Images. (tr) Yurchyks/Shutterstock. 600 (bc) Mostovyi Sergii Igorevich/Shutterstock. (bl) Randy Hjelsand/iStockphoto. (br) DigitalStock/Corbis. (cl) PhotoDisc/Getty Images. (cr) Monkey Business Images/Shutterstock.

(tc) Gallo Images/Getty Images. (tl) Carmen Martínez Banús/iStockphoto. (tl) Image Source/Photolibrary. (tr) laurent dambies/Shutterstock. 601 (bc) PhotoDisc/Getty Images. (bl) Rob Marmion/Shutterstock. (br) ERproductions Ltd/Jupiterimages. (cc) morganl/iStockphoto. (cl) Steve Smith/Photodisc/Alamy Images. (cr) Eric Kamp/Index Stock Imagery/Photolibrary. (tc) Pinkcandy/Shutterstock. (tl) Pixelbliss/Shutterstock. (tr) Digital Vision/Getty Images. 602 (bc) Donna Day/Stone/Getty Images. (bl) absolut/Shutterstock. (br) Morgan Lane Photography/Shutterstock. (cl) Corbis/SuperStock. (tc) GoGo Images Corporation/Alamy Images. (tl) Rob Byron/Shutterstock. (tr) Photodisc/Getty Images. 603 (bc) Digital Vision/Getty Images. (bl) Catherine Yeulet/iStockphoto. (br) Anton Vengo/SuperStock. (cc) Anton Foltin/Shutterstock. (tc) Simon Watson/Getty Images. (tl) Bruce C. Murray/Shutterstock. (tr) Petrenko Andriy/Shutterstock. 604 (bc) Patricia Hofmeester/Shutterstock. (bl) North Wind Picture Archives. (br) Urban Zone/Alamy Images. (cc) Cheryl A. Meyer/Shutterstock. (tc) Davis Barber/PhotoEdit. (tl) Anthony Harris/Shutterstock. (tr) Kathleen & Scott Snowden/iStockphoto. 605 (bc) Stefan Glebowski/Shutterstock. (bl) John A. Rizzo/Photodisc/Getty Images. (br) Andy Z./Shutterstock. (cb, cc) Artville. (cl) The Granger Collection, New York. (cr) RoberMichael/Corbis Super RF/Alamy Images. (ct) Stockbyte/Getty Images. (tcl) Creatas/Jupiterimages. (tcr) Stockbyte/Getty Images. (tl) Somos/Veer/Getty Images. (tr) David Young-Wolff/PhotoEdit. 606 (bc) Kenneth C. Zirkel/iStockphoto. (bl) Brooks Kraft/Corbis. (br) Monkey Business Images/Shutterstock. (cc) Forest Lane/iStockphoto. (cl) Loretta Hostettler/iStockphoto. (cr) BananaStock/Jupiterimages. (tc) Fancy/Alamy Images. (tl) Kathleen Revis/National Geographic Image Collection. (tr) Kerstin Klaassen/iStockphoto. 607 (bc) yung photographer@gmail com/Shutterstock. (bl) graham s. klotz/Shutterstock. (br) Jose Luis Pelaez Inc/Jupiterimages. (cc) PhotoDisc/Getty Images. (cl) Jack Hollingsworth/Photodisc/Getty Images. (cr) DigitalStock/Corbis. (tc) Media Union/Shutterstock. (tl) SW Productions/Getty Images. (tr) John Lund/Drew Kelly/Sam Diephuis/Blend Images/Getty Images. 608 (bc) Jupiterimages/Comstock Images/Getty Images. (bl) NASA/Corbis. (br) Michael Ochs Archive/Getty Images. (cc) Martin Poole/Jupiterimages. (cl) Brand X Pictures/Jupiterimages. (cr) Digital Vision/Getty Images. (tc) Rob Marmion/Shutterstock. (tl) Digital Vision/Getty Images. (tr) BananaStock/Jupiterimages. 609 (bc) Denise Kappa/Shutterstock. (bl) Michael Shake/Shutterstock. (br) Andrey Stratilatov/Shutterstock. (cc) Pete Ryan/National Geographic Image Collection. (cl) James L. Amos/National Geographic Image Collection. (crb) PureStock/SuperStock. (crt) Jason Edwards/National Geographic Image Collection. (tl) Alessio Ponti/Shutterstock. (tr) Beverly Joubert/National Geographic Image Collection. 610 (bc) Eyecandy Images/Photolibrary. (bl) Palani Mohan/Reportage/Getty Images. (br) SW Productions/Getty Images. (cc) Photodisc/Getty Images. (cl) HuntStock/Getty Images. (crl) Monkey Business Images/Shutterstock. (crr) digitalskillet/iStockphoto. (tc) James L. Stanfield/National Geographic Image Collection. (tl) Ted Horowitz/Corbis. (tr) Cleve Bryant/PhotoEdit. 611 (bc) Colorblind/Getty Images. (bl) Vstock/Alamy Images. (br) PhotoDisc/Getty Images. (cc) Yarinca/iStockphoto. (cl) Ken Goff//Time Life Pictures/Getty Images. (cr) Michael Newman/PhotoEdit. (tc) Jim Arbogast/Photodisc/Getty Images. (tl) Tongro Image Stock/Alamy Images. (tr) Jerzy Jacek Gładykowski/iStockphoto. 612 (bc) PhotoDisc/Getty Images. (bl) Jupiterimages. (br) Siri Stafford/Getty Images. (tc) altrendo images/Getty Images. (tl) Jim Craigmyle/First Light/Alamy Images. (tr) rotofrank/iStockphoto. 613 (bl) Ronnie Kaufman/Larry Hirshowitz/Blend Images/Getty Images. (br)

William R. Minten/iStockphoto. (cr) Zurijeta/Shutterstock. (tc) Imagestate Media. (tl) Daniel Pangbourne/Digital Vision/Getty Images. (tr) Gene Chutka/iStockphoto. 614 (bc) Mohamed Al-Tantawi/iStockphoto. (bl, br, crt, tl) John Foxx Images/Imagestate. (cc) Peter Horree/Alamy Images. (crb) Nick Norman/National Geographic Image Collection. (tc) Andersen Ross/Stockbyte/Getty Images. (tr) Digital Vision/Getty Images. 615 (bc) David Tipling/Getty Images. (bl, br) Jupiterimages. (cc) Royalty-Free/Corbis/Jupiterimages. (cl) jamie cross/Shutterstock. (cr) Digital Vision/Getty Images. (tc) PhotoDisc/Getty Images. (tl) Hale Observatories/National Geographic Image Collection. (tr) Denise Kappa/Shutterstock. 616 (bc) Ana Abejon/iStockphoto. (bl) GK Hart/Vikki Hart/Getty Images. (br) PhotoDisc/Getty Images. (cc) Kayte M. Deioma/PhotoEdit. (cl) John Howard/Getty Images. (cr) microstocker/Shutterstock. (tc) Monkey Business Images/Shutterstock. (tl) Dennis MacDonald/PhotoEdit. (tr) iNNOCENt/Shutterstock. 617 (bc) Digital Vision/Getty Images. (bl) Joel Sartore/National Geographic Image Collection. (br) Image Source. (cc) Corel. (cl) Creatas/Jupiterimages. (cr) Kris Butler/Shutterstock. (tc) offiwent.com/Alamy Images. (tl) Tracy Ferrero/Alamy Images. (tr) John A. Rizzo/PhotoDisc/Getty Images.

Illustrator Credits

Cover Joel Sotelo, Visual Asylum. 3–4, 6, 8–9 TSI Graphics. 32–33 John Kurtz. 36–37 TSI Graphics. 50–51 (map) Mapping Specialists. 63, 65 TSI Graphics. 68, 70, 72–73 TSI Graphics. 100, 105, 132, 133 TSI Graphics. 135–136 TSI Graphics. 137 John Kurtz. 138, 140–141 TSI Graphics. 142–156 S. D. Nelson. 162–162 Nic di Lauro. 166–168, 170–171, 197, 198 TSI Graphics. 201–204, 206–207 Chris Vallo. 208–221 ("Aeosop's Fables") Janie Bynum. 230, 232, 235 TSI Graphics. 236, 239 (maps) Mapping Specialists. 251 (globe) Mapping Specialists. 257, 258, 262 TSI Graphics. 263 Chris Vallo. 265–266, 268, 270–271, 290 TSI Graphics. 295 (globe) Mapping Specialists. 297, 298, 302–303, 318, 330–331 TSI Graphics. 334, 336, 338–339 Chris Vallo. 340–354 ("Domino Soup") Dani Jones. 359–365 ("Stone Soup") Sonja Lamut. 368, 370, 372 Chris Vallo. 191, 374, 376, 391 (maps and globes) Mapping Specialists. 401–403, 405, 406, 408, 410–411 Chris Vallo. 412 (globe) Mapping Specialists. 438,469, 470–471, 473, 474, 476, 478–479, 495, 504–505, 506, 508, 541, 542–543 Chris Vallo.